FOOTPATHS *of* FRANCE

For the Tourer, Camper and Caravanner

Michael Marriott

The Crowood Press

First published in 1990 by
The Crowood Press Ltd
Ramsbury, Marlborough
Wiltshire SN8 2HR

This impression 1993

British Library Cataloguing-in-Publication Data

A catalogue record for this book is available from the British Library

ISBN 1 85223 773 2

Dedication
To the memory of Martin Rolfe, cameraman, kindred wanderer and lifetime
friend.

Illustration Credits
All colour and black and white photographs by the author; except on page 107
(bottom right), supplied by Hutchison Library; all maps by Malcolm Walker.

Typeset by Butler & Tanner Ltd, Frome and London
Printed by Butler & Tanner Ltd, Frome and London

Contents

Foreword

Mike Marriott has an enthusiasm for the outdoor life that is totally infectious. Mere enthusiasm isn't enough, though, when it comes to writing a book like this. To do the job properly you need expertise in many fields. To judge walks you must walk them; to vet campsites you must stay at them; and to know a country intimately you must possess a wealth of knowledge built up over many years. Mike Marriott has this expertise, coupled with two valuable gifts: an ability to convey his enthusiasm in words, and an eye for a good photograph.

After his native Britain, France is the country Mike knows best. Countless visits have taken him to every region of this vast republic, and here he divulges a wealth of knowledge that will have you rummaging for your walking boots and booking the next cross-Channel ferry. As the first book of its type to cover the whole of France for walkers, campers and caravanners, it may have been a long time coming, but this is one that was well worth the wait.

Barry Williams
Executive Editor, Caravan
and Motor Caravan

Preface

The drift from passive time-passing to positive-pursuit holidays is steadily escalating in the western world. The 'Great Outdoors' has never been more knowledgeably appreciated than by this generation so acutely aware of the natural wonder of a finite planet. The free-ranging independence, the endless scope for exploring away from saturated holiday areas, and the high standard of contemporary touring parks all contribute to the appeal.

No country in Europe can offer more to the nature seeker than France. The largest country in western Europe, France boasts a road system that is without peer, and scenery that is extraordinarily varied, beautiful and spectacular in places. It is a treasure-house of the past, with a network of camp grounds and footpaths of incredible diversity. The drive-and-walk potential of France is almost limitless.

The brief of this book is to reveal just how fulfilling this form of active leisure is to those who have yet to discover the delight, and perhaps even to uncover hidden corners of the Republic for confirmed Francophiles. Compiling has been a labour of love. Although I have been aware of the danger of seeing through rose-tinted glasses, I must admit it is hard to quarrel with that eighteenth-century quote of Mirabeau. 'Every man has two countries – his own and France ...'.

Mike Marriott

Introduction

The Allure of France

For those who relish open-road travel, France is supreme. Since the dawn of the motor age, the *pilote* and his *voiture* have enjoyed priority kudos, and even today there is a distinct feeling of liberation for British drivers as they disembark from the ferry on to French soil. A *frisson* of that Gallic attitude towards motoring endures, formed during an Edwardian era of dash and *élan*. The French were eagerly promoting city-to-city car races, while British drivers were restricted to following a marcher with a red flag. This utterly contrasted level of acceptance of the internal combustion engine says much about the psyche of both nations. Whatever else, it does mean that if you enjoy motoring, you will love France.

Opening on the subject of the motor car may seem odd for a book devoted to footpath exploration, although in this case it is apt, since the object is to open regional gateways of discovery for the driver–walker throughout the length and breadth of this marvellous land. With luck it may wean you increasingly from wheels to walking, no matter which of the twenty-one mainland regions of the Republic you may be visiting. This is no specialised treatise on walking, driving or camping in France; rather it aims to be a weave of the pertinent strands of these compatible leisure pursuits. While millions of words have been written about all three sub-

jects, there is still a book-shelf intelligence gap for the traveller whose interest in each overlaps. A modest claim may be made by *Footpaths of France* for closing that gap; for providing within one volume the potential three-strand pleasure available from Calais to Cannes, from Biarritz to Besançon.

Britons already *au fait* with their nearest Continental neighbour will know only too well that France is one of the most tolerant and liberal-minded of lands. Do what you like, wear what you fancy, be as eccentric as you wish, and no one will give a second glance. Provided you pay your bills and respect the law (in that order), you really are free. The minority of visitors who find France and the French irksome are invariably those who expect mythical perfection, who make no attempt to learn even the basic courtesies of the language and who then level accusations of rudeness, closeness and arrogant self-interest. There *is* a national characteristic which reflects an ostensible indifference to the rest of the world; Jacques and Jeanne do go about their own business in an earnest manner which leaves little enthusiasm for outsiders, French or otherwise. Their consuming interest is for themselves and those who are nearest and dearest. Perhaps they are simply more sincere than other nationals!

For those who are already lovers of this land, such attributes are almost virtues. The

5

Principal walking areas shaded in green.

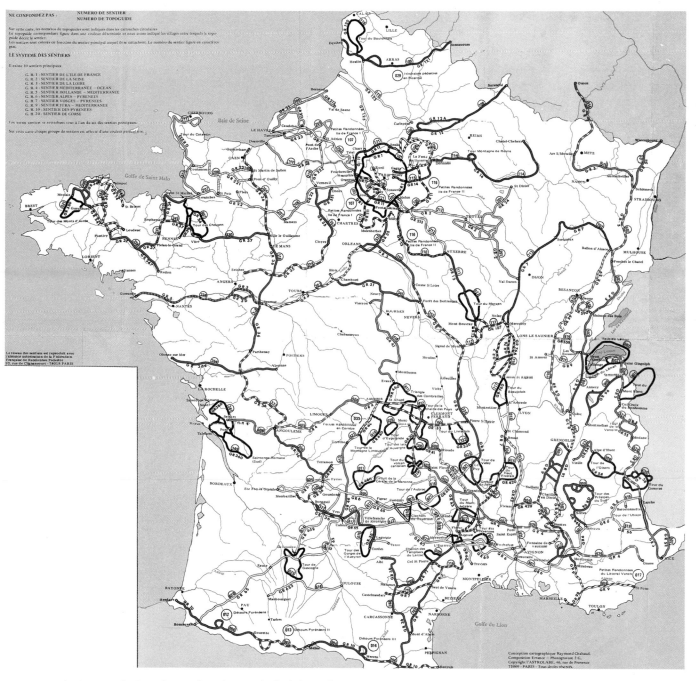

The Sentiers de Grande Randonnée, *interlinked throughout France. (Map supplied by L'Astrolabe, Paris.)*

other side of the coin is a minimum rather than a maximum of bureaucratic contact as a motorist, a casual and carefree ambience on the camping ground, and seldom (if ever) irate shouts from farmers whose land you may be traversing. Perhaps this is a direct throwback to the French Revolution – the belief in the citizen's right to wander at will, within reason, provided he does so with no mischievous intent. If you really do want friendly acceptance, then learn at least a smattering of French. No matter how atrocious your accent, you will be awarded marks for effort!

The footpath system of France, enthusiastically embraced within the great national plan to improve the quality of life, is grati-fyingly wide and handsome. Within three decades pedestrian routes have been officially established, waymarked and mapped, not only in all the recognised beauty areas, but throughout this vast country as long-distance trails. This is a truly staggering achievement, and is even now being further improved and extended. It represents just a part of the Second Renaissance which has totally transformed France since World War II. The turnaround from a predominantly agrarian society to one of sleek, high-tech affluence now rivalling West Germany, is nothing short of miraculous. It can only be fully appreciated by those old enough to remember the French countryside of the 1950s, when roads were primitive and drunken driving was rife; when

The reward of minor road motoring; Vitre, a feudal stone-pile of exquisite beauty.

8

men rarely shaved and women favoured the standard black dress. Footpaths were almost non-existent, since hardly anyone walked for pleasure; camping ground facilities were rudimentary, and signposts and pavements rare. Colourful but crumbling, with governments being formed almost weekly, France was lack-lustre, disillusioned and exhausted.

This old France was nostalgically romantic for some old-timers perhaps, but it has now been erased utterly and completely. Yet, with astute intelligence, the French have protected and preserved their land against the worst excesses of rapid advancement. Of course there are ugly areas where industrial or commercial excess has scarred savagely; regrettably, much of the coastline – Atlantic and Mediterranean – has suffered brutal exploitation. However, this is not the case for most of the mighty hinterland, away from the relatively few major conurbations. The quality of country life enjoys increasing emphasis and, for the outdoor-orientated French, determination to keep rural France unsullied is total. The result is a skein of camping grounds unequalled in any other European country; access roads are just as good, and there is an extraordinary total of 37,000 kilometres of long-distance wanderways (the *Sentiers de Grande Randonnée*), plus countless shorter footpaths awaiting the contemporary visitor. The seasonal influx of outdoor-life enthusiasts into France swells annually, for nothing succeeds like success.

Behind the Wheel and on Foot – the Practicalities

The footpaths selected within each region, the roads taken to reach them, and the camp grounds alongside are, of course, a personal choice. Inevitably, a one-person view may be coloured by factors such as the weather, the terrain and the type of natural or man-made attractions. Objectivity may be the aim, but subjectivity is sometimes unavoidable. I can only hope that you like, more or less, what I like. Optimism prompts the suggestion that if you are a self-sufficient seeker of pastoral France, there may be new terrain revealed, even to veteran travellers. For first-timers, I hope to show that there is far more to *la belle France* than motorways, cramped camping sites and beach-lazing *en masse*.

Documents

Formalities for the British visitor are minimal now, with just one or two documents needed to comply with the law. Obviously, a valid passport, either the full or limited period edition, is the first thing you need; check to ensure that it won't expire during the period abroad. A camping *carnet* is advised, since this is acceptable to campsite operators as proof of identity. It also saves surrendering your valuable passport each time you check in (*see* Useful Addresses page 221).

Drivers must be in possession of a full driving licence and the registration document for the car, plus an approved 'GB' sticker, issued free with ferry tickets. Insurance cover is compulsory. Since Britain is a full EEC partner, the standard policy is perfectly valid and the only legal requirement. The Green Card is no longer obligatory, although most drivers do feel happier having this document. It must be said that it is the most easily recognised proof of insurance cover should the worst happen, either through accident or illness. By completing Form E111 – available

No 'Chunnel' can compete with the ferry approach to France on a fine summer's day.

from any DSS office – you become eligible for the reciprocal EEC Medical Benefit Scheme, which entitles you to a refund of any treatment costs on your return home.

Currency

There are no currency restrictions and you may take an unlimited amount of French francs, cash English cheques when you present them with a bank Eurocard, or use traveller's cheques. The latter are still favourite, and probably the safest convertible asset for the holiday traveller. Banking hours in France are usually from 8.30 a.m. to 12 noon and from 2.30 p.m. to 4 p.m., but there are regional variations. In rural areas banks sometimes open only on selected days (usually market day).

The Car

In France car seat belts must be worn and young children must be back-seat passengers. The carrying of a red triangle is compulsory in case of accident or breakdown, unless the vehicle is fitted with hazard warning lights – both are preferable really in a country where driving is rather more 'robust' than it is in Britain. Speed limits are: *autoroute* 130 kmph (80 mph); dual carriageways 110 kmph (68 mph); other roads 90 kmph (56 mph); built-up areas 60 kmph (37 mph); or as directed.

Unless you intend to do a great deal of night driving, there is no need to convert to yellow headlights, nor tamper with the dipping system. However, do ensure that the vehicle is thoroughly fettled, particularly the tyres, brakes, clutch and radiator hoses, which may well be more heat affected than usual. If you are travelling at peak season, it may pay to install a summer-grade thermostat in the radiator.

Driving on the right swiftly becomes second nature; just be wary first thing in the morning when you may not be at your sharpest. As you are exiting from a camp ground it is possible to forget momentarily, especially if the road is seemingly empty.

Finally there is the ferry choice, to be supplemented at some time in the future by the Channel Tunnel. The latter may prove a time-saver for freight and business traffic, but will it hold any great attraction for the traveller beginning a holiday? 'Fair stood the wind for France' may no longer apply, yet there is still some romance in boarding a ship – coupled with a touch of style, if the publicity about the new generation of jumbo-ferries soon to be launched is to be believed. Drinks under the stars in sky-lit bars, grand curved staircases in ocean liner tradition, huge leisure areas and duty-free shops, plush lounges and many more attractions are promised. Both P&O and Sealink are determined to enter the lists, while we who never intend to emulate the mole anyway will certainly benefit.

Already the short sea routes are pleasant, speedy enough and efficient. Apart from during obvious peak periods you can arrive casually at Dover Eastern Dock nowadays,

Captain P J Wearing, master of the P&O 'Pride of Kent', on the bridge with Chief Officer M. Gearing. They are part of a huge team now providing a cross-Channel super service.

ROUTE	COMPANY	SEASON	TIME
Dover– Calais	Hoverspeed	Year round	35 mins
	Sealink	Year round	1 hr 30
	P&O European	Year round	1 hr 15
Dover– Boulogne	Hoverspeed	Year round	40 mins
	P&O European	Year round	1 hr 40
Folkestone– Boulogne	Sealink	Year round	1 hr 50
Ramsgate–Dunkirk	Sally Line	Year round	2 hr 30
Newhaven–Dieppe	Sealink Dieppe	Year round	4 hr 15
Portsmouth– Caen	Brittany	Year round	5 hr 45 day 6–7 hr night
Portsmouth– St. Malo	Brittany	Feb–Nov	9 hr day 9–11 hr night
Portsmouth– Le Havre	P&O European	Year round	5 hr 45 day 7 hr 15/8 hr night
Portsmouth– Cherbourg	Sealink P&O European	Mar–Oct Mar–Dec	4 hr 45 4 hr 45 day 7 hr 30/9 hr night
Weymouth– Cherbourg	Sealink	Mar–Oct	3 hr 55 day 6 hr night
Poole– Cherbourg	Brittany (Truckline Les Routiers)	May–Sept	4 hr 30 day 6 hr 15 11 hr night
Plymouth– Roscoff	Brittany	Year round	6 hr day 6 hr 30/8 hr 30 night

pay for your tickets and be driving in France within a couple of hours. For those of us who can remember when vehicles were actually netted and craned from shore to ship and ship to shore at Dover and Calais, the contemporary ferry crossing is sufficiently smooth. Stabilized, king-size vessels and the number of departure points available should outweigh a claustrophobic undersea route which can never qualify as an enjoyable overture to any leisure journey.

Currently, the Britain to France ferry links are as above.

Finding Your Feet in France

Leisure walking in France is more or less the same pursuit as it is in Britain, with one or two notable differences. Extreme northern regions apart, the French land mass is drier than ours, considerably warmer and infinitely less wind-battered. Selection of basic walking gear may therefore be adjusted for maximum efficiency and comfort. For example, heavy walking boots and thick over-socks – so necessary to combat the soggy peat bogs of northern England – are not nearly so vital in central or southern France, especially in high summer. Training shoes (preferably of a design providing good ankle support), are perfectly adequate for short- or medium-distance forays, and even for long-distance trekking, provided any accompanying rucksack is modestly filled. Backpackers may prefer to retain heavy footwear if they need to offset the carried weight of camping gear.

What you wear above your feet depends very much on personal choice. The wind-chill factor, a constant consideration in Britain, is far less important in France, except possibly in terrain above the snow line. Therefore,

Etretat – the dramatic high point of the Alabaster Coast, with fine cliff walking in either direction.

lighter and less bulky clothing will generally suffice. Heat, not cold, and dehydration, not drenching, are the hazards in France in high summer. In the southern regions, shorts and a singlet are seen far more often on footpaths than anoraks and over-trousers. The answer is to dress lightly for comfort, but to carry a warm pullover and waterproofs in your rucksack. Consider a wide-brimmed floppy hat too (preferably of natural linen), as a shield against a summer sun than can be surprisingly fierce.

Distances between watering holes are frequently if not invariably greater than in diminutive Britain. On long-distance routes particularly, a great deal of road walking may be necessary, which can be fatiguing in unshaded terrain. Many French pedestrian routes are laid with true Gallic pragmatism, and if long sections of tarmac are charted to link natural paths, then so be it. In Britain,

path planners do their level best to avoid roads altogether; in France there is no such aversion. In this guide emphasis is on green routes but, while prolonged tarmac tramping is not favoured, it is unavoidable in places.

Be reasonable when setting personal distance targets. It is not the kilometres you cover, but the time spent enjoying your walking that is important. Here a word must be said about the sketch maps which accompany the relative text. While they provide outline guidance to selected walks, including distances and duration, they are only approximate and no substitute for those two vital components of any walker's kit – the large-scale map and compass. While some of the paths described are obvious and easy, others, particularly in forest country, do require a modest knowledge of basic navigation. When you have learned the theoretical rudiments put your new-found knowledge to practical use whenever you can. Like so many other pursuits requiring a degree of skill and interpretation, pedestrian navigation is often very different in the field from the way it seems in the armchair. Trust only your compass, your map and your own common sense, bearing in mind that the map-maker's task is made increasingly difficult by the frantic speed of the spread of new roads and urban development. In the countryside you can only *assume* that an arrow nailed to a tree or a combination of colour flashes are accurate, and you should never accept such signs as concrete evidence. If you have a choice whilst at the learner stage, walk northwards on the outward leg of any excursion. This will enable you to correlate map and compass position while reading the map the right way up on the trickiest part of the walk. When you turn south eventually, your own in-built homing instinct should help you.

It is very important to learn, to a reasonable

Fortunately for the walker many of the camp grounds of southern France are cool havens. This is Seranon in the Provence Alpes high above Grasse.

degree of accuracy, your personal miles per hour walking speed, on the level, going uphill and going down. This is not quite as simple as it sounds, for much depends on landscape, personal physique and metabolism, air temperature, altitude, angle of terrain inclination, and so on. Experience is the only way of assessing walking speed, so test yourself frequently on local walks at home, between known mileage markers on tarmac, over rough ground, on hills and through woodland – the more variety the better. A pedometer may (or may not) help. Eventually, with the aid of your watch, you should be able to assess quite precisely the distance walked over any terrain over any given period of hours. The value of this will be appreciated soon enough in practice when, for example, you come to an unmarked fork in the trail, and the map shows not one fork, in the area you *think* you are traversing, but several. If you know, more or less exactly, how far you have walked, the decision on which one to take is infinitely easier to make.

During your initiation – and even later on prospective forays which you suspect may be challenging in part – it pays dividends to mark up your map the night before in kilometre divisions, allowing for any stiff up and down sections as indicated by the frequency of contour lines. Going over the proposed route with a powerful magnifying glass in the comfort of tent or caravan can also be surprisingly revealing, eliminating surprises or even shocks, which might otherwise remain unnoticed until the next day. Another simple way to eliminate anxiety is to get into the habit of glancing backwards occasionally, just as an insurance back-up. It is always comforting on any walk (if you have to abort a venture because of weather conditions, loss of intended direction, or whatever), to have your homeward route confirmed through the sighting of a familiar misshapen tree or a distinctive rock outcrop. These are views that you would not have known existed had you not turned around for a second or two on that outward leg.

Check your map and your compass frequently, remembering that any *ballisage* (waymarking), is only an aid to pedestrian navigation. Sometimes it is excellent, sometimes desultory, and occasionally it is positively misleading, especially where several trails converge. Don't worry too much about being super-accurate with your navigation to the point where it affects enjoyment, just keep on trusting your compass implicitly, with the comforting thought that if you started out from your base on a north-westerly course, your return route home *must* be to the south-east.

On any lengthy walk reasonable proficiency with a map and compass is essential. Navigation not only helps to keep you on the correct course, however; it can also become an absorbing part of the pedestrian venture – hence the popularity of orienteering as a sport. The fascination of periodic position-finding for the long-distance walker often culminates with an intense satisfaction when a wide forest tract or a long mountain ridge is completed without going astray. Certainly your senses are heightened and your awareness of your surroundings sharpened when you are consistently obliged to observe, detect and deduct. It is without doubt a great joy to

In mountain country you should be careful to take the necessary equipment. Hope for the best but prepare for the worst, especially if you intend to overnight alongside the trail.

be fully stretched, not only physically but also mentally.

In France, in southern latitudes, it pays to start any walk worthy of the name early in the day – 7 a.m. is not too early in high summer. Walk only for three to four hours maximum before taking a very long – but light – lunch break of at least three hours. Always carry a drinking water bottle unless you are in really high mountain country where the natural supply will always be bountiful. Lastly, if you are walking in company, the walking pace should always be that of the least athletic. The moral is, choose your hiking partners with special care if you yourself are not to suffer either impatient exasperation or premature exhaustion!

15

Alsace

Départements: Haut Rhin – Bas Rhin
Préfecture: Strasbourg

It is perhaps ironic that the region of France that is alphabetically first should be, in many ways, so untypically French. Alsace is the smallest region in France, and almost minute when compared to the other twenty mainland areas. Small is beautiful, however, and Alsace contains an almost disproportionate percentage of splendid rambling country, most of which traverses high-level terrain. Alsatians themselves call the region the 'Heart of Europe', not without some justification, for it is visually and atmospherically French, German, Swiss and Austrian. It has certainly been shaped by a turbulent history, and is a place of distinct individuality where the French language is still spoken with strong guttural overtones.

The landscape, like the people, is friendly and delightful throughout the southern département of Haut Rhin, and not so pretty in the Strasbourg area, or north-east towards the German border and Karlsruhe. For the very best of the high country, the classic approach route from the west is via the D417 through Münster to Colmar. Pause for a spell in Münster, pretty as a picture, still reflecting illustrious and very ancient beginnings. The town is small enough to make strolling around it a real delight, and is centred upon a monastic abbey which has been in existence since AD 650. There is a good 3-star municipal camp ground here, some 19 kilometres from Colmar, called Du Parc de la Fecht, with some pretty waymarked walks direct from site.

Rich and meticulously-tended farming country, alternating with the pine forests of the Vosges mountains, spreads wide to either side of the road, from the regional boundary almost to the heart of Colmar. An opulent and proud city, this administrative capital of the Upper Rhine is situated on the great Plain of Alsace, but close to the Vosges foothills. The old town, lovingly restored by the city fathers, is a mass of charming squares, narrow cobbled streets, many sixteenth-century half-timbered houses and a thirteenth-century art museum, the *Unterlinden* (incidentally, the most visited in France outside Paris). One special son of Colmar is accorded the highest esteem – the sculptor F. A. Bartholdi, the creator of America's Statue of Liberty. The house where he was born in 1834 is now – of course – a museum. Car parking is not too difficult in the vicinity of the *Unterlinden*, the very heart of the old town, if you wish to explore the attractive, lately much extended, pedestrian precinct.

Just ten minutes' drive from Colmar centre, going south along the N83, is the celebrated Wine Route of Alsace, some 100 kilometres of wine production between Strasbourg and

Colmar is half French, half Germanic, and a real pleasure to explore on foot.

Mulhouse, encompassing some of the most northerly vineyards in France. There is a succession of fascinating villages, many of which are medieval, half-hidden among rows of nurtured grape vines, all along the flanks of the Vosges foothills. Capitalising on this hitherto largely unvisited area, the regional tourist board now supplies a hand-out map and guide pamphlet, highlighting not only the villages and vineyards, but also a network of eight marked footpaths. These vary between one and two hours' duration, and pass in and around some of the most attractive settlements. Information boards along each path describe the work of the growers, the skills involved in wine making and the differences between the wines. Should you wish to know more about the production of the world-famous Riesling, Muscat d'Alsace, Ger-

wurztraminer and others, this less trodden part of Alsace is the ideal place to visit.

Pfaffenheim, between Colmar and Rouffach, is a particularly picturesque hamlet with a hallowed history; an erstwhile place of pilgrimage, it is marked with some historic monuments, and the wine is excellent too. Other notable regional products are kirsch, sauerkraut and – surprisingly – tobacco. It is very Germanic, including the local dialect and at times even French visitors find it easy to forget that they are still in their homeland.

For those of you who are eager to stretch your legs, the Alsace of the high Vosges is the main attraction. Leave the N83 at Guebwiller and take the D431 for Le Markstein and the Route des Crêtes (the ridge road). If the Alsatian scenery was impressive before, it now becomes sublime, especially in the vicinity

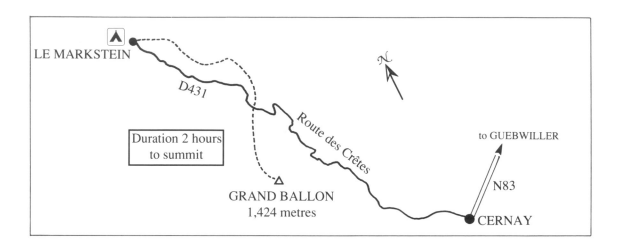

of Lautenbach and the Petit Ballon which landmarks the skyline. If you enjoy top-of-the-world walking, Le Markstein should hold strong appeal. An isolated summit above the tree line, this is a ski resort with an *auberge* that also provides rudimentary camping *à la ferme*. There is a popular high ridge walk of 2 hours or so, from here to the summit of the Grand Ballon, at an altitude of 1,424 metres. There is nothing much in the way of facilities at Markstein, at least not outside the ski season, when it reflects that rather forlorn picture which afflicts the majority of ski resorts when they have no snow. If you seek nature, you might be a bit miffed at the number of excursion coaches which still converge on this lofty bald patch in the height of summer. My preference is for somewhere less frenetic, so, after a spell of high-level walking, with some sweeping panoramas, the following is recommended.

Descend the Route des Crêtes via the D431 to Willer on the outskirts of Thann (an unremarkable spread of industry and commerce, although with a fine medieval church), then turn west on the N66 for the short distance to Moosch. From this village, take the signposted minor road to Camping La Mine d'Argent, which is situated some two kilometres along the richly-wooded valley of the Haute Thur. There is a municipal 2-star camping ground here, which is small but carefully manicured with pristine facilities and close-mown lawn pitching. Apart from the odd French Air Force Mirage in training, the loudest noise here is the rushing of the River Thur or a nearby woodpecker. The site, which is totally restricted to touring units, is open from May to September, and the resident warden is both friendly and efficient. In the small site office there is a good choice of local literature, including some excellent maps of the immediate area for walkers. As a point of interest this campsite is a base for the Mulhouse Camping and Caravanning Club, which organises group walks into the nearby mountains during the season, of 3 to 5 hours' duration. Visitors are welcome to join in if they are there on any of the appropriate dates, according to the warden.

Petit Ballon (1,268 metres) rising above the village of Lautenbach, south of Münster.

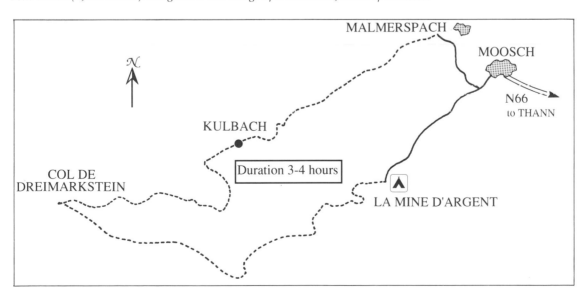

Camping à la ferme *near Lautenbach – an idyllic spot close to the GR5 in the Vosges mountains.*

However, you don't need company to find the natural riches here. There is a wide choice of pedestrian routes, almost the *raison d'être* for the camp ground's existence – patronage is primarily by those eager to explore the surrounding high country on foot. Waymarking is prominent throughout the region and the district walking maps, to a scale of 1:25,000 or 1:50,000, are first-class.

The recommended ramble is quite literally on the doorstep of Silver Mine Camp. Follow the blue triangle route west through the Forêt Communale de Moosch, ascending to the Col de Dreimarkstein. From here, turn sharply eastwards, continuing along the ridge then dropping down to the hamlet of Malmerspach. Prominent on a hillside, if you are walking before 24 June, you will see here a lattice tower of pine, filled with kindling ready for the Alsace Bonfire Night, this one honouring John the Baptist. These wooden structures mark many valley slopes. Of course, if you are walking after 24 June you will see nothing but a pile of ash ...

From Malmerspach hamlet there is lane walking back to the camping ground via the outskirts of Moosch. The walk takes from 3 to 4 hours, depending on how much time you take to stand and stare; you do have to find first gear for the opening 20 minutes or so, especially if you aren't acclimatized to altitude plodding. After this the path, which is beautifully defined, levels out more or less to follow the higher contour. The forest, a mixture of oak and pine, is a joy to cross, and if you aren't already a convert to hill walking, this will surely convince you.

Another attractive pedestrian route – again direct from the Moosch camp ground – goes to the Belacker, where there is a farm *auberge*.

20

This walk is waymarked in red and takes about 1½ hours. Belacker is an odd-sounding name, not unlike the Gaelic Bealach Na Ba (Pass of the Cattle), near Applecross in the Highlands of Scotland. Presumably it is Old German for 'pass'.

At the end of any walking day in this part of the Vosges mountains you will certainly develop a thirst and an appetite. While the Alsace beer and wine is of superlative quality, the water is also some of the purest and lightest in France – there is no need to buy the bottled variety hereabouts. The local gastronomic speciality is fried carp and you should spoil yourself with a sample of this dish if you can as it's delicious. There is even a Fried Carp Route, to complement the Wine Route – in the south of the region around Altkirch, in a district known as the Sundgau.

Seppois-le-Bas

If the mountain weather is particularly fickle, it could be that a lowland base with more settled skies might eventually be preferable. If so, consider Sundgau in the very south-eastern corner of Alsace, and Seppois-le-Bas in particular. At the gateway of three national frontiers, this is a village tucked away in a green and pleasant valley within a landscape rich in forests, small lakes and streams. An interesting if not spectacular area, it is dotted with half-timbered houses, feudal ruins and many wild flowers during spring and early summer. Again, it is a place which is not over-visited, despite the relative proximity of Belfort, Mulhouse and Basle just across the border in Switzerland.

In 1984, a new camping ground was opened called Les Lupins. A 3-star municipal enter-prise, this is a very spacious, level and nicely landscaped site covering some three and a half hectares. Super-modern facilities include a swimming pool, tennis courts and a common room with television. With plenty of options for open or tree-shaded pitches, the season is from 15 April to 15 September. There are some very pleasant woodland walks in the vicinity, plus a village (almost a small market town), which boasts a supermarket and restaurants dispensing those fried carp. To get there, take the D25 south from Altkirch, turning west along the D463 at Feldbach.

The Ballon d'Alsace

In the far south-western corner of the region, the lofty Ballon d'Alsace commands the landscape. Pine and beech are so densely packed that it seems almost as if you could walk across the tree-tops which clothe this and the neighbouring domes of the Vosges mountains. The *ballon* itself reaches an elevation of 1,247 metres. It is the highest point of the southern Vosges range, and is geologically composed of some of the most ancient rock formations on our planet, estimated, in places, to be some 400 million years old. The summit col is something of a regional (and indeed national) landmark, not yet spoiled (I hope it never will be) by commercial over-exploitation. The dominant man-made feature is 'Les Démineurs', a striking sculptured memorial to bomb-disposal sappers who lost their lives in World War II. This is an appropriate place for such a monument, since some of the heaviest fighting of early 1945 was in this region, when the summit was a strategic radio station and observation post high above the Rhine. Of course, countless mine-fields had to be cleared in this area.

The Masevaux municipal camp ground; comfortable and not too cramped.

These days, at the point where three regions of France meet – Franche-Comté, Lorraine and Alsace – assaults of a much more peaceful nature take place each summer on the high country trails of the *ballon* summit. All of these routes, whether *grandes-randonnées* or more local paths, are very well waymarked by that most admirable institution and silent friend of every leisure walker, The Club Vosgien. This club has probably done more than almost any other association or government department to promote pedestrian pursuits in this and neighbouring regions of eastern France.

One of the closest and most comfortable base camps to the Ballon d'Alsace is the municipal site at Masevaux on the D466, some 22 kilometres east of the summit, in the Doller Valley. Much quieter than the Lor-raine side of the mountain to the north-west, which is afflicted by the busy N66 and its heavy commercial traffic, Masevaux has a French name but is, to all outward appearances, as German as Alsace beer. It has a predominance of attractive half-timbered houses, hosts of manicured and colourful flower boxes, very clean and well-ordered streets, yet the town is marred by what must be one of the lumpiest, ugliest church buildings in all France. The municipal camping ground, however, merits its 4-star-rating, for the park-like setting, the full and well-maintained facilities and the restful ambience which prevails, despite a good number of perimeter weekend units. The site is open from Easter to October and is a five-minute stroll from the town centre.

With some 200 kilometres of waymarked

footpaths waiting to be explored at higher levels of the Vosges mountains, plus the GR7 which traverses Masevaux and numerous local walks to both north and south of the town, there is no shortage of pedestrian options. There is even an unusual tarmac link between Masevaux and Sewen, some 8 kilometres along the Vallée de la Doller. Only for the exclusive use of cyclists – and of course walkers – this route makes it possible for you to stroll through part of the picturesque river valley away from motorised traffic. To find this route from the municipal camp ground, walk towards the town centre, turn left at that unmistakable church and join the D466 Ballon d'Alsace road. Just past the Masevaux town limit sign you will see the tarmac trail. When you come to a carefully made brick-wall culvert, just before the first village of Sickert, realisation will dawn that this is no specially laid tourist trail, but the conversion of a disused local railway line, much like those in England's Peak District. This is an interesting and easy walk, however, amid hill scenery of consistent visual delight, and leading almost to the foot of the mighty *ballon*.

Parc Naturel des Vosges du Nord

Typical of the many old-world villages which adorn the flanks of the northern Vosges mountains is Oberbronn to the north-west of Strasbourg. There are three very sound reasons for selecting this area of northern Alsace to explore – the ancient agricultural village of Oberbronn for its delightful atmosphere and string of very ancient houses; the surrounding countryside for its richly-wooded beauty, made splendidly accessible for walkers by the Club Vosgien; and finally the municipal camping ground 'Eichelgarten',

which provides a very comfortable base with first-rate modern facilities and good leisure amenities. This municipal enterprise boasts solar-heated toilets, a large common room, adjacent tennis courts, two swimming pools (one child-sized), a putting green and a health and fitness course laid out in a wooded section of the site. There are also chalets for hire. This 3-star ground is completely rural, being surrounded by wooded mountains and cereal crop farms. There is a preponderance of static caravans, so touring units have to be content with pitches between weekend non-mobile homes, but this situation is made tolerable by the excellent facilities, the generally peaceful atmosphere and the other advantages. The site is open from 1 February to 31 December and is within the bounds of the Parc Naturel.

Eichelgarten is just 1 kilometre from the interesting village of Oberbronn, improved by the industrious Club Vosgien who have tabulated some of the more historic houses and included them in a descriptive hand-out pamphlet (free from the camp ground office).

Ex-railway route for walkers through the Doller Valley – Sickert village.

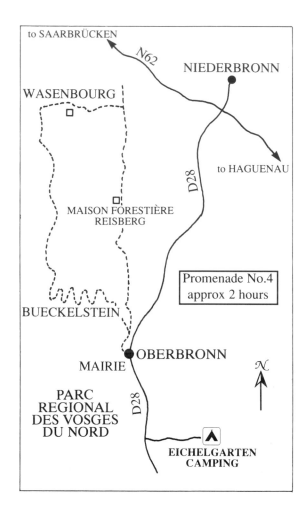

to SAARBRÜCKEN

N62

NIEDERBRONN

WASENBOURG

D28

to HAGUENAU

MAISON FORESTIÈRE
REISBERG

Promenade No.4
approx 2 hours

BUECKELSTEIN

OBERBRONN

MAIRIE

N

PARC
REGIONAL
DES VOSGES
DU NORD

D28

EICHELGARTEN
CAMPING

Wasenbourg Castle, along a foresters' route, before turning to follow a track through beautiful beech woods high above the village, descending eventually via a steep, short zig-zag around the Bueckelstein – a massive sand-stone outcrop – almost overhanging the roof-tops of Oberbronn. There are some superb high-level views across the green valley to the camp ground and beyond. This is a two hour walk and the waymarking is very easy to follow.

For sterner, high-altitude hiking, there are any number of alternatives in this area, some starting from the village outskirts, others from designated parking areas at the Col de l'Ungerthal and the Col du Holderheck – 5 to 6 kilometres from Oberbronn. If you prefer a more sophisticated setting for your camping, close to a gambling casino and opulent thermal spa surroundings, you might consider nearby Niederbronn-les-Bains, which has a 2-star site on the town outskirts, open all year round. As with Oberbronn, the foot-path routes from here are both wide and varied. Full information is available from the Office du Tourisme, Hotel de Ville.

La-Petite-Pierre

Long and thin in outline, Alsace is almost entirely dominated by mountain ranges down its western side and densely wooded above the wide Rhine valley. While the most dra-matic heights are undoubtedly around the Ballon d'Alsace in the south and the Grand Ballon in the centre, the northern sector has its own scenic treasure – and that is La-Petite-Pierre (sometimes called the Rocamadour of Alsace), to the north of Saverne. As well as being one of the celebrated regional beauty spots, La-Petite-Pierre is also the principal

There is a nicely mapped short walk around the village (with two variations), taking in all the most intriguing buildings, some of which date back to the mid-sixteenth century.

For more prolonged and country walking, there are no less than fourteen waymarked pedestrian trails to explore, many of which start from the tiny and venerable *Mairie* in the village centre. One of the many scenic paths is that which winds north to the ruins of

A path near La Petite Pierre, where walking without luggage is a new attraction.

regional dynasties, like those of the Counts of Lutzelstein. Even now, within the stout protecting ramparts, the tiny old town has the air of a medieval bastide, albeit a modern and peaceful one.

There is some splendid hill walking in the vicinity along a variety of marked paths, including the GR53. An exciting new scheme has recently been launched through the Club Vosgien to allow parties of up to twenty to explore, free of luggage – or *levez le pied* – the long-distance route between Saverne and Wissembourg, stopping at pre-selected *gîtes* on the way (*see* map). For further information, contact Mme Haudenschild, Syndicat d'Initiative, Mairie, La-Petite-Pierre, Parc Naturel Régional des Vosges du Nord, Alsace, France.

There is a camping ground close to Petite-Pierre, but it does not come recommended. The nearest congenial base, to the south, is just outside the park – this time perversely not in Alsace, but in Lorraine – at the little town of Phalsbourg. Phalsbourg is a most atmospheric and historic place, a thorough mix of French and German, both in people and in architecture. There are a number of intriguing buildings, not least the camping ground and youth-hostel complex, once the residence of a count and a princess. All around there are many buildings and streets with military overtones, for Phalsbourg was once a fortress garrison, at the head of the Zorn river defile. The campsite is only small but it is attractive, with a variety of shops almost adjacent and with well-kept, clean facilities. It is open from 1 April to 30 November, and very convenient for *auto-route* users, being just a couple of kilometres from the A4, midway between Saarbrucken and Strasbourg.

administration centre of the Vosges regional park, a marvellous mixture of terrain covering some 120,000 hectares of forests, lakes, heath and some regal ravines. One of the most imposing of these plunges almost vertically, below the ancient walls of Petite-Pierre, another of those fortified redoubts imposed on more ancient defences by Vauban-influenced military engineers.

The magnificent château-fortress, a Maison du Parc since 1977, was once a formidable and feared bastion guarding the link between the plains of Alsace and those of Lorraine. The feudal fortress was originally built during the twelfth century and was subsequently the headquarters of the powerful

Aquitaine

Départements: Dordogne – Gironde – Landes – Lot-et-Garonne – Pyrénées-Atlantiques
Préfecture: Bordeaux

The Atlantic-facing land mass of Aquitaine holds within its boundaries some of the best backpacking routes within France, plus a copious selection of more leisurely walking trails. Nearly all are concentrated in the north and south of the region, since the immense spread of central flatlands below the Gironde river and right through the *département* of Landes holds little appeal for most walkers. The exception is the coastal GR8, which runs north/south for some 100 kilometres from the Gironde estuary to St-Brice on the Arcachon Basin. When you compare the vast, almost featureless vine- and maize-growing plains of Landes with the acknowledged walking areas, you can hardly conceive that these hugely contrasting landscapes are in the same country, let alone in the same region. Landes and its neighbour the Gironde are the largest départements in France and together they cover such an enormous area that it seems incredible that the region could contain such diverse scenic beauty elsewhere. That it does is more proof of France's great size. And it has that beauty in glorious abundance, as anyone who has enjoyed Périgord or the Pyrénées will acknowledge. So distant and so different are these two areas of distinction, that each must be considered separately.

Northern Aquitaine

The dazzling 'Golden Triangle' of ancient Périgord province is formed by Périgueux, Libourne and Sarlat-la-Canéda. Each of these towns reflects those images of past glory which are now sought by the contemporary visitor surfeited with twentieth-century uniformity. The first two are ancient cities: Libourne is a thirteenth-century fortified port on the Dordogne; Périgueux was a thriving city in Roman times, capital of Périgord, and is rich still in architectural treasures with an inspiring twelfth-century cathedral. However, Sarlat-la-Canéda is the town which really resonates with impressions of medieval life. Despite the crush of cars and the even greater crush of people on high days and holidays, and the inevitable overtones of commercialism, it is in parts sublime. If you wander away from the conducted tour crowds around the cathedral, you can turn corners or duck under archways where ghosts of the sixteenth-century are almost tangible.

The countryside around Sarlat has gentle wooded hills dotted with stone-roofed Périgord houses. There are several circular lane walks varying between 2 and 5 kilometres in length, starting from the town centre. All are

St Front Cathedral, Périgueux.

waymarked and full information is provided in the relevant booklet, available from the tourist office near the cathedral. The nearest touring site to the old centre is Camping les Périères, a well-run 4-star ground located off the D47 road, 1 kilometre to the north-east. It is open from Easter to 30 September.

The Sarlat surroundings are attractive but not spectacular, sandwiched as they are between the Vezère and Dordogne rivers, and for the best of the area, you have, predictably, to get yourself alongside the celebrated rivers. Beynac and the waterside eastwards towards the regional boundary and Souillac is the best-known stretch. There are many beautiful places in this part of Aquitaine – Beynac itself, and what has been called the 'prettiest village

in France', La Roque Gageac. The steep slopes above the river are covered with oak, chestnut and pine and networked with foot-paths, some of which are very ancient. There are also camping grounds in profusion.

This region is well geared to tourism and there has been extensive restoration of many old villages which have yet to gain a second patina of time; none the less they are absorb-ingly interesting to explore on foot. In and around Beynac there is a choice of short walks, some through the precipitous streets of the town itself; La Roque is similar, only more so! Certainly, this is an area where even a fairly protracted holiday should be amply filled for the leisure walker. There are so many high spots that it could prove profitable

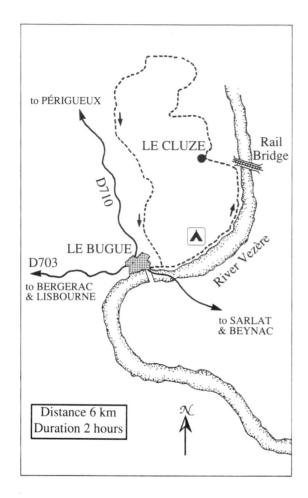

to PÉRIGUEUX

D710

LE CLUZE

Rail Bridge

LE BUGUE

D703

to BERGERAC & LISBOURNE

River Vezère

to SARLAT & BEYNAC

Distance 6 km
Duration 2 hours

N

metres – to avoid the heaviest summer crowding, and there is a choice of camp grounds. The municipal site enjoys a most pleasant location, level and tree-shaded, alongside the Vezère. It is green and spacious, the facilities are adequate if not luxurious, the charges are reasonable, and there is a municipal swimming pool adjacent. A riverside footpath takes you directly into the heart of the pretty little town, which is under 1 kilometre away.

There are several circuit footpaths around here, the most interesting of which is the 2 hour, 6-kilometre Yellow Route. It begins at the town centre, where you descend steps to a newly-constructed riverside promenade, passes alongside the municipal campsite, then turns uphill via lanes to arc on high ground above the town. There are some fine distant views across the bowl of the valley from the wooded ridge. This pleasant walk is almost entirely on tarmac lanes, with just two short stretches of woodland trail, and waymarking is efficient if slightly faded in places. The return to town is via a steepish descent, and the path emerges almost opposite the camp ground entrance.

Le Bugue itself has charm and atmosphere, the shopping facilities are good, and the central tourist office is obligingly helpful. There is a colourful open market every Saturday, when the town becomes packed with cars and people. The picturesque centre is plagued at times by traffic bottlenecks, but the new riverside promenade allows pedestrian access from the camp ground. This is a restful spot in old Périgord where you can keep away from the tourist mainstream. For a glimpse of truly ancient Périgord, visit the nearby caves of Bara-Bahau, a catacomb of prehistoric wall paintings. This place is almost

to circulate daily from a set base with vehicle and walking boots, since distances between the many beautiful areas are frequently quite considerable.

You might consider visiting the epicentre of the 'Golden Triangle', the strategically placed and charming little township of Le Bugue, on the river Vezère. To reach this tucked-away riverside resort, take the D710 for some 40 kilometres south from Périgueux. This is far enough away from Sarlat – some 32 kilo-

as astounding as Lascaux, north of Sarlat, which was discovered only in 1940 and is now closed to visitors. (Lascaux II, however, is a nearby replica cave which is open.)

For long-distance walkers wishing to explore this area, there is the GR6 which passes through Le Bugue, winds around Sarlat to the east, then joins with the GR64 to take in the most dramatic reaches of the Dordogne river. Since Le Bugue is served by the French Railway system it is possible to work out one or two interesting 'walk-out, train-back' excursions.

Basque Country Aquitaine

South-west of Pau green-domed hills escalate into wild mountains along the French border with Spain, the most majestic natural frontier in western Europe. The landscape is as distinctive as the people who inhabit this south-western corner of France; the Basques are even less typically French than their northern compatriots, the Bretons. They belong to one of the most ancient races on earth, and have a language which is almost as incomprehensible to the French as it is to the rest of the world. They are tough, self-sufficient and proud, and it is no surprise that some Basques feel uneasily usurped within their own ancient homeland. Only a small percentage live on the French side of the border and their yearning for independence is less intense than on the Spanish side of the Pyrénées. You will see the odd vandalised road signs and cryptic wall scrawls, but these are the only signs of dissent, perpetrated by fervent youth.

To visitors the Basques are friendly, naturally courteous in rural areas and patiently helpful to any walker seeking guidance. The

place where they live, the Basque hinterland, is beautiful. The contouring is relatively gentle for mountain country; here the Pyrénées although splendidly bestowed, are not as rugged or elevated as they become eastwards above Lourdes. The most revealing approach to the best of Basque high terrain is via Oloron-Ste-Marie south-west of Pau, then via minor roads through Mauléon-Licharre and on to St-Jean-Pied-de-Port. Along this route the scene is almost Swiss with some reflections of the Lake District, scattered with pretty, strangely-named villages and hamlets.

There is a very agreeable 2-star municipal camping ground at Oloron, beside a vast sports stadium, with a tantalising backdrop of the Pyrénées to whet the traveller's appetite. There is plenty of pitching space here, within level hedged enclaves, all mod cons, and excellent shopping facilities at the town perimeter, 1 kilometre away. The site is well signposted from the town (*Stade Municipale*), the tariff is medium, and they are open all year round.

Venture deeper into Basque hill country with two contrasting walks within this green and largely unspoiled territory. The first is in and around St-Jean-Pied-de-Port. This ancient and once-fortified bastion, formerly a pilgrims' crossroad, is now a township full of colour and charm. As the name implies, it is at the foot of a major Pyrenean crossing much used during the Middle Ages by pilgrims *en route* to Santiago de Compostela in north-western Spain. St-Jean was the pausing point below the rugged pass of Roncevaux, and it occupies a gracious sweep of the river Nive valley, amid richly-wooded foothills. The town is massively dominated by a great citadel, built in 1628, then much modified for Louis XIV some sixty years later by Vauban.

A footpath bridge in the Basque country of the Nive valley – rickety but practical.

St-Jean-Pied-de-Port – the path to the great hilltop bastion starts beside the tower.

It is splendidly preserved, with pink granite ramparts, moat vestiges and drawbridges. It towers majestically and is reached by a flight of some 250 stone steps rising almost sheer from the riverbank footpath. Conveniently, this path is immediately adjacent to the walled municipal campsite, itself virtually within the little town centre. A leisurely ascent to the citadel (about one-and-a-half hours) will show you the arrow-slitted walls, the sweeping distant and downward views, and avenues of 300-year-old oak and beech trees. Finally there is a cobbled street descent down the Rue de la Citadelle, where you tread in the footsteps of those medieval pilgrims, past sixteenth- and seventeenth-century houses and a grim but fascinating ancient jailhouse. The walk goes on through the still-gated town portcullis and back along the riverside to a wonderfully preserved Roman bridge spanning the Nive.

If the sun is shining, you will assuredly rate this as one of the most impressive and intriguing places in Aquitaine. For a long time it was the staging post of Compostela-bound pilgrims, today it again witnesses pedestrian traffic, this time tramping the classic Pyrenean high route, the GR10, or the north/south GR65. Apart from these long-distance trails, there are many circuit walks in the vicinity. Detailed information including maps and guides can be obtained from the town centre tourist office, which also provides a list of alternative camping grounds for those preferring to pitch outside the town.

Only 12 kilometres from the Atlantic resort

of St-Jean-de-Luz, not much further from the bright lights of Biarritz or the metropolis of Bayonne, the mountain village of Sare is another world. It is a place of timeless tranquillity, of the pelota court (*fonton*) and the distinctive Basque beret, where the talk centres on sheep farming and country matters just as it has for centuries. There is a sleepy, picturesque square, a winding main street of seventeenth-century character around the prominent old church, and a population of 1,800 within the village and surrounding canton. The whole reflects Basque life almost unchanged since the time of Louis XIV.

At Sare, you will discover just how different Basque culture is from French. Place names, too, sound foreign: you find yourself searching the map for hamlets named Finondoa and Mendiondokoborda and a mountain crest called Souhalmendi, *en route* to the Col de St Ignace on a 3-hour circuit walk from the village. One of three trails in the area (pamphlets freely available from the Sare tourist office), this is an easy if undulating trek which is waymarked (somewhat patchily in places) in blue.

The circuit walk starts with a descent from the village church, winds north into a wooded valley, crosses a small stream bridge then climbs steadily past Finondoa (simply a farmhouse), and continues across wooded slopes via lanes and tracks. Watch carefully for a narrow path immediately beside Mendiondokoborda farmhouse, opposite a

Basque hill country west of Oleron-Ste-Marie; a footpath view near Mauleon-Licharre.

Souhalmendi
301 metres

MENDION-
DOKOBORDA

• Redoubt

Redoubt

to ASCAIN

D4

COL DE
ST-IGNACE

Distance 8 ½ km
Duration 3 hours

to SARE

FINONDOA

Rack rail
to La Rhune

IRATZIA

D4

SARE

N

'Commune de Sare' signboard. The route now veers westwards over the mountain flank below Souhalmendi (an alternative path detours over the 300-metre summit), passing the remains of ancient mountain redoubts, before dropping down through woods to the Col de St Ignace. There is a large car park here, a café and the terminus of a rack-railway which climbs to the summit of La Rhune about 4 kilometres away. From here, after 30 minutes' chugging, it is said you can enjoy the finest, most expansive panoramas in the Pyrénées.

From St Ignace it is all downhill for the walker, taking roughly an hour if you pause here and there to admire the surrounding peaks, solitary and silent after the bustle of the col. The route follows the road at first, then goes along an ancient hill track and metalled Sare back road which winds, mainly parallel to the D4, back to the village.

For a full-day walking excursion, you might consider taking the described circuit route to the col, then the rack-railway, returning from La Rhune along a section of the Haute Route Pyrénées, to Les Trois Fontaines. From here the GR10 ridge route snakes eastwards back to Sare. Provided the weather conditions are favourable, this is an exhilarating trek along the roof of the Basque world.

A few kilometres east of Sare lies Ainhoa, again on the D4. Some 3 kilometres south of here is the hamlet of Dancharia, quite literally astride the Spanish frontier. On the French side, there is a most attractive 3-star camping ground, with a highish tariff, but with facilities to match. These amenities are not readily available on the Sare sites, which are adequate but have few frills. Xokoan, as it is called in unpronounceable Basque, is level and tree-shaded, with water and mains electricity supplied to individual pitches. Within a beautiful wooded valley, this base has a Basque speciality restaurant as part of the same touring complex. There is a choice of waymarked routes around Ainhoa, four circuits varying from one-and-a-half to five hours duration, all of them signposted from the charming old village centre.

Gateway to Périgord

While Sarlat and Les Eyzies are synonymous with Dordogne departmental splendour (and as a consequence are two of the most visited places in France), there are a number of less-heralded settlements alongside the great river, which are no less charming in their way. Sainte-Foy-La-Grande, which lies 22 kilometres west of Bergerac on the D936, is one of these. The tiny town centre is a fine example of the preserved past. The bastide, founded in the thirteenth century was once occupied by the English, which adds interest for visitors from the other side of the channel. There are a number of fifteenth-century houses, some splendid medieval arcades around the site of the ancient keep (now the town hall), and the ancient riverside ramparts, which are still largely intact. Sainte-Foy-la-Grande is a delightful little place and an ideal stopover for those on the north-south route wishing to avoid the great city of Bordeaux. It is certainly an apt spot to begin any east-west exploration of the Dordogne and the first really scenic reach of the river after the Gironde estuary – hence the tag of 'Périgord Gateway'.

Sainte Foy does its best to look after touring visitors by providing a useful tourist office, and a pleasant 3-star municipal touring site and a private enterprise alternative ground close by. Signposting on approach is good, the facilities are efficient (but without frills), mains electricity is available and there are shady pitches – these are very welcome in high summer. The municipal ground is open all year round and is less than five minutes' stroll from the old town centre.

(From the Sainte-Foy-la-Grande campsite, La Tuilerie, there is a riverbank path. This is well concealed although not quite invisible to the observant searcher seeking it at the site entrance. This leads to a small memorial park and the town centre, avoiding road walking. There are short walks on both banks of the Dordogne accessible from La Tuilerie.)

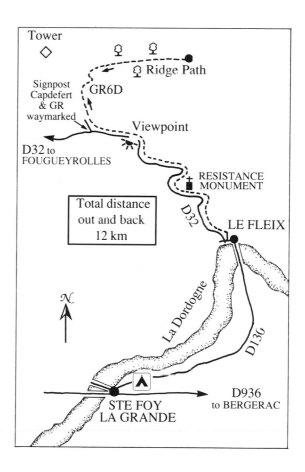

While this area is only on the eastern fringe of the great Bordeaux wine growing region, there is still much devotion to viticulture and pedestrian interest is therefore limited. However, there is a pleasant lane-walking route in the vicinity, beginning at the neighbouring hamlet of Le Fleix, 5 kilometres up-river. There is spacious parking here, in front of the *Mairie*, from where you make a left, right, left dog-leg between the cluster of houses, and then go on to the ascending minor road (more of a lane really), the D32 signposted to Fougueyrolles.

Fleix walk from Sainte-Foy-la-Grande. The path passes close to the transmitter tower.

In about 1½ kilometres you pass a Resistance massacre monument on your right among the trees. This is one of several within Sainte Foy and its environs, commemorating the black summer of 1944. There is a nice viewpoint over the river valley on the opposite side of the road and in 2½ kilometres, still ascending, you take the signposted track on the right towards Capdefert. This is also a loop of the GR646 (the GR6d), which circles through the hamlet of Ponchapt, just to the north. A part-wooded trail now leads past a distinctive red and white receiving tower, above an isolated farm and on along the ridge of the highest contour in the area. Even wider views over the valley open now and the return walk is all downhill.

Perle de la Côte d'Argent

Naturally Mimizan has changed somewhat since 1905 when its baptism as the 'Pearl of the Silver Coast' was officially announced. There is a considerable escalation of development around Mimizan Plage, not all of which is pleasurable to the eye. However, Mimizan town (which does have quite ancient beginnings), is agreeably picturesque with a face-lifted centre. The twin resorts are in the centre of an Atlantic sand beach that stretches almost unbroken between the Gironde and the Adour rivers, so the tag of Silver Coast remains appropriate. It is the straightest and the longest sand-strip in Europe. The great claim of this two-part resort is the therapeutic property of the air. Equal parts of Atlantic and pine forest ozone are guaranteed to be at once stimulating and sedative! Certainly the geography confirms this. It not only has the longest beach, but is also on the fringe of the largest European forested area, the Landes of Aquitaine. If there is a Continental seaside resort which offers a near perfect mix of woodland walking, swimming and beach-lazing, then surely Mimizan is it.

There is an excellent choice of camping parks, with the municipal ground half-way between town and *plage* in a superb pine-wood location. It is on the grand scale and has high-standard well-maintained facilities. There is room for 400 units here, which should give an idea of how popular the place is during the height of summer. There are a number of short strolls and medium-distance trails in the vicinity, although frankly not so many (nor as well waymarked), as one might reasonably expect to find in a region so devoted to outdoor leisure.

However, there are plenty of obvious beach walks, lakeside strolls around the Etang d'Aureilhan, and pine-wood tracks between Mimizan Plage and Contis Plage, some 13 kilometres to the south, where there is alternative camping. One of the more scenic paths begins from Mimizan Plage, close to the Centre Équestre of Le Marina. This route winds its way for about 3 kilometres between pine trees, then joins the foreshore for a return leg along lovely firm sand at the water's edge. There is a huge parking area adjacent to the riding centre, with plenty of room to spare at most times of the year.

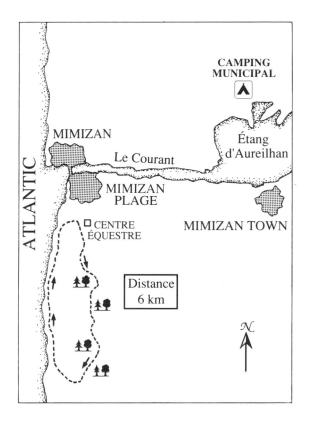

If you have a choice of approach route to Mimizan, make it from Langon to the north-east on the Garonne, via the Landes minor roads. This is a fascinating terrestrial voyage across an ocean of forestry, extending to over 100 kilometres. It represents one of the great agrarian achievements of the French – the taming of a vast swamp wilderness over two centuries and the transformation of a wasteland into a productive, healthy and pleasing wedge of south-western France.

Auvergne

Départements: Allier – Cantal – Haute-Loire – Puy-de-Dôme
Préfecture: Clermont-Ferrand

If a Welshman from Betws-y-Coed might feel an affinity with parts of the Cévennes, a Highland Scot would certainly experience a touch of *déjà vu* in the Cantal mountains of the Auvergne, and particularly in the Pas de Peyrol between Murat and Puy Mary. Glen Coe and Glen Nevis look-alikes unfold along the D680 in a series of green and velvety high pastures virtually devoid of trees, while the dark scree and snow-patched corries of the Plomb Cantal form a sweeping backdrop for long-horned cattle that would look equally at home ruminating in the Great Glen. However, as you penetrate deeper into the gigantic Auvergne rifts that splinter the southern part of the Parc des Volcans, the landscape becomes more dramatic than any to be found in the British Isles. It's a high-altitude world of wild grandeur, with wide horizons embracing such a wealth of open space that it could only be in France – and in Auvergnat France at that. The *parc naturel* embraces the loftiest, most beautiful parts of the region, but Auvergne encompasses almost the whole of the Massif Central, and is still thinly populated outside the Clermont-Ferrand district. It is simply one of the best regions in France for leisure walkers, climbers and winter skiers.

The unique, unforgettable landmarks of the Auvergne landscape are of course the *dômes*. These towering volcanic mounds – green-mantled and inviting now after being dormant for so long – are more or less extinct, although there have been 'burps' and molten eruptions from time to time during the recent past. There are some 60 *dômes* in all, testifying to some terrifying subterranean activity when the world was young. The most famous is the Puy de Dôme, although Puy de Sancy (the highest in the massif at 1,866 metres) and Puy Mary also receive their fair share of pedestrian explorers.

Puy Mary will appeal to many, not only because of its spectacular summit landscape, but also because of the variety of walking that is available within a 20-kilometre radius. An added advantage is one of the most outstanding medieval bases you could find anywhere in France – Salers. This was a fortress town in the Middle Ages and has not been much tampered with since – a film-set cluster of stone, hewn from volcanic rock and capped by those elegant dunce's-cap towers. The perfection of the original is fortunately unmarred by perimeter expansion, and this no doubt contributes to the fact it has the current title of one of the five most beautiful villages in the country. Salers is France preserved in aspic, a place of delight around every tiny corner, of cobbled alleys, miniscule squares and perfectly-proportioned archways. It is quiet,

Typical Auvergne landscape, with Polignac, near Le Puy, on top of its flattened volcano.

fully aware of its heritage value and conscious of its preservation in perpetuity. Yet, with true French pragmatism, a hotel has been built into the ramparts, there is a good choice of shops (even a squeezed-in self-service grocery), as well as, of course, a number of cafés and bars, and outlets for Auvergne cheeses, the famous dried hams and the local wines.

Contemporary life is bountiful here, but this was not always the case. Like the Cévennes, the Auvergne suffered depopulation – perhaps more than its southern neighbour. It has a harsh climate, with long, hard winters followed by short, often oppressively hot summers, caused partially by the subterranean strata in volcanic areas which are still abnormally warm. Topsoil is meagre too and agricultural labour is only grudgingly

repaid. So, not so many years ago people had to be tough and self-sufficient to survive in the Auvergne. It was no accident that the fiercest of the *Maquis* resistance during World War II came from these hardy folk. A study of the historic photos in the Salers bookshop reveals much of life as it was some five or six decades ago; it is marvellously evocative but depressingly a record of existence at subsistence level.

The jaunty and confident locals of today give no such backward glances however – they are too busy catering to visitors in an efficient although politely unobtrusive way. The local council has created a fine camping ground 1 kilometre away, linking it to the village centre and immediate environs by an attractive footpath. Camping le Mouriol is an imaginative hectare of landscaped conifer arbours, providing privacy and shade from that fierce summer sun. Hot showers, mains electric hook-ups and tarmac access roads complete the services, and the whole is maintained in fine condition and reserved exclusively for genuine touring visitors. It is open annually from 15 May to 15 October; both these months, incidentally, are considered by locals to be the best for any walking holiday in the area.

For an opening walk follow the short $1\frac{1}{2}$ hour circuit along the blue-coded path which starts right from the camping ground. From the gateway, you ascend the blue-arrowed lane which presently joins a farm track, the access route to the treeless slopes which are typical of the higher Auvergne. This is the extreme limit of agricultural land, and there is good cattle grazing but no arable farming on this bedrock of ancient lava. Cereal production is evident to the south-west where the land is more suitable, but this, where the

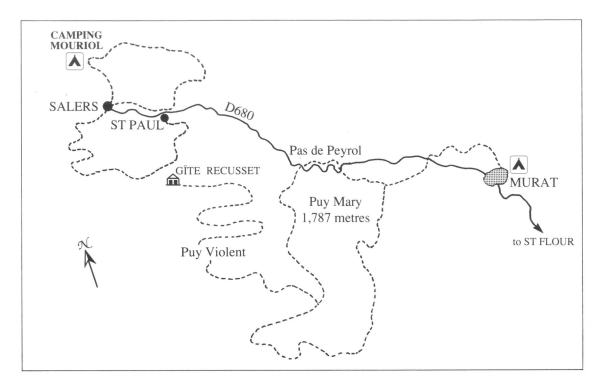

terrain rises steadily, is fell country and it will feel familiar to anyone who has tramped the North Yorks Moors or the Lakeland peaks. It is, almost exclusively, the domain of the buzzard and the adventurous hill-walker.

Eventual descent of the gentle waymarked round route is via a reservoir and an old road to the neighbouring hamlet of Malprangère. The stroll may be extended to 3 hours or so, taking in St-Paul to the east of Salers, another charming *petit bourg* commanding the apex of two valleys. Lengthier waymarked trails may be joined at Salers, notably the one to Puy Violent, just one of the many distinctive volcanic giants thrusting skywards on the medium-distance circuit of the GR400. Here, amid a positive welter of hill tracks, you can take your choice of walks, from a leisurely half-day promenade to a full week or more of wilderness backpacking. Further information is available from the Salers Tourist Infor-

mation office: some is free, and much is found within the pages of the *Topo Guides* on sale.

Puy Mary looms tall in the centre of this marvellous high-country span, topping 1,787 metres, and some 20 kilometres south-east of Salers. The massive semi-circular ridge is a popular objective. There is good access to the ridge path and car parking space can be found a couple of kilometres north-east of the Pas de Peyrol summit. For a fleeting high-altitude pedestrian 'fix', park at the summit itself (1,582 metres) thread your way between the coaches, café and usual souvenir stalls, and take the easy, revealing climb to the crown of Puy Mary. For any extended stay by non-campers, there is a *Gîte d'Étape* closer to the heart of the Cantal mountains at Recusset hamlet, to the north of Puy Violent.

Not everyone wants to tramp the snowline heights of course, and should you wish to sample some of the beautiful wooded country

Le Puy, the other famous volcanic needle in Auvergne, with its Virgin and Child statue.

explosive expansion in recent years, to cope with a western world now on a near-frantic health kick. It is now so crowded, clamorous and costly that the original intent seems to have been negated. Le Mont-Dore, on the other hand, has managed to retain much of its sedate dignity, although it too is heavily patronised, both in summer and winter, being a popular ski resort. The Puy de Sancy, the king of the volcanic peaks, rises just south of here, and is accessible via a wide choice of marked paths. There are also a number of local walks to nearby cascades and other beauty spots with an appeal for those 'taking the cure'. There is inevitable crowding

Vic-sur-Cère, footpath route to the Cascade de la Conche through old town.

of valley Auvergne, you would do well to opt for Murat as a base. Also straddling the GR400, there are many waymarked walks from here into the western forested slopes of the Parc des Volcans. There is a municipal camp ground and two adjacent hills of character to complement the colourful old town, now also an acknowledged resort centre with comprehensive amenities. The first is topped by a huge statue of Virgin and Child; the second is an eyrie for the pretty little church of Bredons, on the opposite bank of Murat's river, the Alagnon.

Northern Auvergne

Two more areas of great natural beauty grace this region, one of which is around the spa centres of La Bourboule and Le Mont-Dore. The former has been assailed by almost

though, especially on camp grounds close to the thermal centre. A better choice for a base in this area might be Lake Chambon on the eastern side of the Col de Morand, a few kilometres away. There are several touring parks in the vicinity of Murol, which is itself a small resort and waterside playground of a smaller and more peaceful prospect than La Bourboule and Le Mont-Dore.

The other great natural magnet for visitors is of course the Puy de Dôme which should (and once did) dominate Clermont-Ferrand. In reality, the situation is quite the reverse. Urbanization of this once-regal green giant is just about total, all of it dating from the birth of the motor car. There is even a motor-racing circuit slicing the lower landscape, while slick new housing development along fresh-cut terracing of the black basalt reaches ever higher from the enormous sprawl of Clermont below the eastern flank. Royat is the recognised visitor base, although again the camp ground here is heavily patronised throughout the season. A quieter touring park will be found at Ceyrat, from where walkers may join the GR forester trails from the sister village of Boissejour.

There is without question still much delightful walking around the Puy de Dôme, but it must be said that the overwhelming influence of Clermont does detract considerably. We who drive cannot carp too much, for most of Clermont's industry is devoted to keeping the world's wheels turning. To the north of the city any mewing of buzzards has long been eclipsed by the squeal of tyres being tortured to destruction on the huge Michelin test track. It may be essential to contemporary life, but it is eminently avoidable if you are seeking pastoral Auvergne.

Tumbling Waters around Vic-sur-Cère

Twenty kilometres from Aurillac, in the extreme south-west corner of the Volcans regional park, Vic-sur-Cère is a recognised portal to the Cantal mountains, the most rugged and regal of Auvergne high country. Vic is a very good base for a park preview, if you happen to be approaching from the south. This small hill resort is at the limit of what might be termed Mediterranean influence, for there is still the atmosphere, scenery, inhabitant attitude and climate (in the main), of the golden south. For many homeward-bound Britons, this is about the highest latitude for basking in southern French ambience, but only in the summer months – Auvergne winters are distinctly *un*-Mediterranean.

For those wishing to tramp countryside which is a little less dramatic than that around Puy Mary for example, in the central park area, Vic should prove an attractive alternative. There is certainly hill walking in abundance, to either side of the wide and fertile Cère valley, but if you want to ramble over reasonably level terrain, the verdant valley floor is very inviting, particularly since there are a number of well-marked local walks starting from the tiny town centre.

Vic itself reflects all the charm and cosy quaintness of most Auvergne hill settlements. It has a very long history, which is indicated by an imposing old residence dating from 1490 and bequeathed to the princes of Monaco, and some finely preserved, more modest houses of the same era, all clustered tightly around and below the venerable church. The tumbling waters of the fast-flowing Cère, together with its feeder-streams, are the great natural feature of the town and its environs. The Cascade de la Conche is one waymarked pedestrian objective – a bit of a hill walk, albeit a short one – and the Pas de Cère another. The first reveals the best of the old-world hill town in a half-hour stroll; the second is a very pleasant valley walk by lane, bridleway and footpath between dairy farming hamlets with distant mountain views, to the towering rock fissure cut by the white-water river which tumbles foaming from the narrow cleft. It is a two-hour walk, out and back, to the Pas de Cère from the high-standard municipal camp ground. Allée des Tilleuls Camping is only five minutes' stroll from the town centre and

has a very convenient supermarket opposite the entrance. It is open from April to September, the facilities are clean, comprehensive and diligently serviced, the riverside setting is generously spacious, and the tariff is reasonable.

The Sentier des Papetiers

Ambert, some 75 kilometres north of Le Puy, is the principal town within that second protected swathe of the Auvergne, the Parc Naturel du Livradois-Forez. Even larger than the Parc des Volcans, it is, somewhat surprisingly, only traversed by three GR routes, yet is one of the most favoured of mid-France walking areas. The country is high and richly wooded in this part of the Auvergne, yet not sternly alpine – it is not just for the fittest of pedestrian explorers. In summer it is idyllic terrain for extended hill walking. The region does have its high-altitude centres certainly, the most esteemed being La Chaise-Dieu on the D906, roughly mid-way between Le Puy and Ambert. At only 1,080 metres above sea level the name ('God's chair') makes an over-bold claim, but the old monks' settlement (now a thriving summer resort), does have an ancient and elegant abbey centrepiece, a comprehensive leisure park with camp ground, and a choice of footpath trails through the pine forests which encircle the lofty location.

A little further north, just to the east of Ambert, the Monts du Forez rise invitingly from the river Dore valley. It is here, among the splendid wooded slopes and world of rushing cascades that you will find the fascinating and unique Museum of Richard Bas. This is the last working paper-making mill in France, dating back, astoundingly, to the

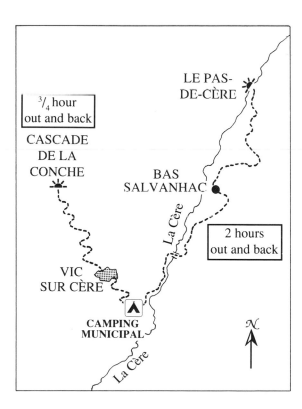

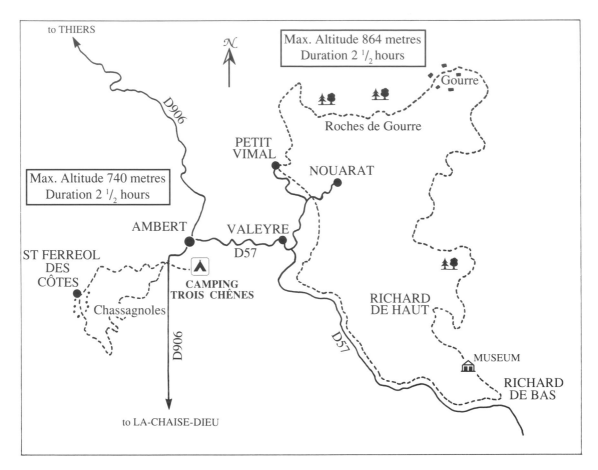

fourteenth century. There is no more appropriate or rewarding way to see this gem of the past than via a pedestrian approach called, what else, but the Sentier des Papetiers.

First, though, you need to find an agreeable base in the vicinity. The Trois Chênes municipal camp ground at Ambert, located alongside the D906 Le Puy road, is a most pleasant wooded and level ground beside the river, with high-standard facilities and adjacent to a covered and heated swimming pool and a fitness course. There is also a supermarket close by. For an immediate leg-stretching stroll, simply cross the road and follow the yellow markers up to the hamlet of St Ferreol-

des-Côtes, some 3 kilometres distant. You can complete the circuit walk (the Chemin des Croix), which takes about two and a half hours, or return when you've had enough along the outward and downward route, for the waymarking is a bit sporadic. There are nice elevated views across Ambert and the Monts du Forez.

For the Sentier des Papetiers, drive to the hamlet of Petit Vimal, signposted from Valeyre on the D57, 3 kilometres east of Ambert. Follow the yellow markers once again, north then east, along a beautiful wooded hill flank via lanes and tracks to the scattering of houses which is Gourre. From here, descend for about 2 kilometres to the splendidly restored rural museum and historic paper-making mill of Richard de Bas. Here, on any day of the year (barring Christmas), you can see one of man's miracle inventions created originally where there was a natural – and copious – supply of wood and water. For many centuries Ambert was the paper-making capital of France, while today the Richard de Bas mill is the last of its kind, dating back to 1326. Here you may still see paper being made by hand in the ancient craftsman's way. The living quarters of a nineteenth-century paper-maker and his family can also be seen in the little museum; another evocative and memorable glimpse into a totally bygone past. The footpath continues north-west from the mill along the D57, before turning north once more for the final uphill leg back to the hamlet of Vimal.

Note: During July and August there are organised rambles arranged for Ambert camp ground visitors by the Syndicat d'Initiative, starting from the town's famous municipal Round House on certain afternoons. The walks are routed through some of the most beautiful Livradois-Forez region and are generally 15–20 kilometres in distance. For solo walkers, there is an information pack available, describing no less than twenty-two short to medium-distance walks in the area.

A Two-Hour Stroll through Medieval Auvergne

It's something of a local joke that tourists often confuse Puy de Dôme with Le Puy, or Le Puy Velay as it is more fully named. To confuse the issue even further, Puy de Dôme is in the département of Le Puy, while

Le Puy Velay is the préfecture of Haute Loire. About 130 kilometres separate the two, and strangers are often aggrieved to find that they are not near neighbours. Both places are high on the sightseeing agenda for Auvergne visitors, and they do share volcanic settings of a most dramatic nature. As far as Le Puy Velay is concerned, it is the man-made embellishment to quirky nature which is the prime attraction and which entitles the place to call itself the 'city of art and history'. It is spectacular enough to warrant a place in the list of Auvergne pilgrimages, not least because the enlightened city fathers have seen fit to colour-code pedestrian circuits around the old, upper town, of two to three hours' duration *and* provide free pamphlets and maps (in English if requested), at the central tourist office. This is not at all well signposted, so drive to the town centre and find somewhere to park adjacent to the taxi rank in Place du

Le Puy – St Michael's Needle and chapel from Camping Bouthezard.

Breuil. A one-way system operates which is simply a mini ring road. After leaving the tourist office, continue to the municipal camp ground (which *is* well publicised) beside the river Borne, adjacent to the sporting complex, which boasts a heated swimming pool and is only five minutes' stroll from the town centre.

Camping Bouthezard is a 3-star site, with a slightly inflated tariff on account of the much-esteemed town it serves; however, it is not prohibitive. A smallish ground, accommodating some 80 units, it is level, well kept, with clean utilities and *very* hot water to showers and toilets. Open from 15 April to 15 October, Bouthezard is virtually surrounded by buildings, yet manages somehow to retain a pleasing rural air. Conveniently, the site is located beneath one of the phenomenal Le Puy attractions, the St Michel d'Aiguille Dyke (St Michael's Needle), on the top of which is perched, most improbably, a remarkable tenth-century chapel of almost perfect proportions. The needle is an 80-metre high volcanic peak which may be assailed almost directly from the camp ground. There is a small entry fee to pay for the privilege of climbing some very steep steps, and admiring not only the outstanding façade and the distant views, but the ingenuity of those medieval craftsmen who built this eyrie of faith.

Not quite so remarkable (or artistically elegant) is a huge statue of the Virgin and Child (Notre Dame de France), cast in gunmetal from captured cannons after the Battle of Sebastopol. This 27-metre figure, topping a volcanic plinth of 757 metres, towers above Le Puy and is an unmistakable landmark for miles around. The great cathedral however is the most magnificent of the lofty structures, built literally on the side of Mont Anis. The

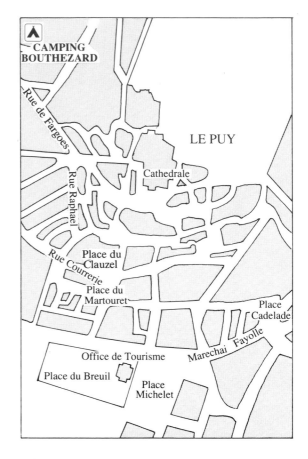

mighty façade plainly echoes the influence of Moorish architecture, prevalent in many of the eleventh- and twelfth-century churches throughout Europe.

Between the volcanic high-rise attractions of Le Puy and the celebrated Crozatier Museum of Archaeology and Lace Work from the sixteenth century, there are many houses, squares and tortuous cobbled streets dating from the eleventh to the thirteenth centuries – a veritable maze of the past revealed to the observant walker following the colour-coded pedestrian routes. While Le

Puy is not a base for lovers of pastoral France, it is worth staying a day or two for an enjoyable ramble around a lovely old town full of atmosphere and character. Particularly evocative is the ancient Porte and rue Goutheron, and the rue des Tables, where medieval stall-holders once displayed their produce above the shining *pavé*.

Other Regional Options

Another Auvergne enclave which must be advocated is a strategic stopover on the N7, about 350 kilometres south of Paris. The Bourbonnais township of Lapalisse is clustered around an imposing fifteenth-century château and is home to some 5,000 people who have, in their wisdom, created a real haven of a municipal camp ground. Situated immediately adjacent to what were once the château gardens and bisected by the gentle river Besbre, the site is modern, impeccably maintained and most reasonable for a 2-star enterprise which provides hot showers at no extra charge. The town centre is just ten minutes' stroll away via the sports complex and delightful riverside gardens. There is good shopping, including a choice of supermarkets, and the château is open to visitors. Many treasures of the past are displayed here including, rather mysteriously, the golden anchor worn by Nelson at the Battle of Trafalgar.

Lapalisse is a little bit of Auvergne heaven,
save for one serious flaw – the flow of countless TIRs that thunder through the narrow centre of this tiny town which is unlucky enough to be sited on a major route between Paris and Lyon. If ever a by-pass were justified it is here, around this lovely remnant of old France. There is relative tranquillity on the camping ground – distanced from the road by tall trees and sports pitches – plus two objectives within reasonable distance which make stopping worthwhile. The first, about 20 kilometres to the south-west, is Vichy – a name to incite disdain with older Britons perhaps, but an elegant (if ostentatious) thermal spa created with no expense spared in the late nineteenth century, the *belle époque*. The setting, on the banks of the wide Allier river, is sparkling. If you haven't seen Pétain's collaborationist capital of World War II before, the diversion is worth the effort.

For another Auvergne walker's delight, take the blissfully quiet and scarcely-used D7 and D25 south from Lapalisse to Châtel Montagne, in the beautiful lower Besbre valley. There are some fine waymarked trails here through forest terrain, including a superb five-hour trek along the GR3 in the main, to St Nicolas-des-Biefs, perched nearly 1,000 metres high. There is *Gîte d'Etape* accommodation here and camping facilities at nearby La Verrerie, a ski centre in winter. This is another little-visited corner of the region, and one which is strongly recommended.

Bourgogne

Départements: Côte-d'Or – Nièvre – Saône-et-Loire – Yonne
Préfecture: Dijon

Parc Régional du Morvan

Synonymous with those exemplary wines from the eastern part of the region, Burgundy's vineyard wealth begins at Dijon and winds south through opulent Beaune, Chalon and Mâcon. Drier and sunnier than the centre, both territory and climate are near-perfect for wine production, a fact that the Romans soon discovered and that the Dukes of Burgundy later exploited.

There have been centuries of affluence and stability for Saône valley Bourgogne, embracing the départements of Côte d'Or and Saône-et-Loire, but not such a happy past for the central départements of Yonne and Nièvre; especially the latter, since it was yet one more area – and a large one – which was beginning to be seriously affected by population evaporation.

The solution was to create another *parc naturel*, extol the assets of the region, make them accessible and attract the new citified generation back to the wide open spaces, if not as residents, then as paying guests.

The Morvan Nature Park was decreed by national government in 1970. It is a huge swathe of land fed primarily by the Cure and Yonne rivers, and the designated area extends from Vézelay in the north, to below Autun southwards, touching on all four regional départements. The heartland is the granite rock region amid Bourgogne chalkstone, known for a long time as the Morvan, giving the young nature park its name. It is not one of France's spectacularly scenic areas, but it is none the less lush green and delightful in its comparative uniformity – a seemingly endless succession of densely wooded hill ranges which unroll one after the other to a French infinity. Where the woods do break for meadow pasture they are dotted with the ubiquitous Charolais cattle, now exported to over 60 countries and as popular as that other Burgundy white, Chablis.

There is no town of any size within this huge landscape and, apart from the N6 which bisects the north-east corner of the park, not much in the way of major roads. The area is ideal, therefore, to fulfil the requirements of an anxious government; namely to give more life to the economy, to develop open air and cultural activity, to preserve historic places and landscape, and above all to encourage visitors.

For the leisure walker few of the twenty-three French nature parks can provide better facilities or opportunities than this one, especially for those pedestrian explorers who enjoy ascending some of the easier hills of France, along tracks frequently tree-shaded from the high summer sun. This is one reason why the GR13, which runs north to south through the entire length of the park, is so popular. The Tour de Morvan, another long-distance trail which touches upon the main lakes of the park, has gained so rapidly in prestige that a chain of ten *Gîtes d'Étape* has been set up at 19- to 27-kilometre intervals, around the entire 220-kilometre circuit. The lakes – Chaumecon, St Agnan, Settons and Pannesière – are great scenic attractions. They are given over partially to leisure activity, where all the usual holiday amenities may be found, but are carefully controlled and limited in extent. The landscape is about as close as you will get, in the heart of Continental Europe, to true woodland wilderness.

The other attractions are the villages and hamlets, most of which appear to be almost untouched by the march of time. Château-Chinon is the Morvan historic jewel; the only real township actually situated within the park boundaries. It enjoys rave notices from the Bourgogne publicity machine, mainly for its 600-metre high setting and the extensive views from the Butte de Calvaire above the small town. It was an ancient settlement of importance, it does have Napoleonic connections and there is an archaeological and folklore museum, but on the whole, it disappoints when compared to Vézelay. It is, though, the capital of Morvan and, apart from a useful information office, it is blessed with a small supermarket which dispenses slightly cut-price petrol. Both commodities are distinctly rare elsewhere in the park. There is a convenient 2-star camp ground, the municipal Perthuy d'Oiseau, which is open from 1 May to 30 September.

North-east of here, via a delightful and almost traffic-free foresters' road (the D37),

is the village of Montsauche; another isolated yet far from immune settlement which suffered badly during the war for Resistance activities. A short distance away is one of the acknowledged centres in the park, Lac des Settons, a 360-hectare catchment created from the river Cure.

There are three camp grounds in the vicinity. I found Camping l'Hermitage the most agreeable – attractively located amid its densely-wooded peninsula surroundings, providing all facilities including a shop and bar, and above all very strategic for lakeside strolling or longer hikes, since it is also an official refuge for the GR13 Vézelay-Autun trail. Marked routes for strollers or trekkers are plainly obvious direct from the site; blue for the former, red/white for the latter. Located on the left bank and signposted 'rive gauche', l'Hermitage is close to the hamlet of Chevigny, 7 kilometres south-east of Montsauche. There is a somewhat tortuous though well-indicated approach road to this $2\frac{1}{2}$-hectare spread, which is open from 1 April to 30 September, and rates the 3-star category.

Apart from the lakeside paths, there is a choice of circuit trails varying from 15 to 38 kilometres in length in the area of the lakes. The nearest to Lac des Settons is the Montsauche Trail, 28 kilometres long but with optional variants of 19 and 16 kilometres. The route winds south-west for some 8 kilometres, mainly along woodland trails but with some lane sections, to Ouroux where there is a camp ground and a *Gîte d'Étape*. It returns east via the high and wooded ground of the Forêt d'Argoulais, reaching 646 metres in altitude *en route* before descending again to the lake shore via the hamlet of l'Huis Gaumont. It is a well-marked and obviously well-used trail, but like

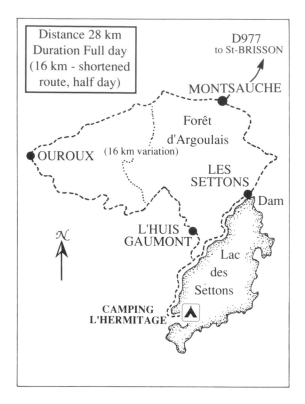

Distance 28 km
Duration Full day
(16 km - shortened
route, half day)

D977
to St-BRISSON

MONTSAUCHE

Forêt
d'Argoulais
(16 km variation)

OUROUX

LES
SETTONS

Dam

N

L'HUIS
GAUMONT

Lac
des
Settons

CAMPING
L'HERMITAGE

so many footpath routes in France you'll find yourself more or less alone with nature outside late July and August (when it is almost too hot for comfortable walking anyway). I spent five hours tramping a section of the GR13 in late June and met just one other walker; and he was Dutch!

For any prolonged stay in this part of Bourgogne, a visit to St Brisson and the Maison du Parc is strongly advised. It is located some 10 kilometres north of Lac des Settons and the minor road route is clearly signposted. Housed within an isolated and rambling old château is a first-class information centre where park brochures are freely dispensed. Tour du Morvan Topo-Guides are also sold, together with IGN maps of the area to a scale of 1:100,000. No walker could wish for more precise local intelligence. The château itself has an interesting character, being sur-

rounded by a deer park and lake, and containing a Museum of *la Résistance*. Watch carefully on approach, for although it is well signposted, the location is secluded and not obviously apparent.

Needless to say, there is a circuit path from St Brisson hamlet which has *Gîte d'Étape* accommodation. A municipal campsite will be found at Dun-les-Places village, 5 kilometres north-west. This circuit, called Dolmen Chevresse, covers 20 kilometres in full, but there are 14- and 11-kilometre alternatives. Again, this path explores some richly-wooded hill country, traversing part of the Forêt Domaniale de Breuil and touching upon some minuscule backwater hamlets *en route*.

Accolay

Camping almost *au naturel* and wandering the wooded hills for days on end, you begin to assume that all Burgundy is Le Morvan. It is largely true that all the best countryside in any given region (for outdoor pursuits at least) is contained within nature park boundaries, but there are exceptions. One Burgundian example is the area around the little hamlet of Accolay in the département of Yonne. Here, the knowledgeable traveller in France may wonder how majestic Cluny, that fount of the tenth-century Christian world could be excluded, or those heady vineyards of Nuits-St-Georges. Well, motorway and main-road motorists will discover both sooner or later, but you could easily overlook Accolay in 30 years or more of traversing France. This is a great pity, for this backwater delight is a microcosm of that bygone France which has now all but vanished. To find it, you have to turn off the N6 between Auxerre and Avallon about 2 kilometres west of Vermenton (itself a pretty enough village largely devoted to the potter's art).

There is nothing spectacular or dramatic about Accolay, but its old-world appeal and timeless tranquillity are seductive. The houses, nestling around the twelfth-century church, are ancient but lovingly restored and maintained. There is just the butcher, baker and one general store, plus a couple of small hotel-restaurants and a municipal camp ground (donated by a local family). It makes a charming diversion worthy of more than a fleeting visit. The river Cure bounces merrily around the outskirts and there is a short section of the Canal du Nivernais, which now carries only the odd pleasure cruiser. Five minutes' stroll along the towpath is all it takes from camp ground to village centre, or you may walk for as long as you wish along the waterside, north or south.

Accolay dates from the sixth century and remnants of its ancient fortifications still exist. In the mid-nineteenth century it supported 1,200 people, mostly boatmen and wine-growers. The population was reduced to a couple of hundred after a disastrous outbreak of vine-pest, and the inhabitants now number just 360. Most occupy the centre, still rich with sixteenth- and seventeenth-century dwellings; although there is a small scattering of modern houses on the village perimeter, these are unobtrusive.

The camping site is simple, but very clean and with all necessary facilities. A 1-hectare patch of level, tree-shaded grass, it is open from 1 April to 30 September. The only other sound to disturb the bird-song here is the village clock, which chimes the hours twice – three minutes apart – as if to emphasise the spirit of French independence.

Two other portals of backwater Bourgogne open at Accolay. The first is a north–south stretch of the GR13 which winds down the pretty Vallée de la Cure, more or less parallel to the N6 though hidden from it, and a local *petite randonnée* loop of optional 21 or 26 kilometres. The other circumnavigates particularly pleasant terrain of low, wooded hills, between easy-distance villages and hamlets like Bessy-sur-Cure (where there is a *Gîte d'Étape*), Mailly-la-Ville and Ste Pallaye. The woods and escarpments of the Vallée-de-Régny, just south of Accolay, are especially scenic.

At Mailly-la-Ville, the immediate scenery changes abruptly from gentle water meadows to miniature canyon country above the Nivernnais Canal. The volcanic upthrust is only very local but is dramatic enough to create a rock outcrop worthy of learner-climbers' attention. The Rochers du Saussois are most impressive, rising sheer from the banks of the canal between Mailly-la-Ville and Chatel-Censoir. For those who fancy a spot of rock scrambling as a change from walking, the views from the top are splendid. For others, the tow path walk from the vicinity of the rock faces, southwards to Chatel-Censoir some 3 kilometres away, is most agreeable.

Avallon and Vézelay

The Accolay camp ground, with its maple tree shade and friendly atmosphere, is a restful base from which to explore those two historic high spots of Bourgogne, Avallon and Vézelay.

Avallon – once a night-halt for Roman legions using the Via Agrippa between Autun and Sens – is a name of fame and the reality

The Basilica of Sainte Madeleine Vézelay, a pilgrim shrine of Burgundy since the ninth century.

does not disappoint. A Duke of Burgundy stronghold, the town is a diligently preserved piece of living history. The new Avallon is not allowed to encroach too much into the original centre, which endured a very turbulent past. There are three splendid rampart walks high above the river Cousin, all clearly waymarked, from $1\frac{1}{2}$ to 3 hours' duration, with street maps and guides (in English), available from the tourist office in the old town centre. There is a pleasant campsite about 2 kilometres along the pretty Vallée de Cousin in a steep-sided rocky amphitheatre. This particular campsite is, rather predictably, extremely busy throughout the summer months.

Vézelay, if anything, is even more popular than Avallon, despite its comparatively small size. Virtually a national shrine and a place of pilgrimage since the ninth century, the setting of the massive basilica Ste Madeleine is superbly striking, with its wooded hill and steep street approach lined with old houses. It was here that St Bernard preached for the Second Crusade and Richard the Lionheart launched the Third Crusade. Today it is one of the most hallowed religious plots in all France. There is a camp ground at Vézelay but again it is usually crowded. It is also very small and distinctly sloping. There is also a Youth Hostel. After you have wandered around the historic heights (car parking is obligatory in the lower square), the restful alternative is to return to the haven of Accolay, roughly 27 kilometres from both Avallon and Vézelay.

Puisaye – Burgundy's By-passed Region

Anyone motoring south-east from the Channel ports, perhaps towards Switzerland, is usually ready for a rest period more substantial than an overnight halt once they are 180 kilometres south of Paris. An ideal place to fulfil this need will be found in one of the prettiest corners of Burgundy, known as La Puisaye. It is to Bourgogne what the Solonge is to the region of Centre – an undesignated *parc naturel*, or, as it would be called in Britain, an area of outstanding natural beauty. This particular swathe of terrain is a richly-wooded and watered one between the Loire and the Yonne to the south-west of Auxerre and the A6 *autoroute*.

The pride of Puisaye, tucked away in a sparsely populated part of central France, is unquestionably St Fargeau, a town which has an historic past and is a true delight to the contemporary eye. A marvellous medieval château, a venerable belfry and a cluster of ancient houses lining narrow, twisting streets compete for visual attention in a very compact central area. All around, beyond the old town confines, are the 'bright and dark waters' of countless *étangs*, as described by the writer Colette, together with regal forest spreads, dominating the gentle rounded hills. Some 6 kilometres south-east of St Fargeau there is a great expanse of shining water, the Reservoir du Bourdon, served by an excellent 2-star municipal camp ground.

Burgundy, watered as richly as it is wooded, has about 200 kilometres of rivers and canals – the region is a catchment area of France's three principal rivers, the Seine, the Loire and the Rhône. From the seventeenth century, a series of canals was dug across the region to link the three river basins. Hence, barraging is commonplace in Burgundy and nowhere in France have they honed the technique to a finer art. Lac Bourdon looks as though it has existed since

The tranquil walking area at Lac Bourdon.

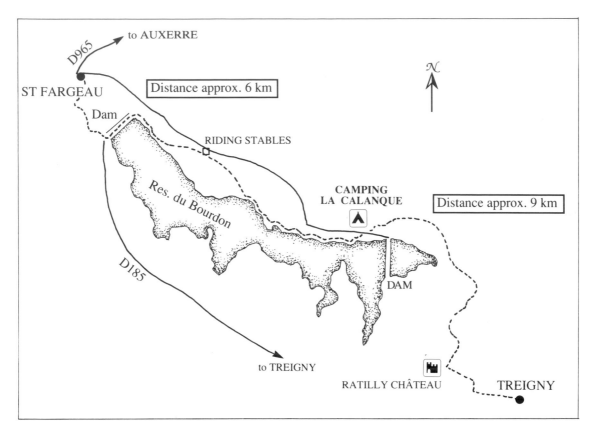

the dawn of time. The sandy shorelines shelve gently, and the irregular shape and encroaching woodland paint a picture of a miniature backwoods Canada. From Camping Calanque, situated at the water's edge, there is a very pleasant walk of about 3 kilometres to the lake dam along a tree-shaded bridle path, barred to motor vehicles after an initial half-kilometre or so. This pedestrian route is a well-marked section of the long-distance Tour de Puisaye, a 220-kilometre circuit of eleven days' duration, with overnight *gîtes* at regular intervals. For those who might consider this as a holiday walk, detailed information is available at the Puisaye park office in St Fargeau.

The short local section follows the shoreline faithfully for a while, then veers to pass a farm and riding stables (from which they organise equestrian *randonnées*), ascending gently afterwards, to give elevated views across the lake and distant forest. The path touches the tarmac road briefly, then returns to the lake shore and the dam, which it crosses, continuing along a valley ridge almost into St Fargeau. The dam, brick-built and mellow-looking to blend sympathetically with the surroundings, is the popular turn-back point, but the waymarking is excellent and you may be tempted to press on to colourful St Fargeau.

For another agreeable walk, turn left at the gates of La Calanque and you will join the south-eastern section of the Tour de Puisaye, which leads past the splendid thirteenth-century château Ratilly and into the time-

The thirteenth-century Ratilly château near St Fargeau, where there is a genuine air of old France.

passed village of Treigny. This is another enjoyable excursion of about 9 kilometres, at first along a bridle path (shared with horses), then through woodland, along an ancient footpath (again, well waymarked, if a trifle muddy in patches). You really need to allow a full day for either the St Fargeau out-and-back walk, or the walk to Treigny and Ratilly château, for there is plenty to savour on either trail of man-made and natural Burgundian beauty.

The St Fargeau camping ground is both spacious and shady, covering some six hec-

tares of mainly level, lightly wooded ground. There are 270 landscaped arbour pitches provided, many with mains electric hook-ups. Three sanitary blocks (with hot showers at set hours), are clean and serviceable, if not exceptional. The site is open from 1 April to 31 October and the tariff is low (considering the beauty-spot setting). There is a restaurant and snack bar opposite the site entrance on the *plage*, but no site shop, so stock up with all necessities in St Fargeau before arrival.

A *Sentier* to the Source of the Seine

Like Old Father Thames, the Seine is held in special national esteem – the mother of France's rivers, if not the longest or the most exciting. It has been inextricably woven into French post-revolutionary history from the moment the Bastille was stormed in 1789 less than half a mile from its water. The vital importance of this premier French river to the life of the capital was recognised during the reign of Napoleon III, when the consul-general of the Seine département, the influential Baron Haussmann, forwarded a proposal to create a monument to its source. In 1867 a significant, slightly flamboyant *grotte* and commemorative garden were created at the place where the most illustrious river of France sprang from the earth, in north-eastern Burgundy. It was of course paid for by the département of Seine.

You can drive direct to the source, but the most romantic way of seeing it is to approach by the GR2 from the village of Chanceaux, which straddles the N71 south of Chatillon-sur-Seine. There is a simple but clean and agreeable municipal camp ground here (open 15 April to 30 September), and the GR is joined in the village centre, to the south of the N71, to follow a well marked country lane route for a couple of kilometres. At a small barrage and *étang*, a track is joined off the D103C and in another 2 kilometres of very pleasant woodland walking the GR leads directly to the site. Like most other worshippers at the shrine, you will probably feel compelled to toss a centime or two into the water, at the feet of the sculptured maiden. This walk is indicated as being of one and half hour's duration, but two hours plus is probably more realistic, unless you happen to be very athletic. At any rate this is a very enjoyable half-day out-and-back excursion from Chanceaux. There is a café, naturally, close to the source for half-way refreshment. Gazing at the tiny trickle of new water welling up from the foot of the statue, it is fascinating to speculate on its imminent journey half across France to spill eventually into that mighty Seine estuary 500 kilometres distant, below Le Havre, and into the English Channel.

'The stairs to the wine cellars lead straight to Heaven' (Burgundian proverb)

Burgundy for many Britons is synonymous only with wine and for passionate wine-lovers, Beaune is Burgundy at its best. The vineyard slopes around Beaune and neighbouring Nuits-St-George are excessively publicised, so that other virtues of the area are often relegated to footnote status. Enjoy the grape of course, but remember that Beaune is a very old Burgundy town indeed, with one of the most splendid and ancient centre-piece buildings to be found in France, or indeed anywhere else in Europe.

The story of the creation of this building – the world-famous Hôtel-Dieu – is almost as fascinating as the glittering structure itself. Apparently it was conceived and built by a Burgundian accountant as an act of atonement for cooking the books! A medieval hospice for the poor, it was a wonderful success and it has survived, gloriously intact, from the year 1443. All around the rainbow mosaic which is the crowning pinnacle of the Hôtel-Dieu there is a maze of charming narrow streets, little squares and semi-pedestrian walks, with evidence everywhere of the town's assured niche in French wine-soaked history. Just a few of the gems are the fifteenth-century basilica of Notre Dame, the wine museum in the Hotel des Ducs, the thirteenth-century belfry and, of course, the ramparts which remind the visitor that this was once the very heart of medieval Burgundy. Allow a full day to see Beaune properly, either by staying at the town camp ground in the rue Dubois (open 15 March to 31 October), or by parking on the extreme outskirts, for vehicle-saturation of the town centre is almost always total.

A very agreeable alternative to seeing both Beaune and the half-hidden delights of the surrounding countryside is to keep right away from the skein of arterial roads and *auto-routes* which now beset the Beaune valley region. Some 8 kilometres to the north-west, for example, on the green route D970, there is Bligny-sur-Ouche and its neighbouring village of Lusigny-sur-Ouche. The former has a clean and simple 2-star municipal camp ground beside a restored section of old railway, now an acknowledged visitor attraction. Lusigny, just 2 kilometres distant, has a picturesque lane and track walk to the source of the river Ouche in the centre of a lovely

Beaune and part of the magical Hôtel-Dieu, one of the most magnificent fifteenth-century buildings in existence.

wooded valley. After overnighting at Bligny (which also boasts a choice of pedestrian high valley woodland walks from above the old village church), you can approach Beaune by the most beautiful of country roads. The narrow D104, which traverses the Monts d'Or and the Hautes Côtes de Beaune, owes nothing scenically to the vineyards which are so ubiquitous lower down the valley. This really is unspoiled high country, all the more remarkable for its proximity to the busiest north–south road artery system of France. Pause at the high point of this short but revealing drive, just outside the old hamlet of Crépey, to look down to the *autoroute* toll booth in its forest clearing – so distant as to

be totally inaudible, and so pointedly alien to the remainder of the sweeping panorama. This road descends eventually to join the D2 at the attractive and surprisingly rural neighbour of Beaune, Savigny-lès-Beaune, less than 4 kilometres from the erstwhile capital city of the Duchy of Burgundy.

Savigny-lès-Beaune, like Bligny, has its speciality tourist attraction, a comprehensive motor-cycle museum housed within a majestic fourteenth-century château, which any driver weaned on the two-wheeled iron horse will find fascinating. Savigny also has a 2-star camping ground which could be a serious contender for the Site of the Year award held by Conques in the Midi-Pyrénées. This

55

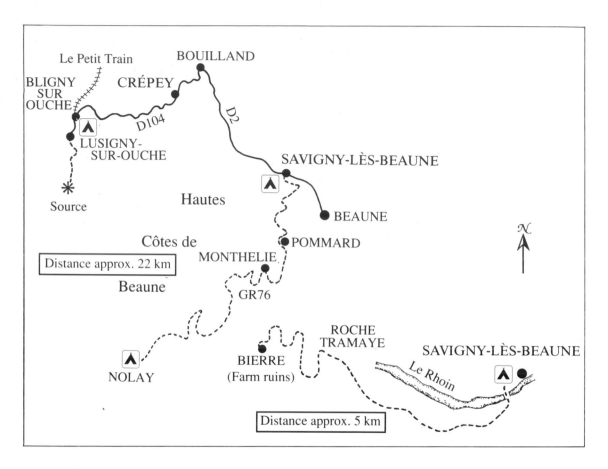

Le Petit Train

BLIGNY
SUR
OUCHE

CRÉPEY

BOUILLAND

D104

D2

LUSIGNY-
SUR-OUCHE

SAVIGNY-LÈS-BEAUNE

Source

Hautes

BEAUNE

Côtes de

POMMARD

MONTHELIE

Distance approx. 22 km

Beaune

GR76

ROCHE
TRAMAYE

SAVIGNY-LÈS-BEAUNE

NOLAY

BIERRE
(Farm ruins)

Le Rhoin

Distance approx. 5 km

N

municipal enterprise is lovingly landscaped and tended, and earns marks on all counts. The toilet block houses facilities which compare with a quality hotel, there is a choice of tree-shaded or open lawn pitching, the ground is level, the noise level is low (despite the minor road forming one boundary), and the distant views are of densely wooded valley flanks. There is a pleasant, largely waterside walk into Savigny (15 minutes), along the banks of the sparkling Rhoin, plus some attractive hill walks near to the camp ground.

One hill walk winds north-west past La Roche Tramaye and Vierge de Poutot to the ancient farm ruins of Bierre, approximately five kilometres distant. Several local footpath routes are helpfully mapped at the camp entrance, while further information is available for pedestrian explorers at the Syndicat d'Initiative, which is situated beside Savigny post office. An excellent long-stay base is Camping Premier Prés, which is aptly named since *premier prés* loosely translates as 'almost perfect'.

Bretagne

Départements: Côtes-du-Nord – Finistère – Ille-et-Vilaine – Morbihan
Préfecture: Rennes

Anyone taking the cross-Channel ferry from Portsmouth to St Malo may anticipate a visual treat. The port is a sparkling anchorage amid a skein of offshore islands, with all the stunning impact of the French seaboard at its most beautiful. It is a natural jewel of northern Brittany on the Emerald Coast, so called for the variety of contrasting green waters. It also boasts a wealth of man-made elegance: St Malo itself is a majestic ancient walled city and fortress in an astounding state of preservation. It is only slightly disappointing to learn that the original was all but obliterated during the last war and that here is yet another restoration miracle of the second French Renaissance. The maze of narrow, busy streets within the great walls is fascinating to wander around, and the seascapes across the narrow waters to neighbouring Dinard are consistently delightful. Indeed, there could scarcely be a more exhilarating starting point to any tour of Brittany.

However, there is an equally pleasing, far more rural patch on the northern perimeter of the coastline, especially for those who relish using their own two feet. To get there, drive south-west to Lamballe, then join the expressway for St Brieuc, there picking up the D786 minor road which winds its coastal way north to Paimpol. Just before you enter the port and town there is Kérity village, with a 2-star municipal camping ground. On the seaward side, hard by the ruined abbey of Beauport, Camping Crukin is a level, hedge-divided site with room for 200 touring units on the edge of the village, and almost literally at the edge of the sea. The toilet block here is modern and well appointed, with hot water for clothes and dishwashing and hot showers for small additional charge. Mains electricity is available and the charges are modest. The site is open from Easter to 15 September. The views seaward are distinctly enticing, particularly since there is a well-marked footpath directly accessible from the site, leading in both directions. This is a recommended base, within a few yards of Kérity village, which boasts a post office, *boulangerie*, store and, of course, a central café.

To satisfy more comprehensive needs, all will be found in Paimpol, some 2 kilometres away either by road or via the coast path and back lanes.

Britanny is a region that is distinctly different from others. The place-names, which unmistakably reflect the Breton language, are, for the most part, quite un-French. Take Paimpol, for example; in the immediate environs there are towns and villages called Ploubazlanec, Plouézec, Plourivo, Kerfot,

St Malo, the most majestic of France's deep water ports. The walled town is a masterpiece of contemporary restoration.

mulating populace in an equally stimulating enclave of France. No wonder Brittany (or Britany, to use its alternative spelling) is so very popular with Britons. After the Côte d'Azur, it comes equal second in the great holiday league, along with the Dordogne and the Loire Valley.

Brittany has that comforting touch of *déjà vu* (important to some who venture abroad), particularly for those who have ever toured Britain's western coastline from the Cornish peninsula, through west Wales, or the western Highlands; plus that French stamp of spaciousness to complement a landscape

Yvias, and Kérity. The names seem to be part Balkan, and part Cornish, with overtones of Welsh. The terrain is hardly typical of *la belle France* either. Both coastal and inland, the landscape is sometimes reminiscent of Ireland or the Western Highlands of Scotland, but seldom if ever identifiable as part of the French Republic. It is not surprising, then, that the people themselves are also subtly if unmistakably different.

Of course, this is a staunchly Celtic corner of France, where the people are still deeply religious, still obsessed with the hereafter and the mystic past, where Bretons come first and French second. It is a not uncommon individualism, and is seen too in the Cornish, the Welsh, the Western Highlanders and, above all, the Irish. The distinctive traits they have of north-west European people are shown in their language, attitude and outlook on life. They are at once charming, poetic, intelligent, a trifle chaotic, wildly optimistic yet often given to sombre reflection – a sti-

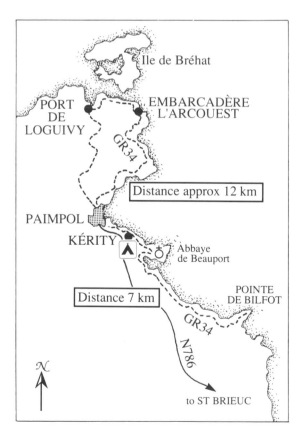

on the grand scale. It is not too far from their homeland, is geared to tourism nowadays, and has some fine footpaths to explore, so it is understandable that Brittany is the first choice with many British tourists.

If you want a spectacularly typical example of the northern Bretagne coast, then Paimpol will provide it. Essentially still a working port, with just a modicum of tourist development, it is a small yet bustling settlement slotted most attractively between low and craggy headlands. In essence it is a fisherman's town, with a fine intake of the fruits of the sea displayed and dispensed from the thronged market stalls. There is pleasant walking in the vicinity, all the way from Kérity through Paimpol, and on to the northern part of the convoluted bay, at Embarcadère l'Arcouest. Here, if you feel so inclined, you may take a launch to car-free Ile de Bréhat, the haunt of countless happy and protected sea birds. This offshore sanctuary is a very popular excursion with French visitors, and there is parking for 1,000 cars at the embarkation point.

A little further west from here another port is tucked away, pretty and quite unspoiled, called Loguivy. From here back to Paimpol,

Paimpol open market. Garlic and seafood are specialities of the area.

it is about 6 kilometres via country lanes, and a possible day-long hike for those who do double this distance via the coast path. If you wish you can follow the tortuous route of the GR34, which is still largely narrow-lane coastal walking, although tracing the many bays and inlets more faithfully.

For a coast path alternative from the Crukin camping ground, turn south at the foreshore entrance and wend your way around the imposing Abbaye de Beauport, towards Pointe de Bilfot. There are some lovely vistas northwards from this route, across the Ile St Riom and Ile de Bréhat. The views to the south-east are equally pleasing, along the southbound section of the GR34 which you are now treading.

It is a natural inclination of the British visitor to compare Brittany with Cornwall, which it does resemble quite uncannily in parts around the northern and western coasts. Central Bretagne, however, is passably more attractive than Cornwall's tree-starved hinterland and is, of course, infinitely larger. Also, the sun shines more consistently.

There are one or two very appealing areas in the Armorican Highlands (Armorica being the ancient Celtic name of the region), including that surrounding Lac de Guerlédan, roughly in the centre of the huge peninsula, due south of Paimpol. There is fairly gentle though richly-wooded terrain here, the centre-piece being a man-made lake created in 1929 to provide the area with electricity. Many years have imparted a natural patina to this expansive water and the surrounding country, now part of the Brest–Nantes canal, which traverses the whole of Brittany from north-west to south-east. There is tranquil towpath walking along this masterpiece of navigation which links the rivers Aulne and Blavet, and some fine paths too, on either side of the barraged lake, through beautiful and serene woodland, with one or two abrupt escarpments above the waterline. The southern shore is traced by a section of the GR341, a well-tramped and well-marked trail, blazed with the familiar red and white markers.

The walking potential is splendid, and there is also a delightful base camp from which to explore, close to the village of Mur-de-Bretagne. Mur lies at the eastern end of the lake, which stretches for about 14 kilometres to Gouarec westwards, while in

Woodland routes of splendour network Lac de Guerlédan and the Nantes-Brest canal.

between lie some 3,000 hectares of a mixed woodland *massif*, criss-crossed by feeder-streams and punctuated with some impressive rock outcrops. From the village, follow the clear signposts to the water's edge and the 2-star municipal campsite, Camping Rond Point du Lac. A genuine tourist site exclusively for transient visitors, the camp ground is set among trees, provides clean, modern facilities, and is quiet (according to the local tourist office) even in August. Pitching is on three spacious terraces, with a choice of shady or open locations; there are hot showers, hot water for dishwashing and mains electric hook-ups are provided. There is room for 133 units, the charges are reasonable and the site is open from 15 June to 15 September. There is a café and small leisure complex at the adjacent lakeside, while shopping and most other needs are met by the village, which also boasts a tourist information pavilion.

Not surprisingly, it is the footpaths that are the major attraction in this area and one of the most enterprising starts immediately from the camping ground. It follows farm lanes for a couple of kilometres then crosses the head of the lake via a sluice gate below the barrage, before turning north then west to follow the lake shore to Les Forges des Salles, about 10 kilometres away. There is a *Gîte d'Étape* at the half-way mark if you feel that an out-and-back trek of 24 kilometres might be too ambitious.

For a short walk introduction to this interesting terrain, turn immediately north from the camping ground and follow the distinctive waterside path for 3 kilometres. This trail eventually meets up with the tarmac perimeter road, although in between is a placid scene of woodland and water harmony. This is another of those seductive corners of France which could well hold you for much longer than you intended. It is not only lovely country, but it is also wonderfully uncrowded, being well away from the main tourist routes, and having appeal, in the main, only for leisure walkers and long-distance backpackers.

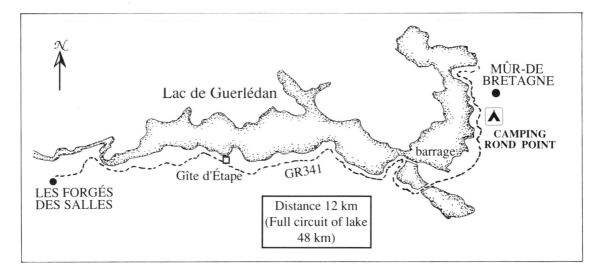

One section of the southern Brittany seaboard is appropriately named the Coté des Mégalithes. At the southern end within the sheltered waters of the Morbihan gulf, is the location of one of the strangest of prehistoric relics in Europe, the Menhirs of Carnac. A silent legion of massive standing stones, clustered in three major groups and littering open heathland just above the town, these petrified avenues run roughly east to west and are as much a mystery to archaeologists as Britain's Stonehenge or Avebury Circle. There is a staggering total of almost 3,000 stones, erected about 4,500 years ago, and including dolmen graves and cromlechs; they are testimony to the ancient significance of the site. It is conjectured that the menhirs originated as places of worship, or as a complex astronomical calendar reference. Whatever they might represent, they are profoundly impressive and somehow appropriate in this Celtic corner of France. They still baffle all the scientific experts.

'Les Alignements' of Menec, Kermario and Kerlescan – assuredly representing countless hours of back-breaking labour – cover an area of 3 kilometres, the serried ranks being 100 metres wide or more. To walk these strange avenues, especially early or late in the day, is an absorbing, almost eerie experience. Protected by law, the area has been left as natural as possible and it creates a vivid contrast to the beach scene a short distance away. Carnac-Plage is a smart seaside resort, as magnetic for its fine-sand beaches and sheltered location as for its unique prehistoric treasure. The township of Carnac is attractively old-world, not much more than an overgrown village, and it is served by no less than twenty campsites in the vicinity, ranging from a 1-star *air-naturel* paddock to a string of

3- and 4-star touring parks offering luxury amenities. A typical and agreeable example is the Moulin de Kermeaux, a spacious landscaped ground amid woodland, with lots of privacy bays and high-standard facilities. One of the closest sites to the ancient stones, which dominate the landscape immediately outside the entrance, Kermeaux is open from 1 April to 15 September and there are 120 pitches. The tariff, as with every French resort of renown, is high.

There are several pleasant short walks in the area, the most significant being that which traverses the extensive site of the standing stones. A modestly-priced itinerary sheet is available from the tourist office at Carnac-Plage, entitled Promenade No 2. This is a 7-kilometre stroll across wooded and heath countryside to the north of the town, taking in the hamlets of Cloucarnac and Kermario. It is signposted with yellow and white markers and the walking time is approximately 2 hours. For more revealing information about the Carnac megaliths, visit the well-displayed artefacts in the archaeological museum. This was founded in 1882 by a Scot, James Miln, who spent much of his life trying to unravel the enigma of 'les Alignements'.

Brittany between Josselin and La Baule

Situated almost centrally in the region, Josselin in the département of Morbihan stands at the northern end of a particularly pretty route to the south and the Atlantic seaboard. It is a spectacular medieval walled town, dominated by the film-set fifteenth-century château of the Dukes of Rohan.

Camping Bas de la Lande, on the western edge of town alongside the N24, is a most

Josselin castle towering above the river Oust; a nice waterside walk from the camp ground.

pleasant starting point from which to explore the place. There are good facilities provided at this municipal ground, including mains electricity, with semi-secluded pitches on a series of tree-screened terraces. From the site entrance there is a readily accessible towpath beside the quiet-flowing waters of the Nantes–Brest canal, a section of the long-distance GR37, which leads you in a couple of kilometres to the very foot of the massive château walls. It is by far the most romantic of approaches. Within the fortifications there are many fourteenth-, fifteenth- and six-

teenth-century houses, plus the church of Notre Dame sporting some very unusual extended water-spout gargoyles. Josselin is a lovely old town of cobbled nooks and crannies, with something of historic interest around almost every corner.

There is more of medieval France awaiting those who have time to take the minor roads south from Josselin to the sea – especially at Rochefort-en-Terre, south of Malestroit. There is a church and clustered houses dating back to the twelfth and thirteenth centuries perched on a granite outcrop, amid low

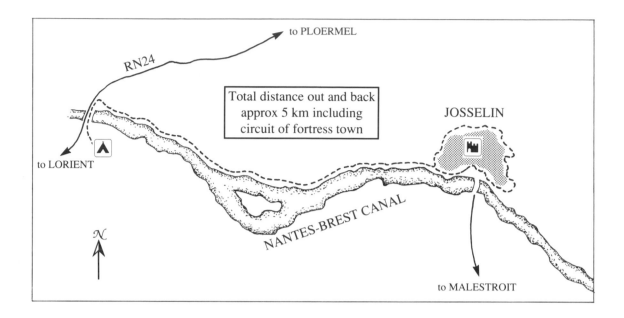

wooded hills. Go south again to another photogenic township, La Roche-Bernard, dominating the heights above the wide river Vilaine. Featureless saltings of the Brière Regional Park stretch to infinity now, until the final regal walled town of fifteenth-century Guerande breaks the skyline just to the north of the famous Pouliguen salt pans and the beaches of la Côte d'Amour.

There is not a great deal for the dedicated walker in this vicinity, although La Baule is Brittany's answer to Biarritz and a much-favoured up-market resort. The La Baule municipal camp ground is of a high standard (and high tariff) and it is within a 1-kilometre stroll of the wide, sandy beach and town centre. The site is located in the rue du Capitaine Flandin and is open from 24 March to 30 September. This route, which begins in Brittany centre and ends on the Atlantic shoreline, is richly blessed with scenic high

spots – perhaps more so than most of the regional hinterland. As in Cornwall, it is the coastline of Brittany that is the main attraction, since much of the inland terrain varies only between acceptably pleasant and almost monotonously bland for the walker (except for the Armorican areas). The marvellous GR3, which traces virtually the entire length of the mighty river Loire, begins or ends at the spectacular old walled town of Guerande, and there are a number of delightful inland enclaves of which just one more must be added – Quimperle and environs, north-east of Lorient. Just to the south of this charming and very ancient town, there is the Forest of Carnoet, where the GR34 meanders alongside the river Laita, down to a once-favoured haunt of Gauguin, the seaside township of Le Pouldu. Here there is a choice of camp grounds, including Le Vieux Four, which is open from Easter to the end of September.

Centre

Départments: Cher – Eure-et-Loir – Indre – Indre-et-Loire –
Loir-et-Cher – Loiret
Préfecture: Orléans

The heart of France is embraced by this massive group of six départements, which extends from just above the level of Paris in the north right down to a point on a latitude with Lake Geneva at the southern extremity. The area is a sweeping canvas of wide river valleys that are richly fertile, and always on the grand scale, creating distant horizons such as are never seen in the British Isles. The rivers dominate the landscape and have long dictated the communication network, population pattern and of course the location of major towns. The watercourses of the Cher, Indre, Creuse and Loir are all worth tracing – as far as this is possible – by the driver or walker keen to find the often unsung quieter beauty of mid-France. The best-known and most majestic of Centre waterways, the Loire, unveils her many charms to the east and west of the 'Maid's City', Orléans. This is the *route des châteaux du coeur de la France,* one of the most favoured of all tourist roads.

The first Loire valley château down-river is that of Gien in the département of Loiret.

Gien and the first of the great Loire Valley châteaux, where there is very pleasant riverside walking.

65

The town is an ancient yet still gratifyingly compact watering-hole at the crossroads of the D952 and D940, about 64 kilometres south-east of Orléans. The château itself is a regal structure, towering tall above the wide tree-lined Loire, mighty and haughty on the site where once stood the fortified castle of Emperor Charlemagne. The château at Gien was built in 1484 by Anne of Beaujeu, a daughter of Louis XI, and you might think from her portrait that she wasn't too pleased with the architect! Perhaps the artist caught her on a bad day. Since then, there has been a succession of celebrity owners and people passing through, including Catherine de Medici and Louis XIV. Latterly it has been a sub-préfecture, a lawcourt and a prison, and today it is a museum devoted primarily to hunting and shooting, open all year round to visitors. So much for Gien culture . . .

There are very good shopping facilities in the small town centre, an obliging tourist office and a congenial municipal camping site on the left bank of the river, with splendid views across the water of the château, which is illuminated in the evenings from Easter to the end of September. The interesting little town is a mere 10 minutes' stroll away, via the elegant twelve-arch bridge. Camping de Gien is a 2-star site of generous proportions, covering about 7 hectares of tree-shaded river bank, with direct access to the sandy *plage* and local bathing place. The facilities are reasonable and adequately maintained, although in truth the enterprise does lack that extra loving touch, as do many municipal grounds created expressly for the touring fraternity. However, there are hot showers, mains electrics and the site is open from 1 April to 31 October. It is plainly signposted from all approach roads.

Once you have been fed, watered and scenically pitched, the prospects for exploring on foot are good. Not surprisingly, there is some pleasant walking along the banks of the Loire. There are three waymarked pedestrian circuits in the immediate vicinity, of $6\frac{1}{2}$, $8\frac{1}{2}$ and $12\frac{1}{2}$ kilometres. The prettiest one is arguably the Circuit de Crocadero, the middle-distance path which encircles the eastern perimeter of the town. The route begins with the crossing of the Loire bridge then turns east along the river promenade from the town centre, and goes through pleasant public gardens. The path kinks around the Gien sports and swimming pool complex before continuing over a sandy spit of river bank and into the wooded Val de la Fontaine. Return is via lanes to Monbricon on the elevated northern side of the D952. It is an easy and pleasant walk, especially in the evening when the summer sun is less fierce.

The longest of the circuits (the $12\frac{1}{2}$-kilometre route) is much more of a town ramble, involving mostly road walking, traversing the higher elevations of Old Gien. The short route, by contrast, is a lagoon and woodland circuit waymarked from the village of Arrabloy, 3 kilometres to the north-east; this is really a drive-and-walk excursion. At this less-visited end of the Loire valley there are two GR routes which converge on Gien – the GR3, threading its way from the Forêt d'Orléans to distant Auvergne, and the GR3C lateral trail wending westwards to Blois, another ancient and beautiful Loire valley town with an outstanding château. The GR3C traverses the area known as the Sologne, much devoted to *la chasse*, a terrain of many lakes and lagoons. This is really reclaimed marshland and best walked – as I know to my cost – outside the mosquito

66

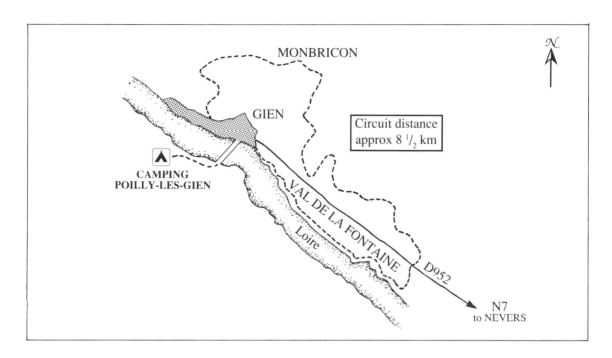

MONBRICON

GIEN

Circuit distance
approx 8 ½ km

CAMPING
POILLY-LES-GIEN

VAL DE LA FONTAINE

Loire

D952

N7
to NEVERS

N

season. There is good waymarking, plus a selection of *Gîtes d'Étape* and camping grounds. The GR3C joins with the GR31 to finish just north-east of Blois.

One other Gien claim to fame is the fine-quality pottery which has been produced here since 1821, when English potter Thomas Hall found all he needed for his craft – limitless clay and sand, wood for firing the kilns, and the Loire for subsequent barge transport. The factory has been turning pots ever since, has won gold medals at international exhibitions and is open throughout the year. The 12½-kilometre walking route passes the factory gates.

A more contemporary installation on the distant outskirts of Gien is the Centre Nucléaire; this one only very discreetly praised. It may be well upstream from the town, but the pluming cloud created by the reactor cooling towers is a constant reminder of its presence as power-supplier supreme to modern-day France.

A still-lovely reach of the river Loire, despite the nuclear neighbour.

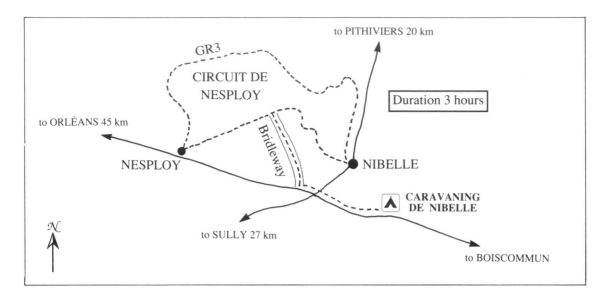

From a stroll along the Loire around one of the river's most historic settings, we move on to Loiret countryside, scarcely changed since the nineteenth century. This is an area of deep, half-hidden rural delight, yet is only 45 kilometres north-east of Orléans. Caravaning de Nibelle is the base camp, and the Forêt d'Orléans the walking terrain.

Nibelle, a *'village fleuri',* is marked only on the largest-scale maps, so its percentage of casual foreign tourists is very small. If you seek the France of the French, you should look here. Coming from the north, the direct and easy approach is from the village of Pithiviers, where you take the signposted road south towards Sully. Nibelle will be found at the 20-kilometre mark. From here, fork towards Boiscommun and follow the international site signs to the camp ground. This is a privately-owned 6-hectare woodland park, most attractively situated in a forest glade. It is not a touring site at all, but really a weekend haven for Parisian and Orléans caravanners. However, there are a number of spaces available for overnighters. The tariff is high, although the nightly charge does include hot showers, mains electricity and unlimited use of the swimming pool. The fact that the owner, Madame de la Planche, speaks perfect English may also be considered a bonus by some.

The tranquillity, spaciousness and limited patronising through most months of the year make this stopping place value for money. The site is permanently open, the owners being resident; drinks and snacks are dispensed from a small bar and there are tennis courts next to the pool. Finally, there are very good forest walks accessible close by, including promenades, half-day hikes or long-distance trekking via the GR3 which passes close to Nibelle.

Nibelle itself has charm and character and is as pretty as a picture. If you want to visit the interesting village Eco-Museum, just ask the butcher — his other function is that of Chef du Syndicat d'Initiative. He will gladly unlock the building by the old church to show you around the steadily growing display of artefacts with pride and enthusiasm. It is a fascinating and telling exposition of ancient pottery and local forestry exploitation throughout the ages, backed up by some splendid old photographs – a composite of long-gone country life and a heritage gem of ever-increasing value.

The Circuit de Nesploy is one favourite walk of those staying at Caravaning Nibelle. It begins with 1 kilometre of road walking to the crossroads, where you take the right-hand forestry track and bridle path signposted *Route Privée*. Continue for another kilometre (ignoring this sign since you are pedestrian), to the waymarked footpath crossing marked 'Circuit de Nesploy', which joins the GR3 just west of Nibelle village. You can walk either south-west to Nesploy hamlet (about half-an-hour), or north-east to Nibelle along forest rides and footpaths.

A Loire Valley Golden Triangle

France does seem to be blessed with a number of unusually beautiful areas, and one of them is the golden triangle that almost every visitor to the region of Centre will wish to explore at length. In a landscape richly endowed with châteaux and castles, encompassed here are three of the most regal – Chinon, Amboise and Loches – lending this marvellous Touraine landscape a touch of enchantment and some wonderful visual evidence of the most formative era of a very long French history.

Chinon, towering high above the river Vienne, has a powerfully dramatic impact as you approach. The welcoming municipal touring site immediately opposite the ancient fortress walls is an ideal long-stay base – it is wonderfully romantic to look from your camp ground pitch upon the floodlit bastion of antiquity. Much more than just a château, Chinon is also a medieval town that Joan of Arc would instantly recognise; the castle

The great humorous writer François Rabelais (1490–1553) was born at Chinon, and his statue sits on the bank of the Vienne.

room where she met the Dauphin, and thus dictated the course of European history, is still in existence. By Chinon standards that event is a comparatively recent one; in April 1199, Richard the Lionheart, King of England, mortally wounded in battle at Chalus, was brought to the fine turreted town-house below the castle, which is still in a near-perfect state of preservation.

Whatever you do, find time here to walk around the old town ramparts; the circular pedestrian tour reveals many delights of the distant past and takes about $1\frac{1}{2}$ hours to complete. The GR3 traverses the town, but is not especially scenic away from the ramparts. However, for a fine distant view of old Chinon, walk a kilometre or so, after turning

69

Chinon from across the wide Vienne; one of the finest medieval stone piles in France.

right at the camp ground exit. From this almost traffic-free farm lane, the fortified walls rising from their natural knoll form a stone cluster not too dissimilar in outline to Mont St Michel.

For more dazzling examples of the medieval stone-mason's art, take the N751 from Chinon to Azay-le-Rideau, about 18 kilometres to the north-east. Here, on the banks of the river Indre, the delicate elegance of the château and the quiet beauty of the surroundings reflect the pinnacle of sixteenth-century formal architecture. While this part of Centre does not have many footpaths, there are a number of forest walks available to either side of the Chinon–Azay road. One worth pursuing is that which circulates from the Carrefour de la Pucelle, about 15 kilometres north-east of Chinon. From the very

spacious picnic area, you can walk via the forester rides and equestrian tracks, to the tiny Abbé de Turpenay (5 kilometres), then return via the Dorothée Duras Crossroads and thus back to Pucelle. The total distance is about $12\frac{1}{2}$ kilometres.

After seeing Azay-le-Rideau, you might well wish to return to Chinon via the D7 which passes the chateau of Ussé. If anything, this is even more breathtaking than Azay. Those with *really* deep pockets may hire a helicopter at the gracious entrance by the way, for an instant aerial view! It is said that Ussé was the original inspiration for Charles Perrault, author of the definitive fairy-tale, *Sleeping Beauty*.

Amboise château-castle, four-square and mightily dominating the wide Loire, was one of the first of the French royal residences.

Azay-le-Rideau – the village is as atmospheric as the château.

The château of Ussé, the original 'Sleeping Beauty' castle.

It was here that François the First invited Leonardo da Vinci, who bequeathed to France one of the greatest paintings of all time, the 'Mona Lisa'. The Italian Renaissance genius ended his days in the nearby manor of Clos-Lucé, today a marvellous museum, dedicated to perhaps the most inventive and far-sighted mind mankind has known. Again, there are local limitations on leg-stretching hereabouts; although the GR3 – which closely follows the Loire between Tours and Chaumont – traverses Amboise, it is mainly road walking.

Loches (south-west of Blois), very ancient in parts, is another fortified town of outstanding architectural beauty – a dazzling white settlement, with the majestic château, castle and twelfth-century church balanced upon sculptured terraces, the old houses clustered below. The Fôret de Loches, just to the east of the town, is the favourite walking ground, notably around the Pyramide de St Quentin and the Pyramide de Montaigu. The GR46 follows the river Indre from Tours, passing through Loches, although again, the walking is largely along tarmac.

The Cher Valley

If you are a keen leisure walker, who may also aspire to château-collecting, seeking a really fruitful base in this area, you should try Bléré, about 20 kilometres east of Tours on the N76. Tours itself is the recognised hub of France's château country, but there is a limit to how much modern city hassle you can take for art's sake, despite the seductive charms of the Touraine capital and its reputation as the birthplace of the French Renaissance. Bléré is near enough to enjoy a spin-off of Tours bustle, modernity and affluence, yet

small enough to make the visitor feel at once welcome, comfortable and instantly oriented. This self-contained little town, ancient enough in its own right and with a documented history going back to Roman times (when it was called Blerium), has enough to make it a favoured alternative to Tours.

There is a well-signposted and really expansive camping ground, reserved exclusively for touring units, about 500 metres from the old town centre. It has a park-like setting, covering over 4 hectares of plumb-level lawn grass and shady trees, with every modern convenience provided inside the ground and a large supermarket just outside it. Above all, however, the setting is strategically sublime. Right on the banks of the quiet-flowing Cher is a magnificent section of the GR41 towpath, going eastwards towards Chenonceaux about 7 kilometres away. The château here, which straddles the river Cher on grandiose arches, is considered by many to be the finest and most beautiful in the world. And if that were not enough attraction, there is also Amboise and the da Vinci manor-museum less than 10 kilometres to the north on the neighbouring Loire, as well as a skein of historic châteaux within easy driving distance at every point of the compass, including Montpoupon, Montrichard, Montbazon, Nitry Leugny and Montrésor. These jewels of the past, and others like Loches and Valencay, may all be seen by following the famous Route des Dames de Touraine.

In between visiting châteaux you may well wish to go walkabout amid slightly less illustrious surroundings. The Bléré municipal fathers (in conjunction with the Comité de Touraine de la Randonnée), have done what they can to keep enthusiast strollers on their patch, by providing three colour-coded local

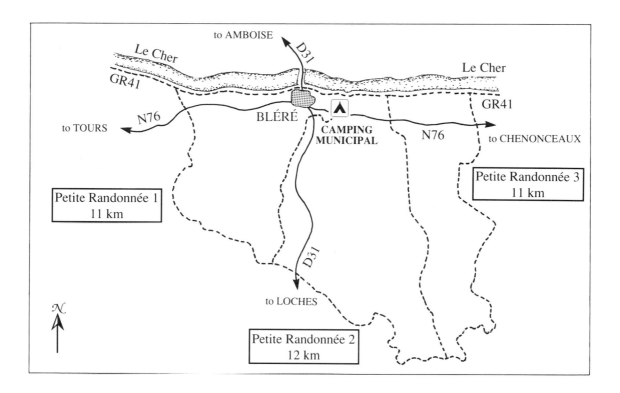

circuit walks of around 11 kilometres in length, all of which start and finish at the 3-star camp ground. A descriptive leaflet and detailed map is available free from the site office. Bléré municipal site is open from 3 April to 15 October, and as a base close to major trunk routes like the A10 and N10, and the massive urban spread that is now Tours, it must be warmly recommended.

There is nothing better after a spell near any great metropolis than to decamp to quieter pastures where nature is the dominant feature. In this case go eastwards, via the beautiful Cher valley, following this fine river either along the N76, or on the tourist route (which takes you part way on the opposite bank), to the great natural treasure of this

region – the Forêt de Vierzon. This 'ocean of trees', as it has been called, is an unbroken forest wedge extending almost from Bourges to the outskirts of Orléans over 150 kilometres away. There are countless beauty spots within this huge forested tract, and nearly all of them are geared to visitor needs, offering a variety of outdoor leisure pursuits, principally walking. There is space here for just one location – the village of Ménétréol-sur-Saulde, deep in one of the most secluded enclaves of Cher département.

To get to Ménétréol from Vierzon, take the D926 north-east to Neuvy-sur-Barangeon (a pretty little forest village), then north again on the D79 to Ménétréol. There is an inviting woodland glade camping ground, a 2-star

Montrichard château-castle in the Cher valley.

municipal site open from Easter to the end of September. Simple, clean facilities are provided in a most attractively designed utility block, there is mains electricity, and the village is just a five-minute stroll away, as is a fine section of the GR31. Just within the area known as the Sologne, the GR31 today is one of the notable routes laid down across the forest and heath of this now-tamed marshland wilderness. The relevant section, which is very well waymarked as a 'Chemin du Sologne', begins almost at the Ménétréol camp ground entrance and winds its way south towards Neuvy some 17 kilometres away. The signpost indicates, with accuracy, that the Neuvy road is 1 hour 20 minutes' walking time away. Vigorous walkers might well wish to continue to Neuvy, which is an agreeable lunchtime objective. The out-and-back hike will provide a very pleasant day and fine sample of one of the great forests of central France.

A shorter alternative, varied and interesting, is the footpath which joins another *chemin rural*, starting immediately from the camping ground along the river bank westwards. Follow the well-trodden route around two large *étangs* to the obvious forest ride which is the CR10. Turn right for Souesmes village, about 1 hour's easy walk away. This trail traverses typical Sologne country, a lush mixture of variegated forest, marsh and heathland.

Other Regional Alternatives

One of the quieter north–south transit routes of France, avoiding Paris, is that via Rouen, Chartres, Blois and Châteauroux. This is particularly favoured by out-of-season travellers and winter migrants to Spain, since there are camping grounds at strategic distances, open all, or most of the year. Châteauroux is one good stop-off place, boasting a very pleasant

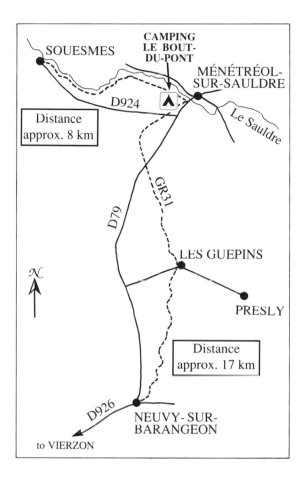

South-west of Chartres alongside the N10 lies Vendôme, with another pleasant municipal camp ground almost inside the town boundary, within a parkland setting, yet very conveniently located for shopping and strolling. Vendôme has a surfeit of old-world charm; straddling the Loir (the narrower tributary of the Loire), it has the mix that makes certain places in France so memorable. There is a fourteenth century ruined château surmounting a rocky bluff, rich Renaissance architecture, a beautiful if flamboyant church, a Bénédictine abbey, and a maze of twisting narrow streets giving delight at almost every corner. Honoré de Balzac (1799–1850), the gifted and prolific writer, spent seven school years at the imposing Collège des Oratoriens. Happily, he would still recognise this ancient fount of scholarship, as indeed he would most of this finely preserved old town.

With a past as rumbustious as any of France's fortified towns, Vendôme is the kind of place which may tempt you to stay longer than you intended. There is some revealing town walking, which you can enjoy by following the arms of the Loir which all but encircle the centre. There is also good local rambling country amid the wooded hills just to the north, bisected with local trails and the GR35 which passes through the town. The tourist office is at Tour St Martin, in the rue Poterie.

Practical yet unpretentious, the Grands Prés camping ground on the banks of the Loir covers some three hectares of level, tree-shaded lawns. The toilets are acceptably clean, hot showers are included in the modest charge, and there is mains electricity if required.

municipal touring site (closed at the end of November) under tall trees, secluded and yet within easy strolling distance of shops and town centre. The location is particularly attractive since it is also adjacent to an extensive leisure park, complete with large lake and an islet café-restaurant. Certainly there is only limited rambling terrain, but if you take in the park, lakeside footpath and historic old town centre, it can occupy almost half a day of pedestrian interest at any season.

Champagne-Ardennes

Départements: Ardennes – Aube – Marne – Haute-Marne
Préfecture: Châlons-sur-Marne

If you seek an interesting touring ground, not too far from the Channel ports, wishing to savour what might be termed 'nearby France' there are countless places to choose from; that is, if you are prepared to enjoy scenery that is subtle rather than spectacular, weather that is sunny if not sizzling, and a pastoral France that is simple rather than sophisticated. One such area is Champagne-Ardennes, about 180 kilometres from Calais. The great attraction for countless outdoor-life enthusiasts is not so much the wine (for which the region is justly renowned), but the water, which sparkles in even greater abundance.

Champagne-Ardennes is a region of lakes – albeit mostly man-made – with eight in all, one of which is the largest in all France, covering an incredible 18 square miles. It is called rather oddly, Lac du Der Chantecoq. Such watery expanses can only be created where there are bountiful rivers, and Champagne-Ardennes has a copious share of these. The Meuse, the Marne, the Aisne and the Seine all link together with their respective tributaries to form a glorious skein of waterways all over the region. One other, the Aube, a beautiful offshoot of the Seine, springs east of Fontainebleau in neighbouring Ile-de-France and courses through some really splendid Champagne country above Troyes and Chaumont. Nestling between the great north–south arterial roads, the Aube flows swiftly yet quietly through a landscape of lush forest and farmland, networked in the main only by secondary roads and punctuated with old villages. Within a reasonable day's drive of Calais, it is, in aspect, character and atmosphere, a million miles from Dover. It represents a rewarding objective for anyone seeking the pastoral heart of France that the French themselves love so much.

The Mountains of Reims

In the midst of the great Champagne vineyards, and frequently bypassed by those heading south or east for distant parts, the Mountains of Reims are rather grandly titled. However, the name is perhaps justified when you consider that they are the dominant feature of the Champagne landscape, which is mainly rolling plain. In truth, the *parc naturel* (designated in 1976) is a triangle of wooded hills rising to some 288 metres, immediately to the south of Reims, extending to the outskirts of Épernay on the N51. To either side of the main road there is an impressive and unusual mix of vineyard and forest, cool, green and shady, and a delight on a hot summer's day.

There is no town of any size within this

190-square-mile expanse, but simply 68 hamlets and villages, all of which are devoted to wine production or forestry. The area is served by narrow winding roads, not at all typical of central France, many of which have been laid for forest exploitation. These back lanes add greatly to driver interest, and form sections of the increasing number of pedestrian routes which are being established in the park. Within a relatively small area there is also some very varied vegetation, due to the many contrasting soils, the diversity of the terrain, and the climate, which is an odd combination of Continental and oceanic. It is an unusual enclave of France, not only because it produces the unique true Champagne wine, but also for a most peculiar species of ancient beech tree known as 'faux'. These arboreal oddities are very slow-growing, exceptionally long-lived and grotesquely distorted, often with two trunks, snake-like branches and gravity-defying off-shoots. They are found at only two sites in the world, and Verzy, on the eastern side of the park, is one of them. Now a national historic site, the Faux de Verzy is the last vestige of a Bénédictine settlement created in the seventh century. It now has a waymarked walk, revealing many of the more remarkable of these gnarled ancient trees, some of which are over 500 years old.

To reach Verzy, a pretty hill village amid a sea of grape vines, turn off the N44 south of Reims, along the D26 signposting the *parc naturel*. Wend your way through this village with eleventh century beginnings and, just past the hilltop Observatoire du Sinai, leave the car at Chapelle St Basle for the 5½-kilo-metre forest circuit trail. This is just one of 14 waymarked paths within the park, which really does have constantly changing scenic

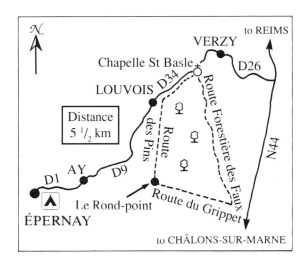

surroundings. There is, too, a host of medieval villages, many of which have tangible Roman origins. For detailed local information, make for the Maison du Parc, which will be found at Pourcy. For this information centre, turn west off the N51 south of Reims, along the D26 and D22 via Sermiers and Nogent. The centre, which is also an eco-museum, distributes a variety of brochures and sells a useful booklet for walkers entitled *Promenades à Pied*. This contains detailed maps and descriptions of the 14 paths so far established. The centre is open on weekdays from 9 a.m. to 5 p.m.

For *aficionados* of bubbly, a visit to Hautvillers, just north of Épernay, is almost an obligatory pilgrimage. It was here in the Bénédictine abbey that the seventeenth-century magician monk, Dom Perignon, perfected his wizardry and the subsequent technique of champagne making.

Should you wish to indulge in any extensive wine-tasting around here, there is a choice of *Gîtes d'Étape* – farm or private-house accommodation – in the vicinity of Courtagnon and Fontaine-sur-Ay. A list is available from the Maison du Parc office. There are no organised touring sites within the forest confines, although 3-star camp grounds will be found at Reims (avenue Hoche), and at Epernay (Municipal Camping, Alles de Cumières).

The Aube and the Orient Forest

The N77 from Châlons-sur-Marne to Troyes is 77 kilometres of almost dead-straight, once Roman road, slicing a seemingly endless agricultural plain; it is one of those ruler-lines of tarmac that is now uniquely and unmistakably French. There is however, a charming little oasis at Arcis-sur-Aube, birthplace of the ill-fated revolutionary, Danton, complete with a camping ground on a picturesque peninsula of the river, beside a tumbling weir and sandy bathing beach. The 2-star Camping de I'lle is clean, shady and agreeable and is open from early April to mid-October.

This is a congenial, interesting and quiet base from which to explore Troyes, one of France's most striking yet compact cities. Park in one of the many gracious squares and just amble where your feet take you. There is rich reward in every direction, with some really stunning squares like the place de Préau, where centuries-old trees surround an ornamental lake, which in turn leads to pedestrian precincts stamped with the patina of time. The spire of the great cathedral of St Peter and St Paul and the chequered glazed-tile roof of St Nizier church rise gracefully amid medieval-width streets, which also house museums, art galleries, one of the country's richest libraries and a scattering of Gothic statuary unequalled outside Paris.

If you like *la France ancienne,* you will assuredly love this little city of living history. There is a municipal camp ground off the N60 at Pont Saint Marie, but it is invariably crowded and over-used throughout the summer months. Arcis-sur-Aube, just 27 kilometres to the north, makes a much better base, and is also conveniently placed for discovery of the natural riches of the Forêt d'Orient.

One of the most successful nature parks, established in 1966 from a reservoir area, the Parc Naturel d'Orient spans some 13,000 hectares of majestic forest around a vast lake covering 2,300 hectares of an erstwhile valley floor. It is now the weekend and holiday target of countless cyclists, walkers and city-based families seeking waterside relaxation. There are numerous waymarked circuit footpaths for those seeking solitude, plus sections of the GR24 and GR24b long-distance routes. There are actually about 12,500 kilometres of footpath routes within the Champagne-Ardennes region, some of the most scenic of which are within the département of Aube.

At the heart of the forest there is a Maison du Parc, sited in an ancient oak wood first planted by the Knights Templars in the

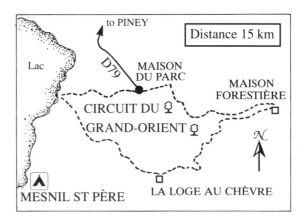

Arcis-sur-Aube. Since 1939 (150th anniversary of the Revolution), Danton has been gazing from his plinth at the fifteenth-century town church.

twelfth century. It, too, contains an interesting eco-museum displaying flora and fauna of the area which is actually part of the vast Forêt du Der. *Der* is Old French for oak which explains the odd title of Lac du Der Chantecoq, the near inland sea south-west of St Dizier. It is 85 kilometres from St Dizier to Troyes and this fact is an indication of the immense stretch of unbroken forest that once must have covered this part of France.

There is an interesting short circuit walk from the Maison du Parc, which touches upon the lake shore in one direction and an old forester's cottage to the other. A camp ground will be found at Mesnil-St-Père on the southern shoreline in what may be termed the fun area. Heavily patronised throughout the season, and noisy with Gallic bustle, its appeal may well be limited. Happily, it is just 1 kilometre from the silent beauty of the forest and its trails. Quieter camping facilities will be found at Brienne-la-Vieille, in the northern part of the park, reached via the scenic D396. There is a lovely old watermill here and one of those simple 1-star touring sites along the river bank just outside the village. Brienne-le-Château lies just north of here, and the massive château where Napoleon Bonaparte spent six years as a military academy student. It is not open to visitors, but you can browse around the interesting Napoleon Museum.

79

Colombey-les-Deux-Eglises

South of St Dizier is the small township of Joinville. Leave the N67 here and take the D960 then the D2 to visit a shrine to another national hero, the tiny village of Colombey-les-Deux-Eglises. Buried amid a rolling landscape devoted to cereal farming, it is as sleepy, dignified and independent as it has been for centuries, an understandable choice of home for 'Le Général', the very embodiment of France visually and spiritually. Distant enough, yet not too far from Paris, Colombey was the de Gaulle home, and is now as much a place of pilgrimage for Frenchmen as Churchill's grave is for Britons. Like many military men, de Gaulle's personal tastes were simple,

as the rooms open to visitors of La Boisserie show. He was buried in the churchyard in 1970. A huge Croix de Lorraine now looms over – indeed almost dwarfs – the village at the foot of a wooded knoll. Stark, powerful and remote, the cross echoes the character of the man with uncanny accuracy, and the rose-hued granite monolith loses nothing of its dignity in close-up. It is a pleasant half-kilometre walk from the obligatory car park beside the N19 to the hilltop column.

Bar-sur-Aube, not far away, is an agreeable stopping place with a camping ground sited amid a wealth of tall trees alongside the river. It is quiet and secluded, and yet within easy strolling distance of the town. Bar itself is steeped in history, with many timber-framed

The luxuriant tree shading of the Bar-sur-Aube touring site. There is nice riverside walking here, yet the site is just a short stroll from the town centre.

houses, a twelfth century church and an enormous tree-shaded square. The latter is a relic of times past, when the little town was one of the centres for the great trade fairs of the Middle Ages, attracting merchants from all parts of the Christian world. Less than 2 kilometres away, via the CD4 minor road, a path leads to the hill of Sainte Germaine. There are some fine views from the wooded summit which is over 1,000 feet high. There is also pleasant strolling along the banks of the Aube from the camp ground.

A Stroll to Belgium and Back

At the extreme northern tip of Champagne-Ardennes it becomes very clear how this region gained the second part of its name. 'Ardenn' in Celtic means 'deep forest', and the description is almost as fitting now as it must have been in pre-Christian times. Probably no part of western Europe is more richly endowed with tree density or variety than this swathe which cuts through Belgium, Luxembourg and Eastern France. Where France thrusts deepest into Belgium along the north-eastern frontier is another charming, less-visited corner. It is here that the Ardennes high country is at its most attractive – a succession of deep and twisting river valleys between tree-clad domed hills, some of which are much higher on close acquaintance than they appear from a distance.

In parts there are often first-rate skiing winters – not so much for downhill enthusiasts as for those who enjoy *ski de fond* (cross-country skiing). When winter turns to spring, the same *pistes* make excellent footpaths, especially when they are carefully colour-coded and distance tabulated, as they are in the northern French Ardennes. The summertime walker owes a vote of thanks to the winter-sports enthusiasts hereabouts, and expressly to those who created the marked *pistes* through the high-country forest of Château-Regnault.

The easiest and most direct route to this fine walking area, is north from Charleville-Mézières, at first along the D988, then the D989, until Monthermé is reached, a pretty and tucked-away little *station verte* town filling an almost full-circle loop of the river Meuse. Among other attractions, Monthermé boasts a very nice 2-star municipal camp ground which is *almost* exclusively reserved for touring visitors. This in itself is relatively rare in a quite heavily-populated belt of north-eastern France. It is also well administered, yet without fuss, and is in a lovely setting, a spacious and level woodland glade about $2\frac{1}{2}$ kilometres from the town centre and alongside the Semoy, a tributary of the Meuse. It is open from Easter to the end of September. There are a number of alternative camping grounds, at Monthermé and nearby Joigny-sur-Meuse, but there are really none to better Camping des Rapides des Phades. Facilities are clean and serviceable, if without frills, and include good hot showers and mains electric hook-ups. Shaded or open pitching on regularly mown grass is left to visitors to select for themselves and there is, consequently, a good feeling of space, freedom and tranquillity. When other sites in this area were packed with weekenders (and none too salubrious), the Monthermé municipal was a wonderful mid-June discovery; there are, of course, no guarantees of what it may be like in July or August. The D4 passes quite close to the ground, but traffic is not heavy and the noise is largely muffled by dense woodland.

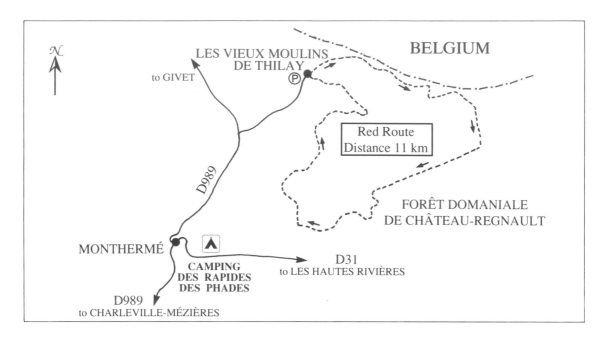

Adjacent to the campsite is the Sentier des Rapides, a bridle track which passes the entrance and follows the river Semoy in a south-easterly direction, passing the modest rapids, after a small river barrage, about 2 kilometres distant. This is a pleasant evening stroll along a track that continues for about $2\frac{1}{2}$ kilometres before joining the tarmac road. The Semoy valley (following the winding river faithfully between Monthermé and Haute-Rivières) is now classified as La Route des Légendes, and reveals some spectacular high-spots and viewpoints with enigmatic names like the Rocher des Quatre Fils and Roche à Sept Heures. Literary buffs can follow the Route Rimbaud Verlaine, the heritage trail of the most famous, and controversial, Ardennais poet (1854–1891).

For some invigorating high-country walking, one objective – the 'Old Windmills' – will have top priority. Les Vieux Moulins de Thilay, lies 11 kilometres north of Monthermé and is reached via the D989. After 9 kilometres, take the minor road right-

Colour-coded route markers Les Vieux Moulins, forest of Château Regnault near Monthermé.

Roc la Tour above Monthermé; one of many such outcrops in this Ardennes high country.

hand fork and in a further 2 kilometres you will come to the end of the tarmac and the tiny frontier hamlet of Thilay. There is easy parking here beside the cottages where there are also prominent coloured direction arrows displayed beside the forest trail. Simply choose the appropriate distance to suit your personal taste and set off along the shortest green trail of $3\frac{1}{2}$ kilometres, or the black route of 14 kilometres. The red route is the most popular, since it winds north-west at first, near the Belgian border for a kilometre or so, before turning south-west via forestry tracks and footpaths, back to the starting point of the 11-kilometre circuit.

This forest route, like all the others, leads the pedestrian explorer through very attract-ive pine forest at an average altitude of around 500 metres, where the air is pure, the silence golden, and the only other people around are walkers or forestry workers. It is Ardennes country at its secluded (though not isolated) best. For any traveller *en route* to Luxembourg and Germany from the Channel ports, a stopover for a day or two is a must, both for the base camp, and for the quality of the leisure walking on offer.

A short distance south of Monthermé lies the busy and expanding township of Charleville-Mézières. This is an important Ardennes crossroads, now almost encircled by autoroutes and major roads and not an instant attraction on any traveller's road map. In reality, however, it is a nice town, the *autoroute* is non-*péage,* the signposting in and out is excellent, and the gracious old town, much rebuilt after wartime damage, is full of atmospheric colonnades, semi-pedestrian precincts, smart shops and a fashion-conscious citizenry, all of which creates a stimulating scene for the observer. Close to the centre, in the rue des Paquis, is 3-star Camping du Mont Olympe. Town and city campsites are not really the brief of this book, but there are the odd worthy exceptions and Charleville is one of them. Naturally well patronised, there is none the less usually ample room for touring visitors on this 2-hectare municipal ground by the Meuse, which is park-like, agreeable, well maintained and with all mod cons. Open from 15 April to 15 October, it provides a pleasing contrast – for a short spell – to pastoral pitching, while the window shopping and café life is of high quality! The fact that Charleville was also the birthplace of Rimbaud adds zest for many visitors.

Arc-en-Barrois – Haute-Marne High-Spot

Although it has some notably dense pockets of population – mainly around Reims, Chalons and Troyes – Champagne-Ardennes also has its quieter corners. One of these is the département of Haute-Marne, where only St Dizier, Chaumont and Langres form sizeable conurbations. The area is delightfully uncrowded, and a true pleasure to move around for the leisure driver or walker. For every inhabitant of the département there is a handsome *three* acres of forest. Haute-Marne is something of a vast nature reserve, as the regional tourist board claims, with no less than 240,000 hectares of forest (one of

the largest in all France), almost all of which has local footpaths in addition to a choice of GR routes.

There are, as might be expected amid such attractive terrain, a number of recognised forest-walking centres, principally Chaumont, Auberive and Bourbonne-les-Bains. For a tucked-away base in the heart of the countryside, however, consider Arc-en-Barrois, south-west of Chaumont in the Forêt de Châteauvillain et d'Arc. This very charming backwater town is just an oversized village surrounded by all that is naturally best in Champagne-Ardennes. It is an ancient settlement, where the paternal grandfather of Joan of Arc once worked as a forester in the grounds of the fine château, a fact acknowledged by the name. Today that château, a cosily integral part of the village and not isolated from the community like many, plays host to a very un-French sport, boasting a beautiful nine-hole golf course laid out in the park. The game – hereabouts at least – is slowly beginning to win Gallic hearts and minds.

More practically there is also a very welcoming little municipal camping ground, le Vieux Moulin, and this too is within the village bounds. Not plagued with weekend caravans (at the time of writing), the site is neat, clean, level and nicely shaded, with a stream (an arm of the river Aujon) forming the boundaries. The site is tranquil by day and by night, for traffic in the vicinity is light, while toilet facilities are basic but serviceable and there are mains electric hook-ups. A visiting guardian collects the fees nightly and the site is open from 15 April to 30 September.

There are one or two nice cafés and restaurants in the town and comprehensive shopping facilities. The Syndicat d'Initiative

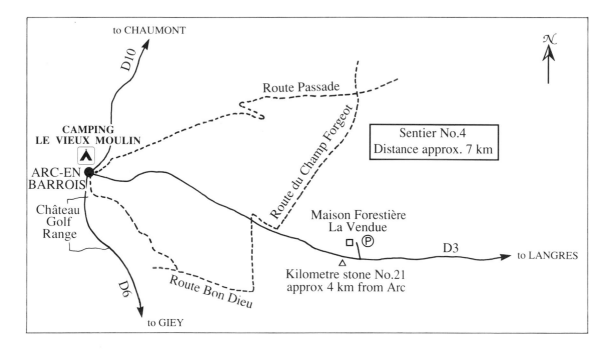

is especially efficient and friendly, dispensing comprehensive information on all the local walking potential, which is wide and varied. There are about a dozen pedestrian circuits around Arc, eight of which start from the central square in front of the château, and four from the Maison Forestière la Vendue, off the D3 Langres road, 4 kilometres to the east. There is an especially friendly atmosphere about Arc-en-Barrois and its inhabitants, who with three statistical acres of forest apiece, really do seem pleased to welcome visitors from afar, and particularly those eager to explore their enviable countryside on foot. One landmark they will almost certainly direct you towards is le Gros Chêne (the Great Oak), reputed to be over 300 years old. It stands huge and proud just off the Chaumont road, living evidence of the ancient forests which extended for miles in every direction from this tranquil spot in Champagne-Ardennes.

Walk number 4 starts on the Giey road, just opposite the château golf club practice range. Take the narrow footpath between high stone walls and ascend past the TV pylon and through the woods south-eastwards. The waymarking on this and other trails in the area varies between sporadic and non-existent. However, with the IG large-scale map reproductions available from the Arc Syndicat d'Initiative (and of course the compass), there is no difficulty in route-finding. All the forestry tracks are wide and naturally easy to follow, while the footpath sections are well trodden. Route 4 winds around arable farmland, via forestry tracks and trails, mostly at hilltop level. The walking is always easy and there are nice views at times over the village, the valley and beyond to the typical wide horizon of Champagne-Ardennes. This route is a particularly pleasant pedestrian venture in early summer as it takes you across little-trodden terrain, where wild strawberries can be seen growing in abundance.

Franche-Comté

Départements: Doubs – Jura – Haute-Saône – Territoire de Belfort
Préfecture: Besançon

This is a region of some singularly spectacular gorges, generally as unspoiled as any in France (save for the area around Belfort), which runs the entire length of the eastern boundary and forms the frontier with Switzerland. Franche-Comté is an agricultural treasure-house and dairy farms particularly seem to thrive under the equal doses of sunshine and rain which are influenced by the Jura mountain chain and the lofty plateau of the Haute-Saône. Increasingly and inevitably Franche-Comté (or 'Free Country') is becoming more and more popular with the touring fraternity, and notably with those seeking a tranquillity almost impossible to find nowadays around France's seaboard. It is also a region much favoured by north–south holidaymakers in transit, especially from Holland, Belgium and Germany. Britons who keep to the main trunk route, through Belfort, Besançon and Lons-le-Saunier, may gain glimpses of green and pleasant Franche-Comté, but the real beauty is less obvious. If you probe a little off the beaten track you will quickly discover how richly endowed and uncrowded this proud and self-sufficient region is.

Franche-Comté is particularly attractive to leisure walkers for three reasons: the landscape in certain areas is beautiful and majestic; the summer climate although certainly warm, does not suffer the stifling heat of the south; and the standard of waymarked footpaths, both circuits and long-distance routes, is excellent, and improving every year. Like its northerly neighbour Alsace, Franche-Comté must therefore be rated highly as walking country. The mountains, although certainly steep enough in places, have that friendly tree-cloaked voluptuousness signifying that walking (as opposed to scrambling or climbing) is the norm. The following is a selection of trails illustrating the wide potential in this region, notably in the départements of Doubs and Jura.

The first trail is from a base camp at the little township of St-Hippolyte, about 50 kilometres south of Belfort, in a deep fissured valley cut by a confluence of the rivers Doubs and Dessoubre. The approach route from the north is via the D437, which becomes progressively prettier as Belfort is left behind. After a succession of green domed hills and pine-forest plantations, the road descends into the sleepy old-world centre of St-Hippolyte, where the signposting to the municipal camp ground is clear and direct. This 2-star site, Les Grands Champs, which is open from 15 May to 15 September, is not *quite* as its name suggests. The fields are quite small terraces, cut into one of the valley's gentler slopes, partially landscaped by the local authority and gravel-covered in places. In an area of sometimes heavy and persistent rainfall, this is a necessary precaution against vehicles becoming bogged down. Facilities are fairly basic but clean, befitting the natural setting, although there are modern refinements like mains electric hook-ups. The advantage of this site is twofold. The town centre is less than 10 minutes' stroll away, where there is limited but adequate shopping with an excellent *boulangerie*, *épicerie* and general store, while directly accessible are two fine valley-top footpaths.

To east and west, high above the river, the 25-kilometre circuits meander along the tops with farming hamlets marking the approximate half-way points on both routes. The bonus here is that detailed sketch maps on the Circuit des Falaises and the Circuit de la Croix de Saussi, are freely available on request at the camp ground bureau. These are good half-day walks in either direction, since there are some fairly sharp gradients in places, especially on the Croix de Saussi. You will see some fine views over the valley, however, particularly from La Grosse Roche.

Grand though these routes are, they are mere appetisers to the main pedestrian attraction in this area, some 20 kilometres to the south-east. To reach Combe St Pierre, drive south on the D437 through Maîche where there is another terraced and prettily located camp ground (some distance from the town centre), and continue to Charquemont. From this picturesque backwater farming town, take the signposted left fork for Combe St Pierre. Along the narrow and winding minor road (the D10E), watch for the signposts, in brown and white, for Echelles de la Mort.

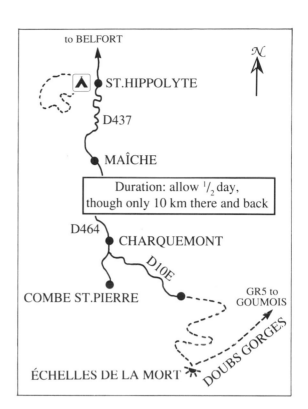

Where the road ends there is a restaurant/café, spacious car parking and the starting point for one of the most dramatic footpaths in Franche-Comté.

Actually a section of the GR5, the path traces a route along the soaring lip of the Gorges de Doubs, affording quite literally bird's eye views across to Switzerland. You may well find that buzzards are your only company in this majestic high and wild place. You can of course, walk for as long as you like either north or south, but 5 kilometres towards Goumois and the Corniche road should prove stimulating enough for all but the most energetic, both visually and physically. Certainly the little café/restaurant at the end of the tarmac road does brisk business with those returning from the edge of the mighty abyss.

Second choice within the département of

Ornans, the tourist centre of the Loue Valley, straddles a delightful reach of the river. Unhappily, modern development is beginning to encroach upon the town.

Doubs must be the splendid Vallée de la Loue nestling in forested seclusion between Besançon and Pontarlier. To get there, drive south from Besancon along the N57, then take the D67 Green Route. Ornans is the recognised tourist centre, a lovely old town flanking both banks of the sparkling river Loue.

The great painter Gustave Courbet was born in Ornans in 1819, and would no doubt still recognise the balconied houses overhanging the river. Elegant, dignified and full of character in the centre, the town today is much expanded and the municipal camp ground, although a 3-star French Touring Club site with all mod cons, is a touch commercial, very sloping and not in immediately salubrious surroundings. High-rise worker flats are the dominant adjacent feature; essen-

tial without doubt, but not an inspiring backdrop when pastoral France is the objective.

For a base camp more in tune with the beautiful countryside, consider Vuillifans or Lods, about 10 kilometres south-east along the D67. The latter, possessor of the odd-looking name which is pronounced 'Lo', epitomises the Loue Valley at its loveliest. The village, not immediately (nor ever totally) revealed from the riverside road, boasts a welcoming 2-star camp ground, which is well signposted and reached by crossing a river bridge. There is billiard-table-smooth pitching below a rocky wooded bluff, with tumbling weir waters giving added charm, plus pristine services including hot showers at no extra charge. For non-campers there is a modest well-run *Logis de France* opposite, called the Golden Trout. On the camp ground visitors are left to cope for themselves and the warden collects fees each evening.

The Lods camp ground really is in a gem of a setting and, of course, it is no accident that a section of the GR595 is routed through the valley. You can follow the river, more or less, for 14 kilometres into Ornans one way, or opt for the shorter $3\frac{1}{2}$ kilometres into Mouthier the other. This is a walk full of variety and interest and it begins at once from the camping ground, from where you make your way south-east along the river path past the extinct Lods railway station to the town bridge. Cross the river here, following the Mouthier footpath signpost, up through the village, past the sixteenth-century château and around the back of the church.

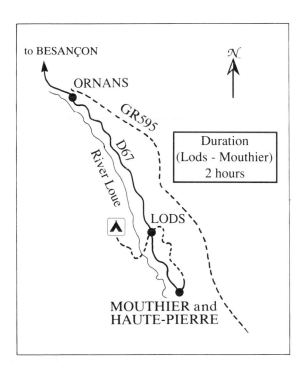

Lods is a village of great character, of impossibly narrow alleyways and arches, all perched somehow on the steep hillside. It has a Spar foodstore to satisfy practical needs, and a good *boulangerie*. From the church a clover-covered track ascends, quite steeply at first, then levels out for 1 kilometre or so before joining a tarmac lane for the eventual descent into Mouthier. From the elevated part of Mouthier, called Haute-Pierre, another cluster of venerable old France, you may return to Lods via the GR595.

A Jewel of the Juras

One long-time personal favourite, tucked away in the far south-western corner of the département of Jura, is St Amour. Pretty as its name, this is a compact country town just sufficiently off the main N83 to retain its peacefulness and escape the worst of the high-season holiday traffic. Among other assets, it has a small but pleasant municipal camping ground, reserved for tourists only, and well signposted along all approach routes. Diligently maintained and providing good amenities with hot showers at no extra charge, the site is open from 1 April to 31 October and is of 2-star category. The setting is adjacent to the sports complex which contains an enthusiastically patronised running track, tennis courts and a heated open-air swimming pool. There is open countryside on three sides, while the fourth is dominated by an impressive, massively-built sixteenth century church. This and the main square are just five minutes' stroll away.

There is much of old France still in evidence at St Amour, not least the church itself, the surrounding square, and the mightily sturdy Guillaume Tower, a relic of the feudal Middle

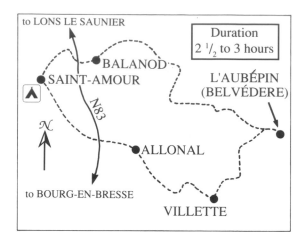

to LONS LE SAUNIER

BALANOD

SAINT-AMOUR

N83

to BOURG-EN-BRESSE

ALLONAL

VILLETTE

L'AUBÉPIN
(BELVÉDERE)

Duration
2 ½ to 3 hours

Ages, surrounded by a number of picturesque arched alleyways. Services are modern, however, with a well-stocked supermarket in the main square and another opposite the Post Office. There is also a tempting *patisserie* that has been granted a national award for excellence. A visit to the Syndicat d'Initiative in the town centre will prove rewarding too. Ask for the pamphlet *Promenades à Pied*, which lists some 20 waymarked walks in the area, all of them circuitous, varying from 8 to 13 kilometres in length.

For a typical example of the landscape scenery, try the 8 kilometre lane and bridle path route which meanders through some small hamlets and takes in the impressive viewpoint of the Belvédere l'Aubépin, revealing a fine panorama of the Jura foothills. The walk takes about 3 hours and is easy going. It begins from the centre of St Amour in the place de la Chevalerie.

This little town can be a very captivating spot, if you have just enough luck with the weather. It is the kind of place you may intend staying just one night and end up staying a week or longer – small enough to become easily familiar, large enough to hold the interest of the enquiring visitor. St Amour is a *Station Verte* well worth visiting.

Often in France, from any town or village

base, there is a degree of road walking before you can tread on more natural surfaces. The pragmatic French mapmakers are not nearly so insistent as the British in avoiding tarmac unless it is absolutely impossible. However, the quickest route to the Jura foothills is via the rue Allonal, where the GR9 footpath signposts are displayed. Some 20 minutes of gentle lane ascent from the town open the walk to the hamlet and old chapel of Allonal. From here there is a farm track to a ridge route which quickly becomes a pastoral hill path, revealing some sweeping distant views over the Juras from the Belvédere l'Aubépin.

Dole

Forty-eight kilometres south-east of Dijon via the N5 lies Dole, clustered above the Doubs river and the Rhone–Rhine canal. Dole was the medieval préfecture of the region (now replaced in this rôle by Besançon), and the regal setting and graceful architecture dominated by the sixteenth century church of Notre Dame testify to that erstwhile importance. The town is renowned for its most famous son, Louis Pasteur. The house where he was born in 1822 can be seen, appropriately, in the rue Pasteur.

Dole is a lovely old town just made for strolling, with many evocative and tangible links with the past. There is a pleasant camping ground on the southern outskirts of the town, Camping L'ile du Pasquier. Here there are waterside tree-shaded pitches, good facilities and pleasant waterside walking.

The Heart of the Juras

The Jura mountains have always been held in special affection by British walkers, partly

Dole, the birthplace of Louis Pasteur; its Notre Dame above the Rhône-Rhine canal is another Franche-Comté delight. There is congenial camping and waterside walking too.

because they overlap from France into Switzerland with the high country that this implies, partly because of the fascinating landscape configuration of the whale-back hill-chain, which seems to beckon seductively from distant viewpoints, and partly because of the rural peace which reigns in this still-untamed high terrain. Britons also feel at home here because it is seldom fiercely hot – and it rains a lot ...

Eastern Franche-Comté is dominated by the Juras, and nowhere is this great mountain range more 'typical' than to the east of the Jura département préfecture, Lons-le-Saunier. About 30 kilometres from here the Hérisson river falls from precipitous limestone escarpments in a series of plunges, to form the famous Cascades du Hérisson. To get there, take the D471 and the D39 from Lons, then the D326 Hérisson valley road from the village of Doucier. This narrow minor road winds alongside two barrage lakes before reaching the end of the tarmac and the beautifully located camping ground of Relais de l'Eventail, named after the most spectacular of the Hérisson waterfalls, 'the fan'. This is a 3-star site, an integral part of a beauty-spot restaurant/bar complex, and it is open from 1 June to 15 September. On the richly verdant floor of a majestic natural

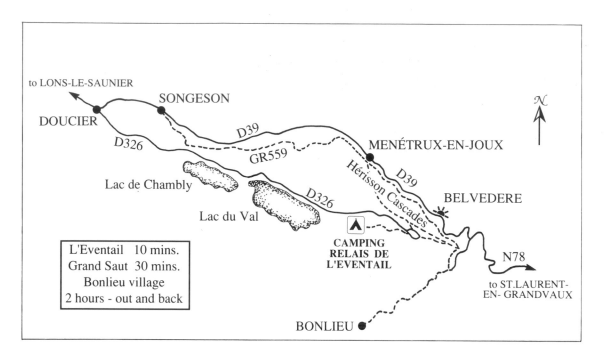

To LONS-LE-SAUNIER
DOUCIER
SONGESON
D326
D39
GR559
Lac de Chambly
Lac du Val
D326
MENÉTRUX-EN-JOUX
D39
Hérisson Cascades
BELVEDERE
CAMPING
RELAIS DE
L'EVENTAIL
N78
to ST.LAURENT-
EN- GRANDVAUX
BONLIEU
N

L'Eventail 10 mins.
Grand Saut 30 mins.
Bonlieu village
2 hours - out and back

amphitheatre, the pitching area is very spacious, dead level and with hedge-divided privacy bays optionally available. The modern toilet block is clean, and well appointed, and there is constant hot water to showers and hand basins. There are also mains electric hook-ups. The tariff, considering both the situation and the amenities, is very reasonable for a privately-owned camp ground. Noise level, both by day and night, is low, despite sporadic bursts of activity around the adjacent car park during weekends and high days. Coach-loads of sightseers do arrive periodically, but they don't stay long, walking only to the nearest waterfall viewpoint and then thronging the car park souvenir kiosk.

Serious explorers of this splendid locality have so many footpath options from the strategic base of the Relais, that it is difficult to decide which to commend. To see the principal (and closest) waterfall at its natural best, arrive early in the season – or at least

early in the day. L'Eventail could not be more appropriately named – the delicate tracery of cascading water tumbling over the sheer rock face looks for all the world like an extended fan. Push on along a rising path (almost over-enthusiastically colour-coded), for a top view of l'Eventail – impressive but not quite so stimulating as the lower – and then on again to see the Grand Saut which cascades unbroken for 60 metres. The rock lip it tumbles from is massive, and is enough to make you feel distinctly small.

For a second foray in this vicinity, consider the hill trail to the village of Bonlieu, which starts close to the lower Eventail viewpoint. This is a superb 3-kilometre walk along a perfectly defined and most diligently way-marked path (double yellow bands), soaring very steeply at first to traverse beneath an enormous overhanging limestone bluff. Glancing upwards during the initial ascent, you may wonder if climbing ropes may not be called for but the scramble is only brief and

The delicate water tracery of L'Eventail at the Hérisson falls.

the route then levels off to meander through beech woods and, finally, along a foresters' track to Bonlieu. Once you join the Bonlieu trail, your only company is likely to be soaring buzzards. This is just one delightful walk among many in the area, both along local trails and the GR559.

Two of Franche-Comté's Finest

Even in a region of France that is so richly endowed with vast forested areas, the Forêt de la Joux is exceptional. The foresters' world of great pine trees thrives here in a way that is not seen elsewhere in the country. Many are extremely venerable, some being over 200 years old, and they are progressively revealed by a fine forest-road journey between Cham-

pagnole and the village of Levier, to the northeast.

The Route des Sapins is meticulously sign-posted off the D471 east of Champagnole, and the drive covers 50 kilometres of beautiful forest, with a wide choice of waymarked walks off the tarmac, including some *sentiers éducatifs* (nature trails). One very attractive pedestrian route leads from the Maison Forestière du Chevreuil, to which you will be automatically directed if you follow the Sapin Route signs. There is good long-term parking here, in a green and pleasant picnic area fronting the Maison du Forêt, and the prospect of a forty-minute ramble to the Sapin Président, the oldest and tallest pine tree in the Forêt de la Joux. It is nearly 300 years old and 45 metres high, and the foresters estimate that it would be big enough to provide 600 cut planks of timber if it were ever felled!

Champagnole, on the Ain river, has a most pleasant and spacious camping ground, open from mid-June to mid-September. A 3-star municipal site, the facilities at Camping de Boyse are first class, and the pitching area is level and well maintained. Champagnole is an attractive town with a well-run municipal park and very good shopping facilities.

From the Joux forest, for north-bound travellers, there is an area of Haute-Saône which is well worth a detour. Continue north to Besançon and Vesoul, and take the N19 to Lure and the Haute Vallée de l'Ognon. Here you are in richly-wooded hill country that is very little visited by casual summer tourists; indeed, it is one of the least-frequented areas in all France, since it is not *quite* as dramatic as neighbouring Alsace. The scenery is stimulating enough, however, especially between Mélisey and Servance – a whole series of grand wooded domes in a very spar-

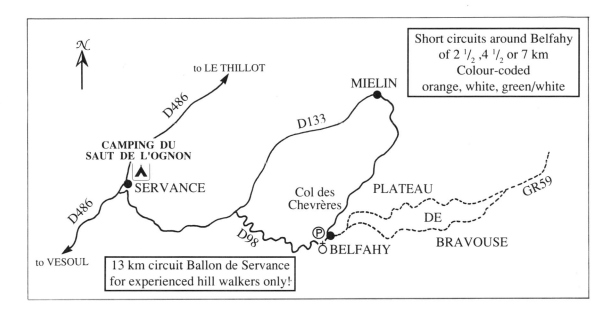

Map labels:
- N
- to LE THILLOT
- D486
- MIELIN
- D133
- CAMPING DU SAUT DE L'OGNON
- SERVANCE
- D486
- Col des Chevrères
- PLATEAU
- DE
- BRAVOUSE
- GR59
- D98
- Ⓟ BELFAHY
- to VESOUL

Short circuits around Belfahy of 2 $\frac{1}{2}$, 4 $\frac{1}{2}$ or 7 km Colour-coded orange, white, green/white

13 km circuit Ballon de Servance for experienced hill walkers only!

sely populated region, studded at higher levels by a host of tiny hill lakes. One village to the north of Mélisey is actually called La Mer, located as it is in the centre of the Plateau of a Thousand Lakes.

Servance is almost an island of civilisation amid a sea of trees, a small town of independent self-containment and boasting a strategic 1-star camping ground located almost in the town centre. A tiny tree-shaded paddock is the pitching area and the facilities are very basic but do include hot showers and mains electric hook-ups. It is privately owned, and the proprietor Monsieur Beretta, makes visitors feel welcome; the atmosphere is comfortably informal, not to say quaint. Good shopping is available virtually adjacent to Camping du Saut de l'Ognon, which is open from 1 May to 30 September. There is room for twenty units, although the site is very unlikely to be fully patronised. Servance is a very convenient base camp for exploring

Left: *Relais de l'Eventail from the rim of the Hérisson valley gorge – the Juras at their most majestic.*

a very convenient base camp for exploring the Haute-Saône region, especially the magnificent higher plains of the Forêt de Saint-Antoine and the Ballon de Servance. As long as your vehicle is of a standard size and in good mechanical fettle, you should be able to make the 6-kilometre ascent from Servance to Belfahy (via the D133 and D98) with ease – the grading is no steeper than Porlock Hill in Somerset, if somewhat more prolonged!

Belfahy is a tiny village with a very large tarmac area beside the church and another (primarily for winter ski visitors), just up the hill on the Mielin road. Park here and take your pick of hill tracks, short and easy for those in a hurry, long and tough for the fully experienced hill walker, or medium-distance circuits for those of average ability and inclination. All of these walks touch upon the Plateau de Bravouse, a semi-alpine height which must be one of the most beautiful in eastern France, right by the Alsace boundary. The pine-scented air around here should send you back to Servance healthily tired, mentally stimulated and ravenously hungry.

95

Ile-de-France

Départements: Seine-et-Marne – Région Parisienne
Préfecture: Paris

If Centre is the heart of the country, Ile-de-France is assuredly the hub. The influence of the capital spreads, web-like, steadily increasing urbanisation of the whole region year by year. There is scarcely a pocket of Ile-de-France landscape nowadays (especially the naturally attractive), that has escaped the effect of that latter-day phenomenon, *le weekend*. Forested terrain, river banks, man-made lakes and any pastoral patch that is green and pleasant all endure the regular inundation beginning every Friday afternoon and ending only at the very tail-end of Sunday throughout the summer. The great escape from stifling city confines is practised by the French with the greatest intensity and enthusiasm, and with good reason, since so many of them come from a recent past that is almost totally pastoral. Touring Britons may be surprised to find that this region is saturated with people and traffic from spring through to autumn, but they forget that for Parisians, still *paysans* at heart, that weekly absorbing of rural France is an essential; and it must extend to two full days and nights. The result of this intense, almost frenetic need for the 'Great Outdoors' is a proliferation of canvas and caravan villages.

In this area the genuine touring site is a rarity. Municipal grounds originally created as traveller havens have long since been taken over, often to an unsightly degree, by touring caravans that no longer tour, but squat, space-stealing and empty, during weekdays. For the foreign visitor, faced with this back-to-nature bustle, the answer is perhaps to confine any Ile-de-France visit to the Monday–Thursday period, or simply enter into the spirit of the game and join in the gregarious fun-making. And it *can* be fun, for, believe it or not, the Parisians are warm, friendly and jolly in their beloved open-air environment; and towards strangers, too, as long as they attempt a little French – no matter how badly.

Certainly it is worth the effort to visit this area, for there are some richly rewarding places within a stone's throw of the capital. However, only those prepared to use their feet will discover the quieter charms of the region. If your only experience of the Ile is the Paris Périphérique or the magnificence of the great capital itself, you have missed some of France's finest natural and man-made riches. There are many possibilities within a 100-kilometre radius of the Arc de Triomphe and the Champs-Elysées.

To the north-west, about 75 kilometres from Paris, in a great loop of the river Seine, lies La Roche-Guyon, the main road approach being via the N13. Within the département of Val d'Oise, there is a lovely

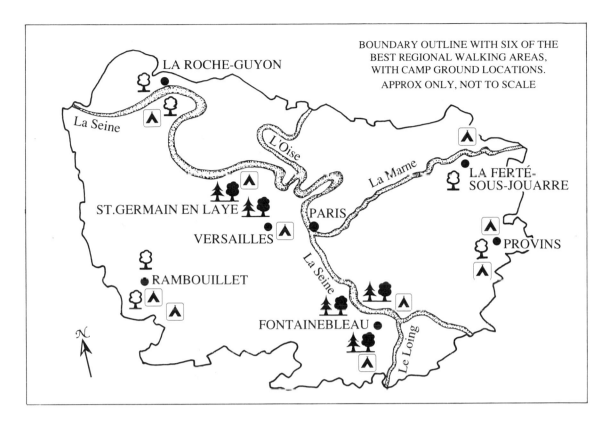

wooded enclave here, studded with bluffs and craggy chines, beside a reach of the Seine much appreciated by small-boat enthusiasts. The historic high-spot is a handsome château, partly medieval, where the architect has made cunning use of the existing rock outcrop. There is an extensive circuit path, diligently waymarked and running largely alongside the river, known as the Promenade du Vexin Français. Haute Ile is the bankside location of many troglodyte houses, and even a cave church. The walk from La Roche-Guyon to Rolleboise, about 14 kilometres, is the most revealing historically and scenically. Some of the caves here have reputedly been occupied since prehistory. This area was much favoured by the Impressionist painter Claude Monet, who lived not far away during the mid-nineteenth century. There is a camping

ground at Freneuse, south of La Roche-Guyon, while the best of the ridge walking lies 2 kilometres north.

The forest of St-Germain-en-Laye, west of the capital, boasts some excellent waymarked paths, and contains, in its south-eastern corner, what is arguably the most famous of European royal palaces – Versailles. Just 23 kilometres from Paris, Versailles is one of the world's greatest architectural and landscape-garden treasures. However St Germain is no less impressive in its way, with a fine château and national early-history museum. The Jardin Anglais here adjoins the surrounding forest where, again, most of the walking is Seine-side. There is camping at Maisons-Laffitte, north-east alongside the river and, for Versailles, at Camping Marcelin-Bethelot, off the N10, 1 kilometre to the east.

The forest of Fontainebleau, so near the capital yet so silent and unspoilt in parts. The GRI is to the south-west of the town.

There is truly ancient forest around Rambouillet, 50 kilometres or so south-west of the capital, alongside the N10. The château here was only completed in the early nineteenth century – quite modern by French standards. It also boasts the once-obligatory Jardin Anglais. All around is marvellous mixed woodland, once the hunting ground of successive French kings, and still a centre of *la chasse* today.

There are numerous marked footpaths and short promenades within an environment that is true woodland wilderness in places.

This is all the more remarkable when you realise that here is countryside within a region containing some ten million inhabitants.

Supreme among Ile-de-France forests is Fontainebleau, covering some 25,000 hectares and claimed – by Parisians at least – to be the most beautiful forest in France. Certainly it is opulently abundant in tree variety and contrasts of terrain, offering great potential to walker, climber and horse rider. Regrettably, if unavoidably, the creeping tarmac has sectioned the vast green space to a degree that would certainly pain those earlier inhabitants

The great Imperial palace of Fontainebleau, where the ghosts of François I, the Sun King and Marie-Antoinette still linger.

of Fontainebleau Palace. The wild boar and the wolf which were pursued obsessively by the French monarchy, and were the original reason for the creation of the hunting-lodge palace, have long been extinct. Much has been preserved, however, and it cannot be denied that, had there not been that royal passion for hunting, there would be little if any forest country close to so many of the great European cities.

Do see Fontainebleau Palace, if only to catch a whiff of seven centuries of history spanning a time scale from the Crusades to the Second Empire. Then explore the natural forest, some of the most interesting swathes of which lie just to the north-west of the Imperial town. There is a mighty sweep of sandstone ridge and steep-valley territory here, regally wooded with oak and beech, and punctuated with water courses, and jutting

99

spurs, irresistible to rock-scramblers and budding climbers. Footpaths and rides also abound, of course. For any extended exploration, a prior visit to the Forest Information Office in the rue Grande, Fontainebleau, is advised.

After the vast, treeless expanses of the agricultural plains, which appear to the car driver to dominate so much of the region, the rock formations that spatter this forest come as a distinct visual surprise. The Apremont Gorges, close to Barbizon, are the most popular rock faces. Barbizon itself is now a much-exploited national shrine to those nineteenth-century mavericks of the art world, the Impressionists. Here are the one-time houses and workshops of Millet and Rousseau, and the artists' meeting place, the Auberge Ganne, carefully preserved and open to visitors.

Back in the forest, apart from the wealth of waymarked short walks from all the tarmac access roads, the forest is quartered by stretches of the GR1, GR2, GR11, GR13 and GR32. While there is the possibility of camping within the forest bounds (beside designated forester houses, with prior permission), casual visitors might be better advised to use orthodox bases just outside the forest confines. There are touring sites at Grez-sur-Loing to the south and just east of the N7, and at Samois-sur-Seine, to the northeast, just off the D116.

La Ferté-sous-Jouarre, 66 kilometres east of Paris, is virtually encircled by some fine wooded country along the Marne valley. The town is on a 'route verte' and is reached via the N3. There is an extensive circuit footpath here, the Promenade des Morins, the prettiest section being that between St-Cyr and Sablonnières (about 9 kilometres). A camping

ground, Les Bondons, will be found at La Ferté. Above the plateau of Brie (where the soft cheese is produced), this town has a fine Bénédictine monastery and is the site of some significant Roman remains. A number of GR routes converge on La Ferté, including numbers 11, 14, 14A, and GR144.

About 90 kilometres south-east of Paris lies the nicest town of the Ile-de-France – Provins. There are no grandiose palaces here, nor extensive afforestation, nor a landscape that is particularly inspiring, yet this little town, just off the N19, seems somehow to encapsulate the spiritual and violent past of the region. Perhaps this is so because Provins is relatively little visited, or possibly it is because of the near-perfect preservation of the lofty medieval buildings; what is true is that it possesses a certain magic. The centre-piece is a mighty twelfth century Caesar's Tower, actually added to by British soldiery during the fourteenth century. They paid heavily for the defensive base which was erected, being caught eventually and put to the sword in a place known to this day as 'the English Pit'.

Joan of Arc attended mass at St Quiriace just by the tower, on 3 August 1429, in a church that was already nearly 300 years old at *that* time! Authentic texts show that Provins was an established centre of major political importance at the time of Charlemagne. A walk around the ramparts of this glorious remnant of the Middle Ages is a fascinating voyage of discovery.

It is no accident that the long-distance GR11 is routed through this, once the third most important city in all France. There are pleasant mixed woodland and meadow undulations along the trail, north and south of the town. For camp ground accommodation Fontaine Riante, 1 kilometre north, is the most convenient, if a little on the small side. For super-luxury lakeside pitching, consider 4-star Les Prés de la Fontains, between Hermé and Gouaix villages, 12 kilometres south of Provins.

Provins is an apt location to emphasise the fact that, although the Ile-de-France region is the most heavily populated in the country, the French people themselves are deeply aware of their natural heritage, and that their policy of preservation is more widespread and more stringent than that of most nations. There is a Gallic determination that the premier region of the Republic will not become totally immersed under concrete and tarmac; that one-quarter of the Ile-de-France land mass will remain afforested, and that 700-plus kilometres of footpath trails will remain – indeed, will be extended – to provide the vital green-space for the first French city.

A King's Legacy on the Perimeter of Paris

If Provins is the scenic jewel of the capital's eastern flank, Rambouillet is assuredly its western counterpart. Evolving from a royal hunting lodge amid an ocean of trees, the famous château is modest as French regal residences of the *ancien régime* go. This one was built by King Louis XVI for Marie-Antoinette, and, though it may be modest, contemporary visitors standing before this fairytale pile may more readily understand the ill-fated queen's attitude towards the breadless peasantry. It is now a presidential residence and summit conference centre, and there is free vehicle and pedestrian access to the gracious parkland and gardens, although you do pay to see the château interior.

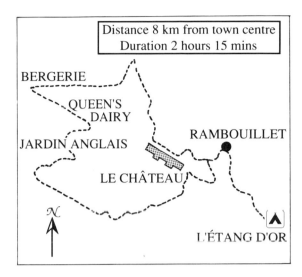

Beyond the manicured lawns, the Forêt de Rambouillet – another of France's most beautiful – covers some 20,200 hectares, a truly vast area, stretching from the Eure river to the high valley at Chevreuse. And all this genuinely rural countryside lies just 40 kilometres from Orly airport, with no immediate threat on the horizon from avaricious developers.

Camping l'Etang d'Or, open all the year round, is the obvious base for the Rambouillet region. This is a municipal enterprise, catering largely for residential and weekend caravans, in handsome surroundings in the heart of a forest enclosure large enough to incorporate a really spacious wildlife preserve. There is ample room for touring visitors and the facilities are basic but cleanly maintained, with good hot water supplies to showers, and mains electricity hook-ups. There is very pleasant walking direct into the forest beside the Etang d'Or (a rather murkier pond that its name suggests), or along one of the many excellent tarmac cycle routes laid

101

throughout the great forest. It is just a couple of kilometres' walk into Rambouillet centre, from where the camp ground is well signposted. From here, there is a wide selection of circuit walks and long-distance trails (including the GR1), especially to the southeast and north-west of the town. For a marvellous 8-kilometre stroll through the Golden Age of French history, consider the 2-hour circuit of the château perimeter. This takes in most of the architectural treasures, including the Queen's Dairy, the *Jardin Anglais*, the *Bergerie Nationale* (birthplace of the world famous Merino sheep), and, of course, the sparkling château itself.

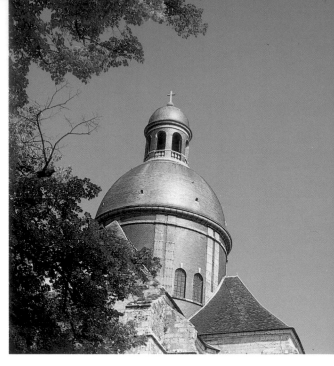

Provins St Guiriace.

The château at Rambouillet. This is one of the most attractive locations in the region.

Languedoc-Roussillon

Départements: Aude – Gard – Hérault – Lozère – Pyrénées-Orientales
Préfecture: Montpellier

Arid, dusty and much-urbanised, the Languedoc coastline in summer is one long shimmer of barren landscape, where only grape vines, developers and sun-worshippers abound. Like the rest of the Mediterranean shoreline (along with most others in western Europe), it is a consistent and uninspiring scene of linear build-up, from the marshlands of the Rhône estuary to the Spanish border below Perpignan. Yet such is the geography and huge size of France that within this same region there is also some of the finest unspoiled high country on the Continent. *Aficionados* will know immediately where I mean; others who love the wilder places will simply have to add the Cévennes to their short lists.

Largely within the départements of Gard and Lozère, the voluptuous and enchanting Cévennes mountain range might have been created solely for the hill walker. It is little wonder that Robert Louis Stevenson's *Travels with a Donkey*, written after his journey through the Cévennes in 1878, became an instant best-seller. Gifted though he was, the Scottish writer could scarcely have had better raw material awaiting him when he set off from low-lying Monastier-sur-Gazeille with his exasperating luggage-carrier Modestine. Ironically, the Cévennes of Stevenson's time were certainly more heavily populated than they are today. The evidence of the hand of man has actually decreased, and the authorities have made a virtue of necessity by creating the whole area a *parc naturel*, encouraging a new influx – albeit an ephemeral one – of visitors to supplant the mass exodus of peasant farmers which reached epidemic proportions after World War II.

As a point of interest, the park is the only one in France to support any kind of permanent habitation – about 500 people. The Cévennes' revenue comes nowadays almost exclusively from tourism. Thankfully, though, they do not suffer the mass kind, but rather are popular with those who enjoy natural pursuits among natural surroundings.

For the walker-wanderer the Cévennes actually become more, not less, attractive as we move towards the twenty-first century. The reclamation (almost a renaissance) of the old sheep-droving tracks has ensured a network of long-distance and circuit trails within the most beautiful of terrain. At higher altitudes above the treeline, notably around Mont Lozère, king of the Cévennes peaks, the air now rings in winter to the swish of skis, while the half-hidden valley villages draw income from the growing trickle of those seeking the 'real' France – the France that was for a former generation simply representative of poverty. The natural grandeur remains, protected by proclamation since 1970. A latter-day development worthy of mention is that Parc Cévennes became twinned with Parc National du Saguenay in Quebec Province, Canada, in 1984. This happened partly through the French connection of course, but also because of a new and significant eco-trend world-wide, which emphasises the necessity of open-space preserves on this finite planet.

The countryside in question lies north-west of Alès and expands ever more grandly as the N106 is followed through La Grand Combe to the acknowledged peripheral park base, Florac. It is a drive in excess of 70 kilometres, which provides an exhilarating scene-setter.

Florac is a hillside market town, not much more than an overgrown village, basking sleepily on the banks of the swiftly-flowing Tarnon, at an altitude of 542 metres. All the facilities that one would expect from a *Station Verte* are here, including three camp grounds. Camping de l'Essi is particularly charming, a modest green patch established by the local Syndicat d'Initiative below a massively regal bluff some 2 kilometres along the D907. There are only basic facilities here on a grassy farm meadow which is secluded though not isolated. Tranquillity amid mountain grandeur is the real attraction; plus the Sentier Corniche du Florac temptingly close to hand. For more comfortable quarters, there is the municipal touring site 2 kilometres along the Mende road, plus one other small and distinctly sloping ground on the town fringe beside the N106. The Syndicat d'Initiative opens from early June to the end of September and carries descriptive wallet maps and route

descriptions of park footpaths called *sentiers de découverte des paysages*. There is a good selection, and the prices are reasonable.

Stretch your legs though with a preliminary amble around old Florac, a marvellous cluster of medieval tumbledown buildings around an ancient feudal château, recently restored and now housing an excellent Parc Naturel information centre. For an immediate unfolding of rugged Cévennes countryside, make the l'Essi camp ground your base and wander down the road towards Florac for some 500 yards. On the right take the packhorse bridge which fords the Tarnon, following the *sentier* signpost indicating the four-hour ramble called La Nouvière Tardonnenche. There is bitumen lane walking for several kilometres (following a stretch of the GR43), which reveals a scattering of houses built in the stout

Florac, the strategic base for the Cévennes mountains and the Gorges du Tarn.

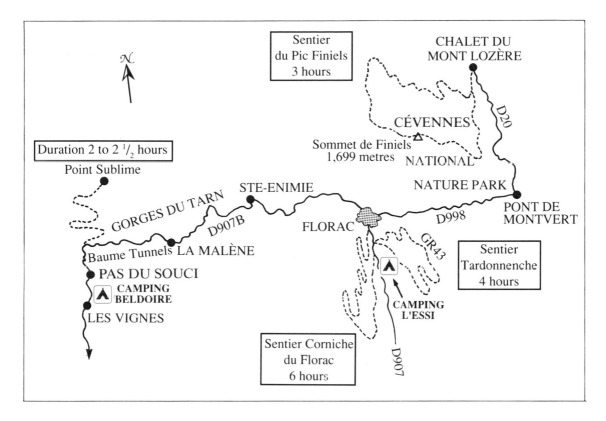

old Cévennes style – thick-walled, with small windows, and with rocks weighing the roofs against the winter winds that sometimes hurtle through the mountain valleys with great ferocity.

The climate of this area – half Mediterranean, half Alpine – is glorious in summer, and savage in winter. This, as well as a meagre topsoil over ungiving granite rock, explains to a large extent the population drift to urban comforts. For the leisure walker in June, it simply adds colour to a route of craggy, steep valley terrain, with the sparkling Tarnon white-water foaming far below.

A more elevated path, that of the Corniche du Florac, starts alongside the D907 between town and camp ground. If you fancy closer contact with those wind-eroded rock sen-

tinels which dominate the skyline above Camping l'Essi, this is the route to take. It is six hours of hard walking, so should appeal only to the fittest and most agile.

For even higher-level Cévennes walking of the most invigorating kind, you have to venture a little further afield. There could hardly be a more exhilarating example of mountain majesty than Mont Lozère, reached via a 20-kilometre drive from Florac. From the Mende road alongside the municipal camp site, take the signposted D998 to Le Pont de Montvert. Here you enter not only the high mountain country, but a place of history and of twofold interest to most Britons. Plumb on the Stevenson Trail (the tubercular scribe arrived here in a state of exhaustion after traversing Mont Lozère), this tiny settlement on the banks of the Tarn

Broom in full colour high above Florac, the Cévennes 'Cloth of Gold' during June and July.

was the scene of savage Protestant revolt against the Roman Church in the late seventeenth and early eighteenth centuries. The inevitable escalation of the rebellion was the eventual destruction of nearly 500 high Cévennes villages and the deliberate slaughter of all their inhabitants. The Camisard Revolt was finally put down after years of sporadic terror, yet still there are staunch Protestant pockets across country between the Tarn and Ardèche Gorges. There must be something about high-country existence that makes men incline to dissent, giving them a healthy freedom of spirit that is much safer nowadays than it once was.

There is another interesting Parc Naturel information centre at Le Pont de Montvert, although it is only open during July and August. There is also a lovely little camping ground within a few steps of the village shops, which carry a limited stock, but all the essentials. All in all, this is a highly recommended base for exploring the surrounding country. From here, you can continue the road ascent along the D20 for 15 kilometres to Chalet du Mont Lozère. This is another splendid drive, through high pasture, forest and steep-sided ravines. Here, high above the tree-line on the very roof of the Cévennes, there is a 3-hour waymarked circuit walk traversing the Sommet de Finiels at 1,699 metres.

For prettier walking, amid a landscape of constantly changing variety, there are alternative waymarked trails lower down the

mainstay of the Cévennes – and the foreseeable end of fossil fuel, life in these marvellous mountains may return almost to how it used to be, within a few decades. It's not an entirely impossible dream!

Gorges du Tarn

West of Florac lies another jewel of the Cévennes crown – the Tarn Gorges, an irresistible draw. As popular with drivers, canoeists and coach-parties as it is with walkers, the Tarn Canyon (like its Verdon and Ardèche counterparts) has been honed and prettied to smooth the way and attract the revenue from the strengthening tourist flow. However, the modernising and improvement programme

Ochre in rock in the Roussillon area.

Le Pont de Montvert, where life is still slow and peaceful, despite the motor car and the creation of a Park Information Centre.

slopes, notably around the tiny hamlet of Finiels. There is more of a Mediterranean influence here. It is a world of rushing streams, pine forests, lush meadows and a riot of wild flower colour through late spring and early summer. The long-neglected tracks along which sheep used to be driven to winter pasture are enjoying a revival, and the classic route from St Hippolyte du Fort to Florac is once again being tramped.

With the restoration of the sheep trails as GR routes, the tentative rebirth of the silk industry – once the other great economical

has had but a minor effect on this Goliath of primeval creation, as a mere few steps from the D907B will reveal. The deep river valley from Quezac to le Rozier, and the great plateaux of Sauveterre and Mejean to either side, are criss-crossed with hiking trails that are both long distance and local. Excellent large-scale maps are available in St Enimie, La Malène and Vignes. They are not cheap, but you will find that they are essential if you are staying a while.

Waterside camping grounds, *Gîtes d'Étape* and bungalow accommodation, exist in profusion all along the great rift, but they do become almost unacceptably crowded during high summer. Also, confined within the precipitous rock walls, the valley floor and flanks can become intensely hot at the height of the season. For these two reasons, most walkers wisely opt for an early or late season visit.

For instant access on foot to some of the most majestic Tarn heights on offer, leave your car between the Cirque des Baumes and Pas du Souci. Take the clearly signposted footpath (also promising drinks and snacks) to the Point Sublime. You may wonder, as you scale this skyscraper path, how on earth supplies are carried to the summit café. Well, of course, as on Snowdon, there is an easy route, in this case a snaking twister of a road which climbs for 13 kilometres to the Point from Vignes. All the way up the pedestrian cliffhanger, and from Point Sublime itself, the views are breathtaking.

The recommended camp ground base for this, the most awe-inspiring section of the Gorge, is Camping Beldoire, on a lovely wide stretch of the Tarn. Despite being adjacent to the road, it is appealingly secluded, yet with Vignes, its cafés, shops and hostelries just a short distance away.

Pyrenean Beauty
Driving or Walking

A little inland from Perpignan (on a less heavily-used summer route to Spain), lies Axat at the northern end of the D118. This is certainly one of the most exciting roads in Languedoc-Roussillon, if not in the entire Pyrenean range. Nearly 60 kilometres of defiles and gorges follow one after the other, as the seemingly endless ascent of the D118 traces the course of the river Aude. Culmination for the driver is a break-out into high mountain-pasture country of prairie-like dimensions, the savanna blanketed in places by great pine-forest swathes. At an elevation of some 1,500 metres, in the veritable heart of this marvellous landscape, lies the tiny village and new mini-ski resort of Formiguères. A scattering of chalets surrounds the original settlement, which is not only Catalan in name, but strongly reminiscent of Spain scenically.

This village can supply all the traveller's needs, including petrol, and there is a small, simple camp ground in a pine wood at the top end of the village (open from June to September). The setting is splendid here, almost totally natural, with a choice of GR routes and local trails to explore, principally through the neighbouring forests of Coste del Pam and Val de Galbe to the north-west. There are two sizeable barrage waters to either side of Formiguères, the largest of which – Lac de Matemale – is circumnavigated by a section of GR which links with a larger loop of the forest-traversing, trans-Pyrenean GR10. Those who love wilderness walking will surely revel in tramping this particular high plateau.

After a spell of comparative solitude there

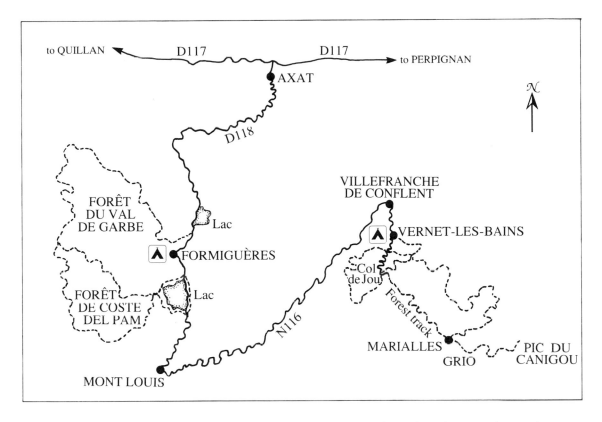

is, by way of contrast, a completely different
but no less interesting base of lower Roussillon, reached by a road route from Formiguères, of memorable grandeur. It starts
with a gentle descent at first from the summit
of the Col de la Quillane to Mont-Louis,
another massive and forbidding stronghold
built by Vauban to repulse Spanish incursions, and continues eastwards along the
N116. From here to Villefranche-de-Conflent
is a snaking downhill run, from 1,600 metres
to 430 metres in altitude, surely one of the
most exhilarating of mountain drives. Not
only are the panoramas superb, but also you
cannot help but admire the intrepid road builders. At the end of this strategic mountain
route, at Villefranche, awaits another magnificent Vauban conversion of an earlier (fifteenth-century) citadel. There is a fine inner

precinct of medieval marvels to be seen
behind the protective ramparts.

Leave the busy trunk road for the D116,
and consider Vernet-les-Bains as a base for
exploring more Pyrenean peaks, this cluster
dominated by the Pic du Canigou, towering
to 2,784 metres. There is a choice of camp
grounds in and around this picturesque
thermal spa, patronised in this case as much
by active, healthy visitors as by those with
maladies, since there is super walking in the
vicinity.

The principal objective is Canigou – if not
the summit, then terrain that will reward the
walker with glimpses of the giant and its
snow-capped neighbours. Try taking your car
south from Vernet along the D116 for some
8 kilometres to the Col de Jou. Here, where
the tarmac ends, you can park and walk

Pic de Canigou, the north face.

several alternative trails. Weather and season permitting, you can continue driving along well-graded if narrow forester trails to Mariailles, then carry on on foot along the GR10 to Canigou summit, passing the Arago refuge cabin half-way. This hike can be arduous and should be considered only by experienced mountain walkers. Whatever your choice of paths in this area there will be no need of the thermal spa after a few days pedestrian exploration.

The Cirque de Navacelles

In France, you are seldom far away from natural delight in one form or another, while occasionally you will come unexpectedly upon a scene not only of memorable beauty but of awesome nobility. One such place is the Gorge of Verdon in Provence; another is the Languedoc Cirque de Navacelles.

The base for this astounding natural sculpture is Le Vigan, roughly midway between Mende and Montpellier. The convoluted

streets of this ancient and colourful town might not seem an auspicious starting point for pastoral walking, but Le Vigan offers a choice of camping sites which are open for reasonable periods each year, while the Haute Languedoc *causse* country and Mont Aigoual, the Cévennes highest peak at 1,567 metres, lie to the south and north.

Camping le Val de l'Arre is about 2 kilometres from the town centre, well signposted off the D999 Ganges road (drive carefully to negotiate the tight turn under the double-arched bridge at the entrance). This is a riverside site, with tree-shaded pitches in the grounds of a pleasant old country house. The setting is agreeable, and the facilities reasonably adequate and clean, although nothing special considering the 3-star grading. A nice peaceful atmosphere prevails. The site is open from Easter to the end of September.

Le Vigan proudly calls itself the Pearl of the Cévennes. It has a park of centuries-old chestnut trees, a fine twelfth-century bridge, and ancient fountains spouting sweet water – 'Les Griffouls'. The town offers comprehensive shopping services and there are a

Beautiful country, so frequent in the Cévennes, around Le Vigan.

The astounding Cirque de Navacelles from the ridge-top relais. *There is a GR7 traverse for bold walkers.*

number of local walks, including a pleasant, lightly-trafficked lane section of the GR7 which is literally part of the Val de l'Arre camp ground. For any extended stay, the 1:50,000 IG map of the area is recommended.

For the road route to the Cirque de Navacelles, follow the Mont Aigoual signs to the edge of town, then the signposts to the Cirque, some 20 kilometres away along a narrow but well-surfaced road. The ascent is through lovely wooded hill country at first, which gradually gives way to the stern, granite-scattered plateau which is the mighty Causse de Larzac. Suddenly, before any hint of its proximity, the Cirque is revealed in the most dramatic manner immediately beside

111

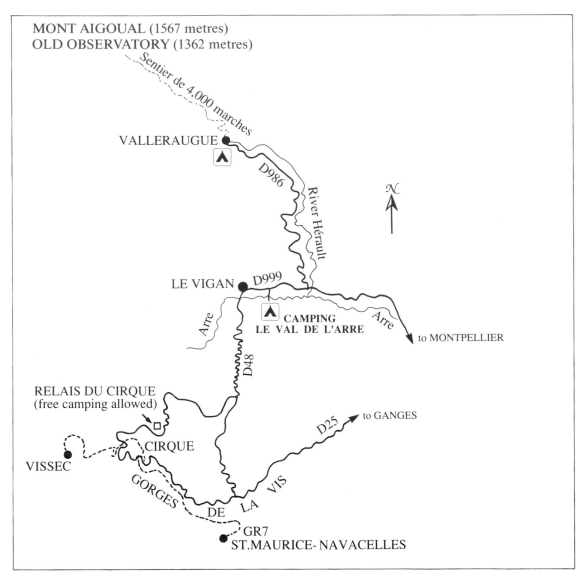

MONT AIGOUAL (1567 metres)
OLD OBSERVATORY (1362 metres)

Sentier de 4.000 marches

VALLERAUGUE

D986

River Hérault

N

LE VIGAN D999

CAMPING
LE VAL DE L'ARRE

Arre

Arre

to MONTPELLIER

D48

RELAIS DU CIRQUE
(free camping allowed)

CIRQUE

D25 to GANGES

VISSEC

GORGES DE LA VIS

GR7
ST. MAURICE- NAVACELLES

the isolated Relais du Cirque. It is a pulse-quickening revelation for two reasons – the boundless force of nature which must have occurred to create such a chasm, and the ingenuity of man to exploit such a steep and mighty amphitheatre. Only the French would have attempted to build a village at the very bottom of the abyss and engineer the unbelievable roads to it!

A popular section of the long-distance GR7 with local young walkers (recommended here to readers with a good head for heights) is that between the hamlets of Vissec and St Maurice-Navacelles. This path takes in both the Cirque and a dizzily impressive stretch of the extensive Vis Gorges. Walking along the rim of this stupendous geological fault, you can understand why locals compare the

112

The approach to Camping le Val de l'Arre, near Le Vigan.

Cirque, quite seriously, to the Grand Canyon of Colorado.

The Drovers' Trail – Footpath of 4,000 Steps

If you drive 22 kilometres north of Le Vigan via the D986 you are on the approach to the highest point in the Cévennes. Valleraugue is typical of Cévenol mountain villages, with its exceptionally tall houses and very narrow streets, and is faintly reminiscent of Le Pont de Montvert above Florac. Here, from the beautifully preserved medieval church, is the start of the Sentier de Quatre Mille Marches, an ancient drovers' route to the high pastures on the flanks of the great mountain.

It is not difficult to visualise the herdsmen and shepherds of the twelfth and thirteenth centuries receiving a last blessing in the church before setting off, perhaps for months, into the savage high country. Their route is preserved to this day, starting with a wondrously contorted stretch up and actually under the village houses to reveal increasingly expansive vistas. If you walk this steep and ancient track for about an hour in good light, you will be able to enjoy a panorama which stretches from the Pyrenees to the Alps; doubtless enjoyed by mountain men around AD 1100 and today the Sentier de Grande Randonnée. There is a choice of simple camp grounds hereabouts for those wishing to explore this trail in depth, the hundred-year-old observatory near the peak, or the summit of Mont Aigoual itself.

Limousin

Départements: Corrèze – Creuse – Haute-Vienne
Préfecture: Limoges

The smallest region of south-western France is Limousin, verdant and pastoral as any in the Republic. Limoges – porcelain capital of the world – is the only sizeable conurbation, and dominates the central département of Haute-Vienne on the river Charente. The rest of the Limousin region, especially throughout Creuse and Corrèze, is almost uniformly lovely. Sparsely populated, with scarcely a major tourist route marring it, Limousin has much pedestrian appeal. The climate is benign, almost Mediterranean, yet with an invigorating touch of freshness. Anyone who seeks a landscape *au naturel* should love the area for its abundance of forest, emerald pastures, and lakes and rivers, all linked by countless kilometres of well-surfaced and lightly-used minor roads.

The leisure traveller – and particularly the leisure walker – is deemed important, since tourism is now an extremely valuable contributor to the regional coffers. Ceramics and timber may still be Limousin mainstays, but the service industry, especially that concerned with tourism, gains annually as the new source of finance. Nowhere is this more apparent than in the vicinity of Vassivière, 50 kilometres or so to the east of Limoges.

Here, amid quiet hill country of pine and chestnut forests, the river Maulde was barraged in 1952 to create a huge lake for the generation of electricity. Today, it is also the acknowledged regional playground, not only for water-sport enthusiasts, but also for nature lovers wishing to explore on horseback or on foot. It is a massive inland expanse of water: over 1,000 hectares form this miniature sea, with such irregular and indented shorelines that it seems almost timelessly natural. There is even a central island of some 70 hectares, kept strictly car-free and dotted with imaginative granite sculptures. Such a natural aspect is a rare achievement for any artificially-created lake, particularly one so young, but the French have engineered the project brilliantly.

Within an enclave known as Monts et Barrages, the surrounding hills are of impressive if not spectacular elevation, notably in the south-east, towards the Plateau des Millevaches. The approach to this Limousin landscape is at its most beguiling east of the D941 out of Limoges, along the D13 minor road between medieval St-Léonard-de-Noblat high above the Vienne river and Peyrat-le-Château. This latter, a small market township (along with slightly larger Eymoutiers), is a much-favoured base for the area. Peyrat, with just 1,500 inhabitants, has a distinctive twelfth-century tower and dungeon, a huge central square out of all proportion to the size of the tiny town, a pretty lake which

laps the walls of the surrounding houses, and some interesting waymarked walks through the nearby forest of Crozat and alongside the river. There are actually seven recognised footpaths in the immediate area, most of which start from Peyrat, varying from 40 minutes to $4\frac{1}{2}$ hours' duration. Pamphlet guides and maps are available freely from the information kiosk in the place de Peyrat. In fact, several specially prepared pedestrian guides cover the whole Vassivière district.

Should you wish to make picturesque Peyrat your base, there is an attractive tree-shaded and terraced riverside camp ground, plus a choice of *Gîtes Ruraux* (bed and break-fast houses). The GR44 passes between Peyrat

Lac Vassivière from Les Sagnes camping ground at Port Crozac. A great walking centre and a preserved pastoral playground of Limousin.

Peyrat-le-Château, the village, donjon and lake.

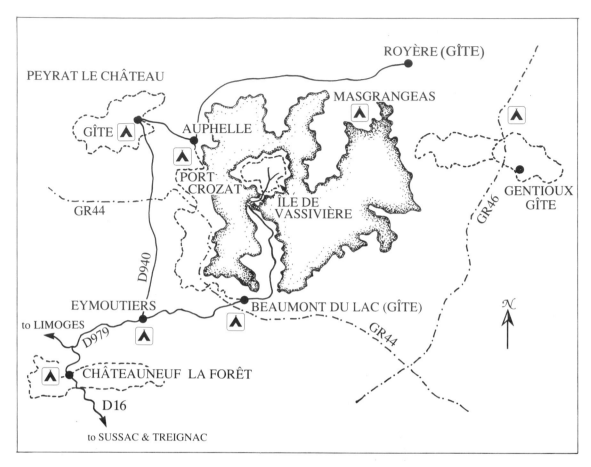

and Eymoutiers, an east-to-west traverse of Limousin, beginning at Limoges and negotiating some splendid countryside, including that around Lake Vassivière. This is a popular backpackers' route in summer, according to the local ramblers' association, largely tree-shaded as might be expected and, though hilly, not fatiguing country to walk.

Eymoutiers is the principal canton township, a *station verte* of old-world aspect, and with 3,000 inhabitants, the largest settlement in the area. Although there is some evidence of ancient France along the banks of the Vienne here, including a medieval church and a seventeenth-century tannery, it is not *quite* as pretty as Peyrat; but then it doesn't boast fortified remains or a 17-hectare lake right in the middle of the bourg. The situation of Eymoutiers is scenic enough, at the foot of the Plateau des Millevaches, but the camping ground is loftily sited with a twisting and narrow approach. It is also narrowly terraced, rather small and a fair step on foot from the town centre. Personal accolade for a base in this area goes to Châteauneuf-la-Forêt which, as its name suggests, is tucked away off the beaten track amid hill country of tall trees, a few kilometres south-west of Eymoutiers. It, too, has its own lake – a 12-hectare shimmer of unpolluted Limousin water – with a most pleasant municipal camping ground overlooking a safe bathing bay. The level, well-run site, is prettily situated within easy strolling distance of the town centre, which boasts good shopping, with much local produce displayed along the engaging main street.

Apart from tourism, much of the livelihood of Châteauneuf-la-Forêt comes from the production of parquet flooring; understandable, since the location is surrounded by a regal mixed forest of oak, beech, birch, larch and chestnut. It is not only the brandy-cask makers of neighbouring Poitou-Charente, who have twigged the value of Limousin timber.

There are a number of local short walks and longer trails hereabouts, notably around the Puy-de-Vaux, the Pierre Andouillère deep in the heart of Châteauneuf Forest, and Puy Venouhant, a wooded dome topping 600 metres. Altogether this is a back-country target of commendable attraction to any walker. The major attraction for the casual visitor to eastern Limousin is the lake of Vassivière, where there are some notable lakeshore and hill country wanderways. There are also some 45 kilometres of ocean-like sandy beaches, and every conceivable kind of sporting activity from sailing, horse riding and windsurfing, to water skiing, fishing and canoeing. Camping grounds and *gîtes* around the principal lake – and the three subsidiary waters on the eastern side – are many and varied, although probably the most patronised are those near the nautical centre of Port Crozac (close to Peyrat), and Royère-de-Vassivière on the north-eastern bank. Again, the great Plateau des Millevaches is the dominant landscape feature, rising sedate and wooded above the south-eastern shoreline. Social and night life is abundant throughout the summer months, with everything from rock and reggae concerts on the 'Island of Stones' and in waterside vacation villages, to artists' exhibitions and classical music evenings. It is, though, the 300 kilometres of waymarked paths that trace their way around the star-shaped water that are the real attraction. From Royère or Port Crozac, detailed pedestrian circuit maps are freely available; you simply take your pick and set off.

One very pleasant 2-hour stroll begins from the municipal camping site adjacent to Port Crozac – Les Sagnes at Auphelle. At first winding alongside the D222, after $1\frac{1}{2}$ kilometres it sheers off into pine forest where twists and turns (always well waymarked) lead the walker in a gentle clockwise circle. After about $7\frac{1}{2}$ kilometres you pass an orientation table at the 729-metre mark (the highest point of the walk), before rejoining the D222 a couple of kilometres west of Auphelle.

For a longer trek, you might consider the hamlet of Beaumont-du-Lac, due south of Port Crozac. This is a tiny place with a thirteenth century church and a population of 150. It also boasts a café/bar, much appreciated by walkers, particularly since it is located at the second highest point in the Vassivière region, at 770 metres. Loftiest of all is the hamlet of Gentioux-Pigerolles, at over 800 metres. With its skein of lakes, variety of interesting villages, and the pedestrian potential amid hill country on the grandest of scales, this is a region which merits a lengthy stay.

The beauty doesn't end at Lac Vassivière. From Châteauneuf-la-Forêt there is a touristic route southwards which is well worth taking. There are of course countless *Routes Touristiques* throughout France, but this one really does excel. It reveals Limousin back-country beauty which is virtually unbroken for 75 kilometres or so through the département of Corrèze. Seemingly endless hills clad with pine, oak and chestnut are populated mainly with rich chestnut Limousin cattle browsing the lush pastures of the Vézère valley and the Monédières Massif. The route passes close to Treignac, which has a medieval bridge and church, and finishes with a glorious visual bang at Uzerche, a majestic sixteenth-century stonepile perched on a precipitous knoll high above the Vézère. There is a fascinating stroll through history here, and, should you wish to stay overnight, there is a camp ground alongside the river, reached via a narrow arch and lane approach.

A Dordogne Plateau Walk

There's a district in the Corrèze département of Limousin called La Xaintrie, and it is one of the most attractive enclaves of Dordogne hill country in the whole of the *massif central*. Much less visitor-saturated than the upper reaches of the renowned river further to the north-east, Xaintrie is the triangle of terrain formed by the Dordogne gorges north-east of Argentat, and a snaking Dordogne tributary, the Maronne, which flows south and east from Argentat. The whole forms a marvellous area of high country, richly endowed with forests, fast-flowing feeder-streams, and a number of imaginatively barraged lakes

Near La Roche-Canillac, La Xaintrie district. There is beautiful combe walking hereabouts.

which actually enhance the effect of nature. One of several such waters is Lac de Feyt, close to the little village of Servières. This old-world hamlet is majestically dominated by a mighty château, and some gigantic rock crags which thrust upwards and outwards from spectacularly steep valley flanks.

The most impressive approach to this Limousin mountain landscape is to take to the minor roads south-east of Tulle, to the villages of la Roche-Canillac and St Martin-la-Meanne. From the latter, follow the D29 to the huge Barrage du Chastang, then ascend the sky-scraping valley ridge to Servières, a superb wooded plateau and the signposted campground about 4 kilometres away. Camping du Lac will be found at an invigorating height of some 500 metres where the pine-laden air is, almost literally, like wine.

This is a glorious setting for a camp ground, promptly exploited by the enterprising Servières council when the barrage project was completed. Camping Municipal du Lac is administered (indeed, 'stage-managed', as the brochure proclaims in English) by Madame Josette Alrivie, whose courteous and friendly manner makes visitors of all nationalities feel instantly welcome. There is open grassland pitching here beneath pine trees or within hedged privacy bays, the facilities are basic but clean and well maintained, and there is a restaurant and a small sailboat centre close by. The main attraction, indeed the only other attraction, is however the natural beauty of the area, and the real mountain tranquillity, the perfect accompaniment to a lake-shore circuit walk.

Surrounded by mixed woodland and just the odd house or weekend chalet retreat, Lac de Feyt is about 6 kilometres in circumference. About 3 hours of leisurely strolling via tarmac lanes, access tracks and footpaths, will circumnavigate it. The going is easy, there are no severe gradients, and only the odd feeder-stream to negotiate. Opposite the camp ground there is a tiny aqua-sport centre where a few pedalo craft are available for hire and where the lakeshore walker can find refreshment.

Servières château (seventeenth century) has a long and interesting history going back to the tenth century, when the site was a fortified stronghold. There is actually a medieval footpath cut through the rocks which links the village, high above the river Glane, with neighbouring Gleny on the banks of the Dor-

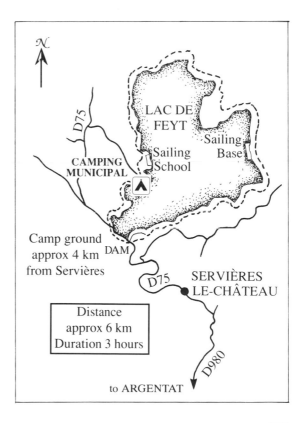

Servières Château near Lac de Feyt.

dogne. The château of Servieres, with its isolated setting, was used as a POW camp for German troops during World War I, and is today a hospital for the mentally handicapped.

Just a few kilometres to the north-west is another less dramatic but no less appealing wooded area of Limousin, in the vicinity of la Roche-Canillac. This is an ancient and atmospheric village, with a delightful tucked-away municipal camp ground, complete with chalet huts for hire and adjacent tennis courts. There is splendid walking hereabouts in beautiful deep wooded combes and valleys, along lanes and forestry tracks, especially to the south of the village.

Round About Bort-les-Orgues

On the far eastern side of Limousin and the département of Corrèze, where the river Dordogne forms the boundary with the Auvergne, is the much-praised resort of Bort-

les-Orgues. Once, no doubt, it was a sleepy mountain village mainly supported by a small tanning industry, but the creation of a mighty Dordogne barrage and lake has meant bustle and modernising which has much enlarged, although not necessarily enhanced, the town.

Certainly there is still the fine twelfth-century church (remnant of a riverside bastide), and from the old Dordogne bridge and place Marmontel a number of narrow, picturesque streets radiate. However, it is the surroundings, both immediate and middle-distant, rather than the town which attract visitors. Bort is a marvellous base for exploring some splendid stretches of the Dordogne, and the Auvergne Parc des Volcans, virtually adjacent. Bort's own celebrated natural attraction is a stern rock escarpment of strange configuration, which looms high over the town to the north-west and from which Bort gains its name. Les Orgues are uncannily like a row of organ pipes; not especially pleasing to the eye (particularly on a grey day), although certainly impressive and indicative of the power of nature at her most violent. The volcanic wall of million-year-old flutes fills the skyline above Bort and, of course, draws most visitors upwards. The view from the summit plateau over the town is as near to an aerial picture as you could hope to gain from an earthly footing. There was a footpath which encircled the outcrop, but this has been closed since much of the surrounding land is now in private hands.

There are a number of alternative marked footpaths in the vicinity, of which number five on the Syndicat d'Initiative list is particularly revealing (free fact sheets available from the tourist office in place Marmontel). This walk takes about $1\frac{1}{2}$ hours and begins with a street and then lane ascent, to a small Notre Dame statue. Pause for a deep breath here, then continue for another half kilometre before turning sharp right past a farm off the tarmac and on to a footpath, just slightly higher than the obvious farm track. Follow the low stone wall through the woods, along the hill flank for some wonderful eagle-eye panoramas – not only of the town, but also the distant Dore mountains of the Auvergne – before descending once more to the town. The tan markers along this route, incidentally, are in distinctly short supply, although the path itself is not difficult to trace.

Bort may not be the prettiest of Limousin towns, but it does possess warmth and character, and if you linger a day or so it does begin to win your heart. Certainly no setting could be more congenial as a base than the camp ground of Toulourou, on the minor road to Ribeyrolles hamlet, about 3 kilometres westwards. This is only a simple 1-star site, but the facilities are clean and main-

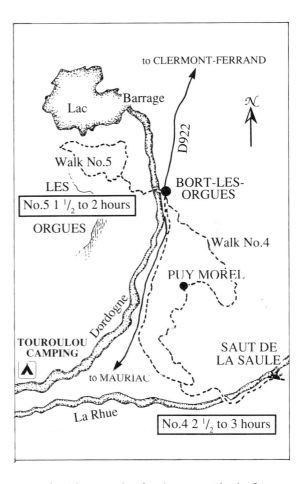

tained with a touch of military pride, befitting for a haven whose archaic name translates as 'foot soldier'. The location is beside a quiet-flowing reach of the Dordogne, with fine pastoral views in all directions. Mains electricity and hot showers are available for very modest extra charges, the atmosphere is comfortably relaxing and – unlike its sophisticated municipal counterpart nearer town which is closed until 1 June – Touroulou is open from Easter to the end of September. There is agreeable lane walking direct from the camp, either

The distinctive fissured wall of nature which dominates Bort-les-Orgues.

along the cul-de-sac to Ribeyrolles, or upwards under the shadow of the looming Orgues pillars.

For a more extended walk, consider number four on the Syndicat d'Initiative information sheet. This takes you to the hamlet of Puy Morel, just to the south-east of Bort, across the Dordogne and thus out of Limousin and into the Auvergne. There is an obvious footpath (green-arrowed), which takes over at the end of the tarmac lane, to traverse a rock-studded and wooded plateau, broken here and there by grazing meadows. The path meanders south-east, descends to the gates of a special education centre (CAT), then goes back to the town alongside the

The plateau path at the hamlet of Puy Morel, near Bort-les-Orgues.

122

railway line. This is a pleasant walk and you get another memorable view of those ubiquitous Orgues. For those with extra energy, there is an extension footpath from the CAT gates, to the Saut de la Saule (1½ kilometres), an attractive cascade on the river Rhue, a tributary of the Dordogne.

The principal attraction of Bort-les-Orgues as a base is not in Limousin, but its natural competitor, the Auvergne Parc des Volcans. Though not strictly within the compass of Limousin, mention must be made of a good 4-star camp ground with a gratifyingly low tariff (considering the scenic setting), close to the village of Lanorbe. Open on 1 June, Camping de la Siauve lies just off the D922 about 3 kilometres from Bort, is super-modern in conception and administration,

The fifteenth-century Château Val on Limousin border near Bort-les-Orgues.

with chalet huts for hire on the shores of the great barrage lake. Among other attractions in the vicinity is a variety of footpaths (both short circuit and long-distance GRs), and a fabulous fairy-tale cluster of fifteenth-century towers that is the Château Val, just a couple of kilometres away.

Two Little Lakes near Limoges

When you have seen the fine old heart of the Limousin préfecture – and probably bought your souvenir porcelain – the contrasting calm of the countryside may appeal to you, especially in the heat of summer. Limoges is one of the major transit cities of the great north-south routes of France and the recognised half-way house between Le Mans and Toulouse. Consequently, all the camp grounds within close confines of the porcelain capital are crowded and over-used from early spring through to late autumn. This is not the case a little further afield, and two camp grounds especially deserve a mention, since they both have many footpaths. They are located, too, amid some of the prettiest of north Limousin terrain, known somewhat grandly as Le Pays d'Ambazac et des Puys et Grand Monts. The rounded granite hills of the Ambazac range are bountifully wooded and watered by no less than five major rivers – the Vienne, Taurion, Couze, Gartempe and Ardour – so it is hardly surprising that the region should be one of the most prolifically lake-studded in all France. The barrage builders have been busy, and their particular pride and joy is Lake Pardoux, dwarfed by Lake Vassivière, but still covering a huge 300 hectares.

Ambazac's water and the camp ground beside it are worth a detour via the D5 if you happen to be travelling south on the N20. A

123

nice little town about 20 kilometres north-east of Limoges, Ambazac boasts a 2-star municipal camp site on the shores of 27-hectare Lake Jonas, where waterside footpaths make for pleasant and peaceful evening strolling well away from all trunk road noise and bustle. The site is open from 1 June to 15 September. There is terraced pitching, although shade is at a premium – a distinct drawback if it happens to be really hot weather. If this is the case, a little deeper into Grands Monts country there is Laurière – about 20 kilometres north-east of Ambazac – which has another picturesque lake with a shoreside camping ground situated amid lush woodland, offering a wealth of shade. This well-appointed 2-star municipal site is open from 15 March to 31 October. You cannot walk with ease all the way around the barrage water of Laurière, Le Lac de Pont a l'Age, but there are some pleasant short paths leading directly from the terraced camp ground located above the leisure *plage*. Laurière itself is an ancient and interesting hamlet, with a feudal past stemming from the twelfth century – an intriguing well-preserved rustic gem of old France, light years away from the contemporary Limousin reflected by Limoges and the arterial trunk routes.

Other Regional Options

For those prepared to brave the traffic congestion and somewhat confusing street layout, Limoges has a fascinating city centre, still thriving in the old way, amid an ever-widening sea of concrete and contemporary development. The art of the kiln is much on display, but it is La Cité, the oldest part on the banks of the Vienne, which is really interesting – an eye-catching delight of half-timbered houses, cobbled streets, colourful squares, open markets and the ancient butchery quarter dating from the fifteenth century. All but obscured now by modern Limoges, it is a cache of unexpected charm worth finding.

Limoges is a vibrant city thronged with people, but nearby lies a desolate ruined Limousin township inhabited only by ghosts; at once horrifying, and strangely compelling. This is no archaeological remnant of the distant past, but a preserved shrine testifying to the darker side of contemporary man. Oradour-sur-Glane was the scene of a reprisal massacre and obliteration in 1944 by SS troops. Today it is preserved exactly as it was on the infamous day in June when the entire population of 642 people was slaughtered, and the village put to the torch. It is untouched to the last scorched brick, with car skeletons of that era, chillingly dated shop signs, a gutted church and, most searingly poignant of all, the skeletal schoolhouse, now a silent memorial to 247 children. It will remain in perpetuity thus, and visitors from all over France, and farther afield, come to pay their respects and shake their heads with incredulity. Old Oradour was quite a sizeable settlement, and it takes an hour or so to walk the haunting perimeters properly. It is a sobering experience. The French nation are determined it will never be forgotten, and it is clearly signposted on all approach roads, about 20 kilometres north-west of Limoges. There is spacious car-parking and access is free of charge. At the charred archway entrance there is a simple notice: *Souviens-toi* – 'Remember!'.

Pays de la Loire

Départements: Loire-Atlantique – Maine-et-Loire –
Mayenne – Sarthe – Vendée
Préfecture: Nantes

Those unfamiliar with France might assume that this region is one glorious wedge of green land to either side of the Loire, studded at regular intervals with fairy-tale châteaux and castles. It is, after all, *the* French river valley extolled by seekers of pastoral beauty. In part, this sort of landscape does still exist, although it is thinly reflected in the region that is named after the famous river. For the best of château country you have to travel eastwards into the neighbouring region of Centre, to ancient Touraine, where breathtaking combinations of regal river and glorious architecture form that sought-after mix of memorable images, or to Amboise, Blois or Gien.

In the Pays de la Loire, outside the capital of Nantes, those château stone piles are more widely scattered and seldom as close to the river as might be imagined. The one stunning exception is Saumur. Here, a majestic fortress-château towers above the river along one of its most dramatic, island-dotted reaches, fully justifying the town's claim to be the Pearl of Anjou. There is too, the unique exhibition of two facets of war, for Saumur is not only the home of the most illustrious and ancient of military riding schools, it also hosts the greatest collection of tank warfare relics in Europe, in a world-famous museum.

Saumur is an illuminating old town to tramp around, not only for its newly-created pedestrian precincts in the most interesting localities, but also because most of the historic delights are within easy strolling distance of each other. There is a camp ground on the Ile Offard, in the centre of the river, should you wish to overnight in a strategic spot. Saumur is also firmly on the long-distance walker's route, since the GR36 and GR3 cross on their east–west and north–south trails here. One of the prettiest routes (virtually all lane walking, since there is little riverside foot access hereabouts), winds north-west towards Angers. *En route* are the acknowledged beauty spots of St Florent, Trèves, Cunault and Gennes. All of these villages punctuate a scenic 16-kilometre stretch of the Loire south bank. All provide good visitor amenities including camp grounds, information centres and a choice of local footpaths. Some of these paths touch upon prehistoric or medieval sites in the vicinity of the river, while others meander through woodland and laid-out leisure parks, or via interesting features of the villages themselves.

Gennes, with its neighbouring hamlet of Les Rosiers on the north bank, is a particularly attractive base area. One of ten touring sites between here and Saumur, the

The fortress-château of Saumur; the essential Loire Valley scene and a fascinating fount of history.

2-star municipal ground of Gennes is immediately adjacent to the river. The Loire is imposingly wide here, and with immense stretches of sandy edging that are so rarely flooded that they are rated as *plages*. The river bridge, which links Gennes with Les Rosiers, is double-spanned, the central supports utilising a mid-river islet which contains a tiny landscaped picnic area. Since Gennes is twinned with Wincanton, this is rather amiably named Wincanton Parc. The view from the bridge, of Gennes and the twelfth-century spire of St Eusebe topping a massive wooded knoll, is superb.

From the camping ground, which is spacious, tree-shaded, level and congenial, it is a short step to the little town centres of both Gennes and Les Rosiers; the latter is somewhat smaller and perhaps marginally prettier than the former. Both provide comprehensive shopping facilities, cafés, restaurants and information centres. The Rosiers camp ground is smaller and more distant from the village, but it is clean and shadily inviting, despite being immediately alongside the D952 which carries more traffic than the south bank D751. There is very limited riverside walking – on either bank – but Gennes has two local promenades of which it is quite proud. The first is within the Parc Municipal de Joreau, just to the southeast. Here are some 200 hectares of typical

The bridge linking Gennes and Les Rosiers.

Saumurois countryside encompassing a small lake, waymarked paths, one of those increasingly popular health and fitness courses (*parcours de santé*) and picnic areas. There is spacious car parking here, or you may walk direct from the town along the rue de Pressoir from Gennes gendarmerie.

This is a modern imprint on the Loire valley, but there are also those created in the prehistoric era, revealed by tackling part of the 15-kilometre circuit route entitled Itineraire No 1 de Saint Maur. This pamphlet, available from the Gennes tourist office, outlines an interesting walk from St Maur, a hamlet located about 6 kilometres from Gennes and reached via the D132 riverside road through Le Thoureil. From St Maur there is a lane and woodland track route south-east, of some 4 kilometres, to the Dolmen de la Bajoulière – just one of several Loire valley megaliths in the vicinity, and one of the largest and most impressive. There are other trails in the vicinity; the one incorporating the finest stretch of the Loire bank is possibly that around St Rémy la Varenne, west again of St Maur and a section of the long-distance GR3.

Between Le Mans and the Loire, the region is green if unremarkable – vast agricultural plains for the most part, except for the splendid Forêt de Bercé south-east of Le Mans which is traversed by the GR36 (see page 132). Long distances between habitation extend across the terrain of north-western Loire, with limited appeal for the leisure walker. South of the great river, however, the landscape, climate and ambience change subtly yet distinctly. Here begins the first of those celebrated wine routes which march across the southern half of the country, where the sun shines more warmly and where living out of doors is more consistently agreeable. The traveller who presses on to the southern corner of the Pays de la Loire is rewarded with a singularly intriguing enclave of France that is part Atlantic and part Mediterranean in aspect and climate – the département of Vendée.

One part of this area has been tagged – with more imagination than accuracy – 'Green Venice', and is a strange wetland of sluggish and weed-choked waters, where cattle are ferried in punts and even weddings are waterborne. A far better place to see is a little-visited forest region just north of Fontenay-le-Comte, where some of the best walking in south-western France is to be found. Mervent is the base, and the dense, beautiful forest around this ancient village perched high above the barraged river Mère is the objective, along with some 2,000 hectares of oak- and chestnut-sided gorges and valleys which now form the Parc Naturel de la Vendée.

Fontenay-le-Comte lies 78 kilometres inland from the Atlantic resort of Les Sables-d'Olonne. From this time-mellowed old town, take the D938 for 6 kilometres and turn right opposite Hôtel Le Lac on to the D99 minor road. About 3 kilometres into the forest of Vouvant is the entrance lane to Mervent municipal touring site.

Fontenay-le-Comte; many famous (and infamous) people have lived here – from Rabelais to Molière, from the Marquis de Sade to Simenon.

Camping du Chêne Tord (the twisted oak), is a 3-star ground extending over 4 secluded hectares of broad-leaf woodland. It is just under 1 kilometre from Mervent village, and offers attractive seclusion, yet without isolation. It is level for the most part, and there is plenty of space on this site for most months of the year. Visitors are free to select their own patch beneath the tall trees. The atmosphere could not be more peaceful, with the noise level being low to non-existent, both by day and by night. The facilities are clean, modern and comprehensive, with hot water to hand, and really hot showers. There are plentiful drinking water standpipes and mains electric hook-ups. The warden is resident, and the enterprise is operated efficiently yet without fuss and it is open all year. The tariff is medium.

The deep forest setting, the tranquillity, and the pure air make this a base with an infectious ambience, where familiarity, especially through pedestrian exploration, steadily increases fondness. It is of course the walking potential that makes Mervent something special. Much of the land and waterscape round the villages of Mervent and Vouvant is man-made, but this in no way detracts from the beauty, or the dramatic impact on any newcomer. For a revealing preview of the terrain awaiting your footsteps, walk the short distance to the village square and wander into the gardens of the old château (now the town hall), which are freely open to visitors. Take a peek over the ramparted garden wall; if the scene doesn't impress you, your pulse must have stopped . . .!

The steep-sided gorges to either side of the barraged confluence of the rivers Mère and Vendée come as a distinct surprise, since there is little indication of such grandeur on the approach from Fontenay-le-Comte. It illustrates in a dramatic way what flowing water over a few million years can do to any landscape. The mini-peninsula far below, by the way, is known as the Ile les Paillottes.

Mervent today is part of a much larger inland peninsula, loftily located high above its elongated lake which, since it was dammed

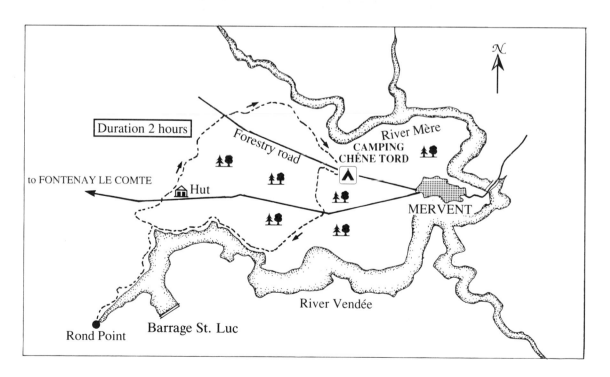

Coastal path near St Jean de Monts; sand, sea and space ...

in 1956, is both a practical asset and a distinctive leisure attraction – twin virtues much approved of by the pragmatic French. So successful was this particular project that they built a second barrage, the Pierre Brune, in 1979. Both of these engineering masterpieces may be visited via marked footpaths from the village, one being 4 kilometres away, the other 5 kilometres. There is also a choice of five waymarked local footpaths in the vicinity, ranging from $1\frac{1}{2}$ to $3\frac{1}{2}$ hours' duration, plus a section of the GR364 which largely traces the banks of the river Mère, just to the north of Mervent.

The 2-hour walk which begins directly from the municipal camping ground is one of the most interesting, since it touches upon both the river Mère and the river Vendée, traverses some deer forest and has a short detour trail at the southern end of the circuit, offering close-up views over the Vendée barrage. *Sentier* pamphlets are obtainable free of charge from the tourist office in the village square, next to the Post Office. Mervent also boasts a good general store and a *boulangerie* which produces delicious bread on the premises.

Atlantic Coast – Mediterranean Ambience

The Vendée marshes have blossom in February, and umbrella pine forest backing on to silver-sand beaches with an annual sun

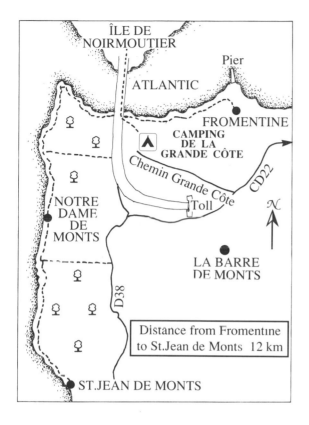

The bridge link between the mainland and the Ile de Noirmoutier.

average (thanks to the Gulf Stream) rivalling that of the Riviera. The vast, distinctive flatlands are relieved along the Atlantic foreshore below the Ile de Noirmoutier by a line of low sand-hills, named successively, La Barre de Monts, Notre Dame de Monts, and St Jean de Monts. The result is an unusually intriguing shoreline in an area that is not over-visited by touring Britons; this is surprising, since there is super camping here, some magnificent beaches, and very pleasant – and extensive – foreshore walking. It represents an attractive combination of leisure virtues which are all at their annual best in spring or early autumn. In high summer the region is best left to the natives, who descend on this coast in force from cities like Nantes and Poitiers.

There are six camp grounds around the tiny resort of Fromentine; the municipal Grande Côte is perhaps favourite for its spaciousness (incorporating almost a thousand individual pitches), and for its direct access to the sandy foreshore. Very good facilities are provided by a positive wealth of modern toilet blocks dotting the huge pinewood spread. The site is open from Easter to the end of September and is about 1 kilometre from Fromentine via the beach route.

Still semi-wild, this coastal stretch remains miraculously unspoiled by high-rise concrete, with sweeping vistas of the Atlantic uninterrupted save for the horizon island of Yeu which can be seen 23 kilometres distant from the Noirmoutier toll bridge. The beach walking is splendid and you can stroll over the motorists' toll road link to Noirmoutier island if you wish. The beaches are far superior to any on offer along the Mediterranean coast, while the Atlantic air alone is worth the visit.

The most direct, and hassle-free route to

131

here from the north is via the St Nazaire toll bridge spanning the Loire estuary. At 3,356 metres this is claimed to be Europe's most imposing. This way you avoid going anywhere near Nantes, which can be a driver's nightmare. What is more, you enter the region of Pays de la Loire in a highly dramatic manner.

The walking potential from the vicinity of Fromentine and La Barre de Monts is so wide and varied, *and* visually obvious, that no elaboration is necessary. Just to whet the appetite, however, there is a 12-kilometre stretch of clean sand beach backed by woods which you will discover simply by walking south along the tide-line – highly recommended for any early or late season visit. By way of a bonus – or black mark, depending on your viewpoint – there are designated nude-bathing sections around the Monts settlements.

You might assume that Les-Sables-d'Olonne, the principal resort of the Vendée coast, is equally worth a visit. Well, bigger is not necessarily better. The forest is there backing those fine sandy beaches, but there is also a surfeit of urban development, and a positive rash of camp grounds and holiday parks, all of which guarantees an almost intolerable level of concrete, cars and *homo sapiens* right throughout the high summer months.

Clemenceau Country

For a base near to the fun strip of Les-Sables-d'Olonne, but on a much quieter stretch of this Pays de la Loire coast, press on along the D949 towards Luçon then turn south in 15 kilometres on to the minor road to St Hilaire-la-Forêt. There is a nice little family-run camp ground in the hamlet, called La Grand Metairie. Tranquillity prevails and it is only 6 kilometres from St Vincent-sur-Jard and the seaside cottage of the French statesman, Georges Clemenceau. His weekend place is now – of course – a museum. There is pleasant foreshore walking as well as forest footpaths around the little bay here, and a simple municipal camp ground in a pinewood setting. The GR364 describes a wide loop from the coastal woods around Jard-sur-Mer, swinging north-west above St Hilaire-la-Forêt and passing close to the giant dolmen of La Frébouchère, one of the most celebrated in all France.

Another Regional Option

Seemingly a million miles from the Vendée coast, yet in its way outstandingly attractive, is the Forêt de Bercé, to the south-east of Le Mans. Unless you happen to be an avid motor-sport fan, the industrial sprawl of Le Mans will hold limited appeal. For the natural beauty of Sarthe, make for Château-du-Loir, south on the N138. Some kilometres south of here, in the village of Dissay, there is a pleasant municipal riverside camping ground in the place de la Mairie.

The great lake and forest area of Bercé spreads wide north of here, traversed by the GR35 and local circuits through some majestic oak and beech enclosures. Despite the busy artery route of the N138 between Le Mans and Tours, this lovely woodland country above the gentle river Loir is a restful leg-stretching objective within a reasonable day's drive of the Channel ports.

Lorraine

Départements: Meuse – Moselle – Meurthe-et-Moselle – Vosges
Préfecture: Metz

The double-barred Croix de Lorraine, symbol of Gaullist Free France in World War II, Verdun and the battlefields of World War I, the birthplace of Joan of Arc, and the power-house of heavy industry around Metz are some of the more obvious associations of this region. Lorraine is not in the premier league of tourism. This is in some ways surprising, for it is bisected north to south by the Meuse and Moselle rivers, with quiet green beauty on a grand scale to the east and west of the Thionville–Epinal artery. While the influx of British visitors remains relatively low each summer, the Dutch and Germans are well aware of Lorraine's charms, especially those who seek the simple healthy pleasures of pastoral France. If you are already an enthusiastic leisure walker you will probably be well aware of the regional potential; if not, then the following suggestions may convert you into a Lorraine lover.

Enter the region via Verdun on the N3/D964 crossroads and you are at once in a place that reflects the best and worst of human endeavour. Magnificent examples of architecture spanning every important era from Roman, through Medieval to Renaissance are here on the banks of the Meuse. In and around this gracious town, however, the visitor is constantly reminded that here was the place where, in 1916–17, a generation of Frenchmen and Germans fought a bitter war. The casualties on both sides were huge and the numerous preserved fortifications, cemeteries and entrenchments around the town are mute testimony to the slaughter.

Turn south for a more peaceful Lorraine, along the D964, following the gently-flowing Meuse to the market town of St-Mihiel. There is a spacious, level camp ground here on the banks of the river, a Youth Hostel and a Syndicat d'Initiative in the town centre. Here you are on the western boundary of the largest of two regional nature parks, the impressive centrepiece of which is Lake Madine. There are two other, more rural campsites at the lakeside, part of a comprehensive leisure complex which includes horse riding, windsurfing and other watersports. The camp grounds are almost adjacent, one a 2-star, the other 3-star, and both are open from April to September. There are footpaths in the immediate vicinity of the lake, but the best walking lies just to the north-west of the water, among some lushly-wooded and rounded hills close to the hamlet of Vigneulles. Waymarked trails vary from 1 to 4 hours' duration, and there is an interesting bird sanctuary just to the north of the hamlet of Heudicourt.

133

The Verdun trenches, which are still a place of pilgrimage for the army. Many of these shrines were preserved by American generosity.

Contrexéville

Vittel and Contrexéville are names constantly seen the length and breadth of France on the ubiquitous bottles of drinking water. The former is an industrious production and distribution centre of the desirable *eau de source*, the latter a more up-market spa. The two towns lie just four kilometres apart in the département of Vosges, and Contrexéville is particularly colourful with throngs of visitors seeking 'the cure', testifying to the therapeutic pulling power of the waters. The number of hotels around the thermal springs is staggering, considering the limited area of the town.

For those of you seeking simpler accom-modation, there is a nice little touring site on the eastern fringe, called Tir aux Pigeons, a 3-star municipal ground located amid woods of tall trees beside the sports stadium. Individual hedged pitches are provided and the facilities are clean, modern and comprehensive. The 1-hectare ground is open from 1 May to 30 September and is well signposted from the town centre.

Before you don walking boots, a visit to the Syndicat d'Initiative should prove profitable. To get there, turn left at the campsite entrance, cross the road and turn right along an obvious footpath at the end of a small group of houses. The path crosses the railway, leading almost directly to the tourist office and thermal station 10 minutes away.

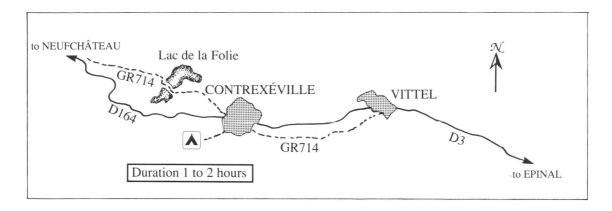

There is a section of the long-distance GR714 which bisects the pleasantly wooded strip of country separating Contrexéville from Vittel, plus another of those health and nature circuits situated just north-west of the town by the Lac de la Folie, together with a number of waymarked circuitous paths. The lake itself is situated just to the north of Contrexéville centre and is signposted via the Chemin des Lacs. There is excellent free parking space here with a small café and restaurant adjacent, plus an open-air swimming pool. Access paths around the water and in the adjoining woodland are clearly marked, as befits this park-like area, all part of the dignified and rather sedate face of this eminent spa resort. Certainly enough to warrant a visit if you are anywhere in the area.

Heart of the High Vosges

The true scenic pride of Lorraine is Gérardmer and the surrounding countryside of the lakes valley. Located deep in the western flank of the Vosges mountains, the landscape on approach from Epinal is quite superb – lush pastures alternate with forested hill slopes, and there is a riot of vivid green in spring and early summer that even the south of France might envy. Gérardmer is one of the great outdoor-pursuit centres of eastern

The hills of Lorraine, a blend of forest and open meadows.

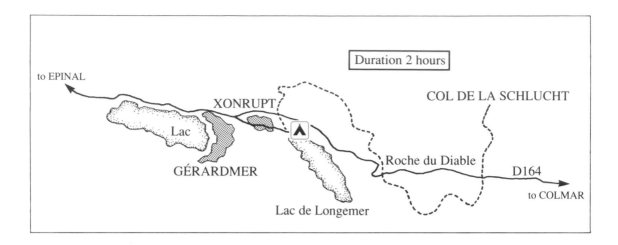

France, and this is reflected in the holiday atmosphere and smart façades of the town, which hugs the shores of the lake after which it is named. It all looks new, shiny and spacious, evidence of a recent turbulent past. Eighty-five per cent of the original Gérardmer was razed by the retreating German army in 1944.

There is one historic claim to fame, however – the Tourist Office, adjacent to the railway station, is the oldest in France. Although the building itself is new, the concept – an extension of the local ramblers' committee, incidentally – was first introduced for visitors in 1875. The parish has been in existence for longer than that – since the thirteenth century to be exact – and legendary connections with Charlemagne are claimed.

The new arrival in this area is faced with a bewildering choice of camp grounds in the vicinity; there are twenty or so around Gérardmer and neighbouring Xonrupt-Longemer. The latter may be difficult to pronounce, but it is popular since it boasts a large, level municipal ground, some hectares in extent, on the shores of lake Longemer. Le Domaine de Longemer is a 2-star enterprise, with a choice of open ground or tree-shaded pitches. The facilities are basic but of accept-

able standard, the atmosphere is easy going and there is room to spread yourself. The charges are reasonable and the site is open all year round, since this is also a popular ski resort. There are more streamlined and carefully tended camp grounds nearby, but this one is particularly strategic for the walker, since there is direct access to one of the many waymarked paths which network the lakes valley. To get there, continue east through Gérardmer along the D417, then turn off right at the Xonrupt-Longemer signpost. Continue through the village to the lake and camping ground.

Once installed, consider the footpath route to the Col de la Schlucht as an appetiser to other trails hereabouts. Make your pedestrian way to the Hotel du Lac àt the camp ground perimeter and take the blue circle ascent path beside it. This route follows tracks, paths and forestry roads via Roche Boulard, Belle Roche and Balveurche to the lofty Schlucht. This is a circuit route of 12 kilometres, with some marvellous high-level panoramas *en route*, and air which is headily therapeutic. For any intensive or prolonged footpath exploration in this area, the specialised walking map, available at Gérardmer tourist office, is recommended.

In this part of Lorraine you are amid true mountains. They may look friendly and benign beneath blue skies, but peaks like the Hohneck, rising to 1,362 metres, can quickly catch out the unwary. This mountain, sometimes called the 'Elephant's Back', is typical of those which form the High Vosges ridges. Richly flanked with beech and fir trees and patchworked by huge granite escarpments it is topped with a bald summit that is not peaked but rounded, one of the many *ballons* which dominate the deep valleys of Lorraine and neighbouring Alsace.

For a short walk, rewarded with a bird's-eye view of the lake and valley, stroll to the village centre of Xonrupt and ascend the lane by the Codec supermarket. This is an easy if sometimes abrupt 2-kilometre circuit, interesting and elevated. For an even easier and very pleasant waterside walk, set off around the left bank of Lake Gérardmer towards Ramberchamp and return via the D417, beside which there is a lakeside path. This is a 6-kilometre circuit, and there are ample car parking spaces in Gérardmer or around the lake.

There is one other camp ground in the vicinity which must be included, since it is not only very strategic for visiting the town itself, or circumnavigating the lake, but is also a charming place in its own right, with lanes and footpaths through forest terrain almost immediately accessible. Camping des Sapins, located about 200 metres from the waterside, will be found in the route de Ramberchamp, on the southern fringes of Gérardmer. It is a 3-star establishment and therefore more expensive than Xonrupt municipal, but with immaculate toilets, neatly landscaped individual pitches, and the sort of cosy and friendly atmosphere that

is only generated in a family-run enterprise. There is open meadow on one side and some inviting forest slopes on the other. The hot showers here are really hot and there are about thirty mains electric hook-up points. It is a smallish ground, very popular of course, due to its proximity to the lake and Gérardmer, but a most pleasant green haven at any time outside the summer peak. It is open from May to September.

You will find that Gérardmer caters well for touring visitors. There are many modern, well-stocked shops, three supermarkets, a wide choice of cafés, and restaurants specialising in local gastronomic delights. It is a favoured watering-hole, incidentally, for those walkers tackling the 100-kilometre Cross Vosges Route. The GR5 actually runs east of the town through the Col de la Schlucht. If the vicinity of Gérardmer and Xonrupt is overly full – as it may well be in high summer – consider Granges-sur-Vologne as an alternative base. This is a very pretty hill village just north-west of the town, reached via the D423. There are two farm camp grounds here, one of which has chalets for hire.

A Short Walk to Germany

In the département of Moselle, about 70 kilometres from Strasbourg, there is an enclave of the Lorraine region that encroaches on the northern landscape of Alsace. At the heart, astride the N62, is the oddly-named Bitche, an ancient town surrounding a mighty sandstone outcrop once crowned by a feudal castle. Vauban modernised this fortress on the orders of Louis XIV, and thus Bitche gained its celebrated citadel; some locals joke that the town got its name too from the heavily

Shoreline camping pitch at Xonrupt-Longemer – a very popular walker's base.

overworked Vauban. Wandering inside the massive walls of the citadel, with its many tunnels and revealing museum, you can understand how the great stronghold was never conquered. Along border country constantly in dispute throughout the centuries, Bitche is just one fortification among many, both ancient and modern, which are scattered in profusion throughout the northern Vosges mountains. These places add to the interest and variety of the richly forested landscape, much of which, even in these modern times, is only accessible to those who are prepared to walk.

There are two other main attractions within reasonable distance of this citadel township. The first is a pedestrian route to the nearby German frontier, the second a restored reminder of the enmity which so recently divided France and Germany.

For any Briton in the middle years of life, it is a strangely evocative experience to approach the German frontier from France on foot – particularly since it is necessary first to drive through a French military zone in order to join the marked footpath. To get there, take the D86 from Bitche to the very un-French-sounding village of Haspelschiedt, close to a wooded, barrage lake, and a military road, where there is parking. The route is waymarked in yellow, winds north-east for about 5 kilometres, past some prehistoric stones and the hamlet of Roppeviller to the Rochers Diane (sculptured Gallo-Roman rocks depicting the ancient gods) on the actual frontier. An extension of this walk is a circuit of about 3 kilometres, inside Germany around the Brechenberg rocks.

There are supposed camping facilities at Haspelschiedt for touring visitors, but the truth is that the lakeside ground is filled to gross over-capacity, not only with static caravans, but with unsightly shed attachments. In this part of Lorraine, sadly, the touring visitor is badly served, both inside and outside the

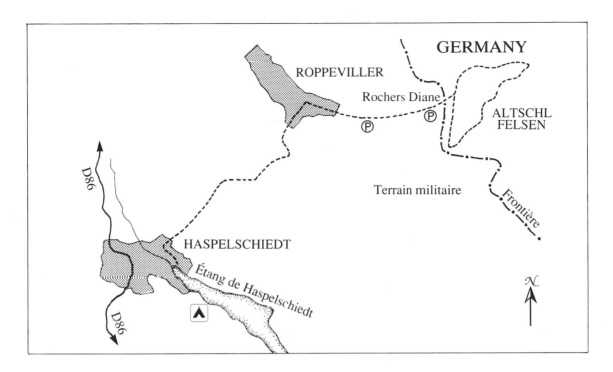

Vosges natural park. Bitche itself had a touring site, which is now closed, Haspelschiedt is best forgotten, while Baerenthal (to the south-east of Bitche), is another lakeside camp ground filled to overflowing with static vans. This one does make a minor concession to genuine touring campers by reserving a postage-stamp patch for those who actually travel. It is not, however, very attractive.

For any prolonged stay in this region (which you might consider with real enthusiasm, for it is a superb swathe of eastern France), there are only three bases that I could recommend. All of them are in neighbouring Alsace and one of those, Oberbronn, is coming close to the limit-line with its allocation of weekend static caravans. The other two are splendid examples of what touring sites should be; hopefully trendsetters for the rest of France. In effect they are an updated version of the *aire naturel*, up till now just a free patch of land, perhaps with water and rubbish disposal facilities, where touring campers could stay overnight. The new-look category still provides that – exclusively for the touring fraternity, it should be emphasised – but with facilities that are perhaps more appropriate to the twenty-first century. Small but modern toilet blocks are built to blend with the natural landscape, complete with hot water to hand basins and showers, mains electric hook-ups and a barbecue shelter. The pitching areas are left more or less natural, although the grass is cut and landscaping is carried out where this is considered desirable. The tariff is low and a visiting camp guardian collects the appropriate fees nightly. There are two of these simple but super sites to the south of Bitche, off the east-west D919 at the hamlets of Wingen-sur-Moder and Hinsbourg.

Back at Bitche, the second major visitor attraction is the resurrection of a section of the famous – or infamous – Maginot Line. This was supposedly the most impregnable of all frontier fortifications, but the invading German army simply went around the elaborate bunker system in 1940. This left much of it intact for posterity, but did little to add to the reputation of André Maginot, the French minister responsible for its creation! At Simserhof, not far from Bitche (off the D35 in the direction of Sarreguemines), you can see one of these World War II underground defences, complete with armaments and an interesting museum of military artefacts. There are guided tours daily (except on Mondays), at 9am and 2pm.

Two more fortifications of very differing eras can be seen if you take the splendid forest road from Alsace into Lorraine from Oberbronn. (*See* pages 23–24 for camp ground details). Turn off the N62 northwards, at the village of Phillippsbourg, on to the D87. Where the road forks for the Château de Falkenstein, look carefully at the bank on the left-hand side of the road and you will see one of the cunningly concealed Maginot Line bunkers, almost in a perfect state of preservation, save for a few shrapnel scars around the tiny entrance. Evidence of a much more distant but equally turbulent past is revealed after a twenty-minute walk from the car park and picnic area deep in this forest, to the thirteenth-century remains of Falkenstein. Here, a great medieval redoubt, on top of a sandstone outcrop of impressive dimensions, still holds lonely vigil over a very impressive and strategic setting. Relics like this old castle, of which there are many, and the beautiful, expansive forest all around make this part of Lorraine very attractive and appealing terrain for those who enjoy exploring on foot.

The Zorn Valley and Dabo

For those who spend the night at the pleasant and historic camp ground at Phalsbourg (*see* page 25 for details), there is a very interesting route south via the D98 and D45. The road winds through thickly-wooded hill country along the steeply-flanked Zorn valley where, near St Louis Sparsbrod, you pass an ingenious giant elevator. This hoists barges using the Marne au Rhin canal system, avoiding the tedium of negotiating a series of seventeen locks, and is a masterpiece of imaginative engineering on the grand scale. If you continue southwards you will soon ascend to Dabo, another gloriously well-situated hill village, providing the most expansive views across the plain of Lorraine from the famous Rocher de Dabo, a thrusting pinnacle of sandstone, topped by a chapel and towering over the village to a height of 664 metres. Dabo itself is pretty enough in a modern way, but the big attraction for nature lovers and leisure walkers is the new 2-star camp ground. This municipal enterprise is accessible only to genuine touring visitors.

About 2 kilometres from the village, off the D45, this site provides first-class amenities in a fine forest setting, actually on the route of the GR53, Saverne–Le Donon section. The pitching area is smallish, but level and on well-kept grass. Mains electric hook-ups are provided and there is attractive *gîte* accommodation adjacent to the campsite utility block. There is also a small, permanent caravan site close by, along with tennis courts, but this is totally separate to, and segregated from, the touring section. Top marks to the local authority here for this genuine touring amenity. Walking maps and guides covering the area (including the GR

Camping du Rocher Dabo – expressly for genuine tourists.

route and the local waymarked trails), are available from the Dabo main street store. The touring site, Camping du Rocher, is open from April to October and is very quiet and peaceful for most months of the season.

More About The Maid

On the banks of the gently-flowing Meuse, the tiny agricultural village of Domremy-la-Pucelle has now developed into something of a Joan of Arc industrial zone. Every shop has a Joan logo and effigies in every material abound. Her house is now a heavily-hedged museum, and next to the war memorial is a purpose-built souvenir shop. Those of a mind (believer or not) can emulate the Maid in one simple way. They can *walk*, in true pilgrim fashion, from the d'Arc family home, following the route of the GR714 (Bar-le-Duc–Neufchâteau section), along the 2-kilometre gentle ascent to the ornate basilique shrine built in the early 1900s. This reputedly is at the spot where the shepherd girl is said to have first heard the voices of the saints. However sceptical you may be, it is an interesting walk.

For those wishing to overnight at

Phalsbourg municipal camp ground and youth hostel, once a royal château. This is an intriguing old town.

Domremy – a statue of Jeanne d'Arc's father, Jacques.

Domremy, there is a small and agreeable camping ground located behind the main street houses. It is just a stroll from the most famous house of all, which is quite a substantial dwelling really for a fifteenth-century artisan family.

Paths of Glory

If World War I had been a nightmare and not a reality, Verdun would still be a very attractive place to visit. Owing nothing to modern history (prior to 1914), it was a fortified bastide on the Meuse in the fourteenth century, with a turbulent history evidenced by the squat towers of the old Chaussée gate through the ancient eastern ramparts. There is natural beauty too in abundance, just to the north-east where the rolling wooded hills of the lower Ardennes begin to rise steadily towards the Belgian and German frontiers. This high ground was once most appealing to military minds schooled in set-battle warfare, while on the nearby valley floor Verdun and the river Meuse were challenging twin obstacles on the western route to Reims and Paris. It is estimated that nearly a million men died, then or later, attacking or defending this pastoral landscape during the middle years of the Great War.

Verdun is now listed, along with Hiroshima and a handful of other distinguished places, as one of the five most famous – or infamous – shrines dedicated to those who fell in war. The whole Verdun area is now a memorial ground on such a vast scale that a special touring route has been laid to cope with the constant flow of visitors. There is a danger that this sacred place will be turned into a tourist industry centre, with coach traffic in particular becoming heavier every year. Fortunately, the authorities have recognised the threat and are now trying to encourage more pedestrian wandering around this sad and yet beautiful Lorraine landscape.

To see Verdun with a vestige of understanding and sympathy, you have (to use military jargon) to plan an assault. The first requirement is a congenial base camp and this is not so easy to fulfil. There is a 3-star municipal site, Les Breuils, which is well signposted on the south side of the town off the D34; it is tolerably acceptable to touring visitors, although heavily patronised by weekend units. Space is reserved for genuine travellers, and mid-week it is pleasantly tranquil. There is a shop and café adjacent, and the site is open from March to October.

To the north, off the D964, there is the most convenient of the battlefield area camp grounds, Sous le Moulin, at the village of Charney. Regrettably, weekend caravans are packed in like sardines here, so it cannot be recommended. Coming from the south a night stop at St Mihiel about 35 kilometres down-river might be considered. Still on the banks of the Meuse, the municipal site here is not of top quality, but it is spacious, usually with room enough for casual visitors, the setting is agreeable, and the old town itself is quite interesting, located as it is on the fringe of the Parc Régional de Lorraine. If you are approaching Verdun from the north-west, then Varennes-en-Argonne on the D38 is not a bad alternative site mid-week. Clean, green, level and well run, its location is almost in the village centre. There is, though, a surfeit of weekend static vans. From either of these camp grounds an early morning arrival in Verdun should be possible: the best time to explore the extensive memorials. If ever there was an argument for the Community of Europe, Verdun is it.

Go first to the great Verdun Memorial Museum, to the north-east of the town, and there collect your selection of Les Circuits Pédestres, available freely on request. These are eleven well-produced descriptive leaflets of walks around the battlefields, of $1-2\frac{1}{2}$ hours' duration, complete with scale maps which will enable you to follow the colour-coded routes easily. The museum itself is a moving and telling kaleidoscope of futile heroism, while not far away is the huge Douaumont Ossuary, where some thirteen thousand unidentified French and German soldiers share a communal resting place. In front of the massive, shell-shaped dome, a further fifteen thousand French crosses form

143

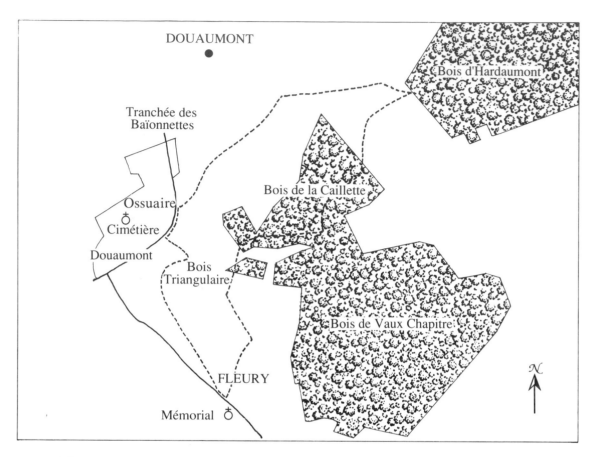

neat, soldierly ranks. To the north of here is one of the earliest of all Verdun battle scars, the curiously-named Tranchée des Baïonnettes, close to the annihilated village of Douaumont. During one of the ferocious skirmishes of that 1916–17 period, a gas attack preceded a bombardment and a company of French infantry died where they stood, with fixed bayonets, ready to go over the top. The subsequent shelling covered the men with debris so that only their bayonets were left protruding above the earth. A few years ago those bayonets remained as evidence of this ghastly carnage but – sign of the times – all have now been looted by souvenir hunters.

Not all the footpaths hereabouts are routes through harrowing history, although one or two do bring home to the observant wanderer the horrors of trench warfare. Near the Fort de Douaumont, for example, there is a snaking footpath section which winds around the rims of countless shell craters, still filled with stagnant water and with odd pieces of unrecognisable metal protruding above the ground. If you tour this region by car, you could easily miss much of its significance. The landscape is kindly cloaked now by tall pine trees and, on a sunny day, and between the sombre landmarks, it is difficult to comprehend the horror. The evidence is here at Verdun, however, most revealingly of all in the haunted expressions of the infantrymen photographed, frozen in that terrible time, and now displayed in the halls of the museum.

144

Midi-Pyrénées

Départements: Ariège – Aveyron – Haute-Garonne – Gers – Lot – Haute-Pyrénées – Tarn – Tarn-et-Garonne – Principauté d'Andorre
Préfecture: Toulouse

Stretching north to south from the foothills of the Massif Central to the high Pyrénées, this huge region embraces more départements than any other in France. No part of the land mars the Midi-Pyrénées, and almost every département – indeed, nearly every canton – has something to interest the walker, either natural or man-made, or an intriguing blend of both. This is a remarkable statement to be able to make about a totally land-locked swathe of this size. However, although it is land-locked there is no shortage of water in the Midi-Pyrénées, for some of the loveliest of French rivers, including the Dordogne, Lot, Tarn, Garonne, Ariège, Aveyron and Adour, are contained here. It is difficult in the extreme to advocate just a few footpaths amid such a bewildering potential choice, but I have done it by opting for high spots in contrasting areas, some northerly, others in the deep south.

The first centres on a fascinating if little-known river in this region of rivers – the Alzou. This watercourse hides its charms shyly amid scenery of rugged, sometimes savage grandeur, where rounded hills explode suddenly into chasms and gorges of dizzying depths. For here, between Brive and Cahors, east of the N20, lie the mighty plateaux (*causses*), of Martel and Gramat. Near the northern rim of the Causse de Gramat, where the snaking Alzou is faithfully traced by a section of the long-distance GR6, is the location of the second most-visited place in France, Rocamadour (only just pipped in the popularity stakes by Mont St Michel). Like Vézelay in Bourgogne, this was a medieval stop-over on the Compostela Trail and no pilgrim sanctuary could be more dramatic or impressive. It hangs, all but suspended, from a south-facing rock precipice, almost too sheer to hold the cluster of ancient buildings beneath a cliff overhang topped with a splendid château. It is much visited and beset by awful traffic chaos at times, but this doesn't detract from its breathtaking impact. It is, as the French assert, the most beautiful religious haven of the Middle Ages.

Certainly, it could have been no leisurely stroll to reach during the twelfth- to fifteenth-century period when the pilgrimage flow was at its highest. The way for foot travellers in those times must have been arduous, and a short walk in the vicinity – or around the near-perpendicular streets of the village itself – will indicate the kind of physical stamina necessary for any pilgrim of that earlier Christian era!

Cliff-hanging Rocamadour, the second most-visited historic site in France. There is fine walking from here along the Alzou river valley.

Even if Rocamadour village did not exist, this quarter of the northern Midi-Pyrénées would be worth visiting, endowed as it is with some glorious rough-hewn landscapes. The limestone outcrops are studded with caves, some revealing evidence of early man that makes Rocamadour appear modern. Les Grottes des Merveilles is one such, while the Gouffre de Padirac, to the north-east, is a staggering fissure plunging deep into the Gramat plateau. The GR6 touches upon both these marvellous natural features which, regrettably, have become over-commercialised. However, there is plenty of uncommercialised natural wilderness for the walker

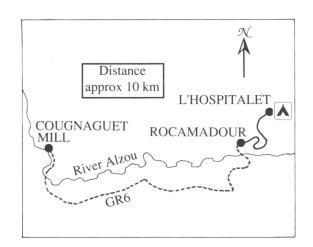

here, especially for those who follow the Grande Randonnée between Rocamadour and the fourteenth-century fortified watermill of Cougnaguet. Conveniently, there is a camping ground high above Rocamadour and about 2 kilometres from the venerable village, at l'Hospitalet.

Fairly level, partly shaded, this is a basic facility ground, with a café and shop adjacent, plus an information kiosk at the entrance. It is open from April to September. From here, with some road walking, the GR6 follows the Alzou eastward more or less faithfully for 9 kilometres to Gramat; westward through Rocamadour to the isolated and picturesque mill at Cougnaguet, 10 kilometres away. There is a *Gîte d'Étape* $1\frac{1}{2}$ kilometres from the mill, which is a popular night halt with backpackers. The GR continues northwards from the mill, passing the famous grottoes of Lacave, before rejoining and re-crossing the Dordogne river again and continuing to Souillac. This whole section passes through some rocky high country; a landscape of haughty sternness, especially arid and mightily fractured away from the watercourses.

In gentle contrast, this same département of Lot also boasts the greener pastures and softer contours of Quercy Province. Dominated by the river Lot valley which is rich and verdant, Quercy is still not far away from the starker plateaux. Gourdon is a recommended objective for those who may prefer a small town touring base. The town is called the 'Gateway to the Causses', lying roughly midway between the plateaux of Quercy and Périgord. At once modern yet medieval, Gourdon contains some surprising gems of ancient France within its old confines, and there are some superb distant views from the flank of the rocky spur upon which this sub-

préfecture stands. A walk round the former ramparts is a pleasant and revealing exercise. The restoration of many old buildings is being vigorously pursued, not least the once-fortified fifteenth-century church of St Pierre. The shopping here is first class, as is the 3-star touring site adjacent to a lagoon on the edge of town. There is a choice of seven waymarked short walks in the vicinity, varying from 1 to 4 kilometres in length. Sketch maps and descriptive leaflets are available free from the Syndicat d'Initiative in the town centre. This is another good night halt for long-distance walkers, since the GR64 and the GR652 pass through the town.

The High Pyrénées

In the foothills of the central Pyrénées, all roads lead to the celebrated religious hub and health spa of Lourdes. For a long time one of the most-visited places in France, this cure-and-curiosity centre suffers rather from overcrowding and ever-increasing peripheral development. The town's 'exceptional destiny' (as it is described by the French Tourist Office), began in 1858 when the peasant girl Bernadette Soubirous saw the first of eighteen apparitions of the Virgin Mary. Contemporary exploitation of this phenomenon ensures that the indigenous Lourdes population of some 18,000 is doubled or trebled almost year-round by pilgrims and sightseers.

If you haven't visited Lourdes before, the strange marriage of religious devotion and blatant marketing will leave a marked impression. Among the 400 hotels and 33 camping sites, the Basilica, Château-Fort and La Grotte des Apparitions retain just a flavour of nineteenth-century rural France. For those who love walking, and mountain walking

147

Gedre, gateway to the high Pyrénées south of Lourdes.

above all, Lourdes is hardly an objective – merely a gateway *en route* to some of the finest high country in France. The area may not seem too promising as you head southwards along the N21, a road lined initially with ribbon development and scarred by the industrial townships of Argelès and Pierrefitte, where sulphur clouds plume from tall chimneys. However, it all improves markedly where the road forks – one way goes to Cauterets, the other to Luz-St-Sauveur.

Both of these minor mountain towns are now major health spas, almost totally reliant on tourism of the therapeutic or active kind.

Luz-St-Sauveur is the more *bijou* of the two; more importantly, it is directly on the route to one of the most beautiful walking enclaves in France, the Cirque de Gavarnie, some 20 kilometres above and beyond. If time is not too pressing, Luz is colourful and charming despite its tourist overtones. There is a very spacious square in the centre of the town, called place 8 Mai to commemorate the end of World War II. Countless squares and streets are so named in France, but this one is especially welcoming to visitors. Along one side, overhanging a white-water torrent, is a well-run Tourist Office and spacious car

148

park; opposite is a grand style restaurant/café and *salon de thé*; on the third side is the main shopping street, and on the fourth, an attractive and extremely well-run touring site called Camping Toy. This is a concentrated comfort station of distinct merit. Two other attractions of Luz are a very rare thirteenth-century fortified church of powerful visual impact, and, just behind it, reached by tortuous and very narrow streets, an information office for the famous Parc National des Pyrénées, access to which is via Cauterets or Luz-St-Sauveur.

There is walking direct from Luz, not least the GR10 with a loop section which traverses some fine high country to the south, much of it right alongside the Spanish frontier. There is local promenading, too, notably to the Pont Napoléon which bridges a steep and impressive ravine, slashed out by the river Gave. The natural beauty is not enhanced by souvenir stalls and coach-party throngs, although it is a pleasant enough evening stroll from Camping Toy. Really, if you intend using Luz as a base, then drive-and-walk excursions are the best idea.

This is not the case at Gavarnie, which is reached by one of the most scenic 20 kilometres of mountain road to be found in the Pyrénées. It is all uphill from Luz, winding through the Gave gorge, and the views become more and more majestic with every twist and turn – towering peaks, rushing waters over a chaos of boulders in places, flower meadows and conifer spreads, and always that mighty horseshoe of summits which is the Cirque, growing ever grander on the southern skyline. Finally, where the valley narrows almost to a defile, you arrive at Gavarnie, where the man-made scene is almost as fascinating as the natural grandeur.

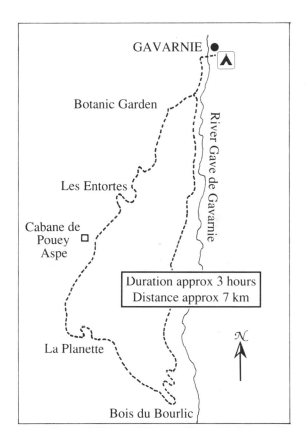

A one-street hill village with a strong frontier flavour; part winter ski resort, part tourist trap with all the trimmings, yet with all the bustle, it hasn't lost charm or character. Perhaps this is because nearly all the visitors are there to explore on foot or on horseback. Indeed, the frontier town boasts a population of horses, ponies, donkeys and mules to rival the number of humans, and for the most part they all wander about just as freely.

One legacy – now fully exploited – has been left by the intrepid nineteenth-century *Grand Tour* élite, who discovered the fun of mountain exploration by taking the mule-

Mountain road southwards from Luz-St-Saveur; on the skyline, the Cirque de Gavarnie.

teers' tracks from the then quite isolated Gavarnie hostelry. Today, you can ride the well-worn short circuit taking about 2 hours. The walker, however, is free to choose any number of routes, some of which criss-cross the valley floor, while others soar to the snow-line beyond. Whichever you choose, the first requirement is a base. Provided you don't mind it *au naturel*, drive right through the main street to the extreme southern end, where the houses finish and there is no more car access. Cross the narrow river bridge and turn into the 1-star café and campsite – the one preferred by most hill walkers of serious intent. Facilities are spartan, but for the self-contained visitor the meadow pitching could not be more strategic. You simply walk out of the gate straight on to pedestrian trails which trace both banks of the river.

You will soon discover why the Cirque de Gavarnie is rated as one of the finest natural jewels in France, along with the Tarn and Verdon Gorges and the high alps around Mont Blanc. Just beyond the village, the track widens into an enormous natural amphi-theatre some 10 kilometres square, carpeted with sweet grasses and wild flowers, broken by pine-forest swathes, divided by rushing, gin-clear streams, and totally surrounded by some of the mightiest of the high Pyrenean peaks. From crevasses and gigantic over-hangs, cascades sparkle and plummet, some of them in unbroken falls of hundreds of metres. For most leisure walkers, day walking anywhere in this region must rate as a truly memorable experience.

The Chemin de Saint-Saud is a typical ex-ample among a selection of beautiful walks. If the sun is shining, this is 3 hours of pure magic, the path tracing its route immediately alongside then partly into the great Parc National des Pyrénées. It begins from the campsite where you cross the bridge and initially join the wide mule track. Shortly, there is a branch path to the left which climbs gently alongside the river to a distinctive knoll, now a partly-fenced botanical garden where most varieties of Pyrenean wild flowers may be seen in season. The path continues south-west, crossing small bridges and ascending through pine enclaves of the Bois de Bourlic, via tumbling cascades and a small plateau, La Planette, where there are glorious views of the peaks above the river which here becomes the Gave des Tourettes.

Here, after some 3 kilometres, you turn north-east again for the equally spectacular return leg, passing a mountain hut, the Cabane de Pouey Aspe, and descending the zigzag trail, the Sentier des Entortes. From here you go via more woodland and grazing meadows back to the village along the wide mule track. This is an easy, well-defined route with no difficult scramble stretches; it reveals the full beauty of the Cirque as a reward for relatively little effort.

For those who enjoy more strenuous walking, the 3½-hour Chemin des Espuges is another fine trail which starts again from the camp ground. This time, however, you do not cross the river bridge. The path traverses a majestic mountain flank section, probes deeper into the circle of summits, then turns again to follow the river bank back to Gavarnie. This one is a route for settled weather and the appropriate IGN map and compass should be carried. Full information on these and other routes into the Cirque de Gavarnie and neighbouring Cirque de Troumouse is available from the National Park Office in Luz-St-Sauveur.

Barbotan – a Back-Road Midi-Pyrénées Haven

About 75 kilometres from Auch, tucked away in the extreme north-western corner of the region, is Barbotan-les-Thermes. Away from the mainstream trunk routes, this green enclave is located approximately half-way between Toulouse and Bordeaux, and is an excellent rest and replenishment base for those dodging the heavily used north–south arterial roads. Here you can take the waters, almost literally from the well run 3-star camp ground, Lac de l'Uby, just half a kilometre from the thermal baths. Spa and campsite are open from April to October and both enjoy

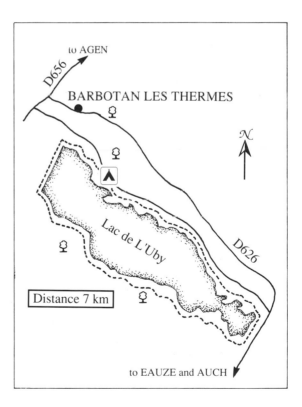

a scenic waterside location. Created from the barraging of the river l'Uby, the site has been attractively landscaped, with a pedestrian circuit of some 7 kilometres around the wooded lakeshore. A sport and leisure complex with swimming, tennis, fishing and boating, is adjacent to the camp ground.

Barbotan is devoted to the cure of ailments, although basic shopping needs will also be satisfied among the boutiques and therapy parlours. There is a pleasant semi-pedestrian precinct, and enjoyable strolling in the wooded parkland surrounding the thermal village, making this yet another recommended transit stop where you can stretch your legs agreeably.

Ariège, la Terre Courage
St Lizier, St Lizier!

One of the finest mountain walking areas in the whole of France is centred upon Gavarnie. That might be considered riches enough for one region; not so, however, for the Midi-Pyrénées, which boasts a majestic second Cirque, not far to the north-west of Andorra, deep within the half-hidden valley of d'Ustou. To find this scenic place, make for St Lizier and St Girons, on the D117, about 45 kilometres west of Foix. Take or make time to pause at St Lizier, capital of Couserans département and a cluster of old France, reflecting some two thousand years of history in the bubbling waters of the river Salat.

Your target, however, is a second St Lizier — St Lizier d'Ustou, a tiny village in a mountain setting of breathtaking beauty. This is a justified *Frontier Sauvage*, to be revealed to the south-bound driver following the Salat river course through the Gorges de Ribaouto to

Seix — itself another old-world settlement and one-time turbulent frontier town threatened by Spanish incursions. About 5 kilometres further south along the D3 is Pont de la Taule, and the turn-off to Vallée d'Ustou. Another 7 kilometres and a second sharp hairpin turn-off leads to St Lizier, and its well-run little camp ground which is open all the year round. This is a near-perfect walking base, right in the centre of the village, and, indeed, an important part of it, since the store serves both residents and visitors. Within a couple of hundred yards on either side of the one-street village and its distinctive church, the GR10 may be joined to explore this lovely high-altitude valley to east or west. The campsite is only small but walkers are assured of a warm and friendly welcome from Claude and Pierrette Guitton.

A long-distance path winds westwards to Couflens, first as a farm track, then as a trail with some distinctly stiff ups and downs. The south-eastern section leads to Guzet-Neige — a true mountain trail from the start with a number of steep ascents and descents. Both provide marvellous bird's-eye views over the valley and panoramas of the high Pyrenean peaks. Guzet-Neige, incidentally, is a ski resort and virtually deserted most of the summer, so no refreshment is available.

There is a second, equally stunning objective waiting to be explored from the St Lizier base camp — the glacier Cirque de Cagateille. Take your car for this one, continuing south on the D38, then turning off at the hamlet of Stillom to the end of the tarmac road soon after. Even if you don't make it to the actual glacier (about an hour's hard tramp), you couldn't pick a nicer spot on the map of Europe to take your exercise!

(These mountains, like all others, should

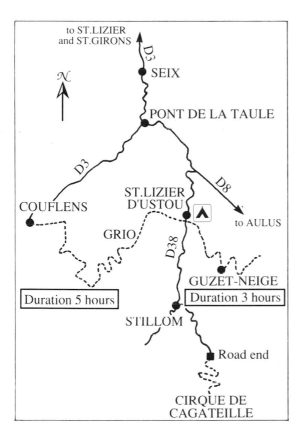

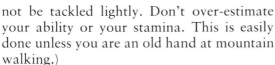

Conques, where there is medieval splendour around every corner.

not be tackled lightly. Don't over-estimate your ability or your stamina. This is easily done unless you are an old hand at mountain walking.)

A Pinnacle of Medieval Midi

When all the elements essential to enjoyable walking in France converge, a little over-enthusiasm must be in order. Conques, pride of Aveyron, the Midi-Pyrénées and, indeed, of France, is the sort of place to inspire such enthusiasm. The road approach to this wooded, hill-country retreat is beautiful from every direction; via the Lot valley to the north, or south from Rodez on the D901 along the course of the sparkling Dourdou (above which Conques basks), a Lot tributary. The village

itself is world-renowned among students of religious history, and the towering treasure of the eleventh-century abbey is one of the finest of all medieval creations, and reputed to have been the favourite of Emperor Charlemagne. Inside the venerable cloister museum is housed the 'treasure of treasures': gold work of the eleventh to fourteenth centuries, displayed around the tenth-century centre-piece of Sainte Foy (she who discovered the relics that made Santiago-di-Compostela the principal pilgrimage centre of the Middle Ages, and Conques an important staging post on that long and arduous trail).

Today, the identical route of countless pilgrims may be walked from this sublime place, which has been preserved almost perfectly in its medieval state. Join it beside the mighty

Val d'Ustou – here in reality is the walking country of armchair dreams.

old-world believers, you have to marvel at the capacity of medieval man to conquer almost any obstacle. 'Foy', incidentally, translates simply as 'faith'.

Converging on to contemporary Conques are three Grande Randonnée routes – befitting of a pilgrimage staging post of such distinguished eminence. There is also a choice of eight local walks varying in length from $\frac{1}{2}$ hour to $2\frac{1}{2}$ hours, and all are described, with accompanying sketch maps, in a booklet available from the tourist office beside the abbey-church.

Without exception, these are all hill routes, but this should be no deterrent to those who are in average health and keen hill walkers. The grandeur of the natural surroundings blends supremely with the man-made wonders of Conques, which is cunningly hidden away within shielding hill flanks, much as St David's cathedral is in west Wales. You have to be right on top of the settlement before it is revealed.

This Midi walking base is made near-perfect by the campsite provided – Camping Beau Rivage. About twenty years ago Mon-

The majestic Cirque de Cagateille near the hamlet of Stillom.

abbey, descend the stony rue Charlemagne, pause at the tiny, perched Chapelle St Roch, descend again to cross the Roman pack-horse bridge, then climb steeply, past the Chapelle Ste Foy, south-west, eventually traversing the Pyrénées and on, to the far north-west corner of Spain. Those who have neither the time nor the energy to undertake this massive endeavour can of course indulge in a rather shorter walk! The route, incidentally, is now called the GR65 and if you tramp only a fraction of it in the footsteps of those devout

154

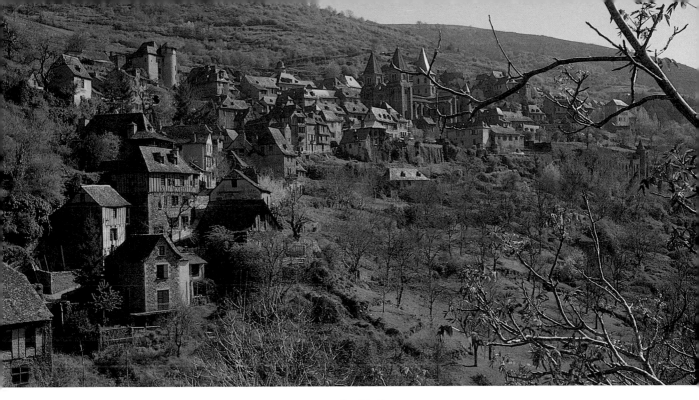

The cluster of Conques from the chapel of Sainte Foy, on the GR65.

Rue Charlemagne, Conques.

sieur and Madame Carles began to create what they hoped would become a traveller haven befitting their modern pilgrims' village. The ultimate accolade for two decades of arduous effort on the part of this ex-quarry worker and his wife was bestowed in 1989, when the Minister of Tourism, Olivier Stirn, presented the Carles with the Camp Ground of the Year Award, 2-star category. These grandiose diplomas are often suspect, but in this case the award is justified. Nature and necessity have been blended with charm, practicality and more than a little artistry. This riverbank ground is level and verdant, studded with a whole variety of trees and shrubs, while all the utilities are spotless and the welcome for the tired traveller warm and friendly. Just two of the imaginative installations here are a motor caravan service bay, complete with an air-line for tyre inflation, and a drinking water supply line for tank refilling, an information room for walkers

155

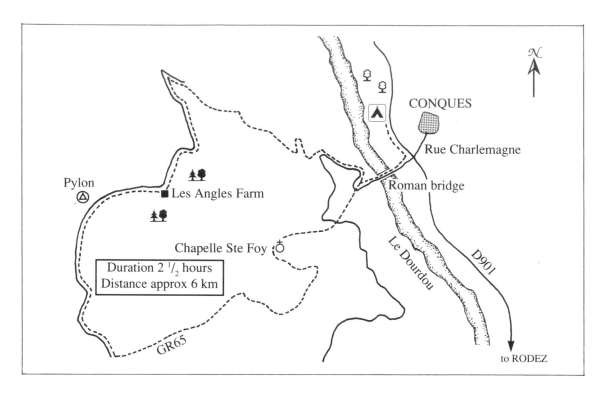

Duration 2 ½ hours
Distance approx 6 km

(with wall maps), and a tiny mineral museum in the reception chalet.

There is nothing extravagant or out of character. It is only a small 2-star site with room for some sixty units, but there is hot water and mains electricity, with hot showers at a small extra charge. Nature lovers should appreciate Beau Rivage. Allowing for the usual disclaimer about peak summer conditions, this camp ground must be considered one of the top half-dozen locations in France for the hill walker seeking the preserved past in beautiful surroundings. If one had to carp – perfection ever an illusion – it would be about the proximity of the D901. Engine noise does tend to be reflected in this ravine setting, but fortunately you will find that vehicle movement virtually ceases after dark.

There is one especially revealing pedestrian circuit, which is a lovely walk to make in the afternoon to gain the full benefit of the western sun upon the Conques cluster. From the camp ground, cross the nearby Roman bridge and ascend the flank of the wooded hill via the tarmac minor road and the GR65 to the chapel of Ste Foy. Dog leg, south and west, to pick up the tarmac lane once again, turning north and ascending to the prominent electricity pylon and on past Les Angles farm. Ascend once more to the end of the tarmac and continue to the summit via the track, which then descends directly down to the D232 and the Roman bridge once more. This is a very rewarding hike, with fine views across Conques, and is well worth the few stiff ups and downs.

Nord Pas de Calais

Départements: Nord – Nord Pas de Calais
Préfecture: Lille

Just 34 kilometres of English Channel (or La Manche) separate France from Great Britain – a short hop that becomes in effect a giant stride segregating landscape, language, attitude and life-style. The aromatic blend of *Gauloises* and garlic, the vast, almost tree-less agricultural plains of the Pas de Calais, and the seeming indifference of the French to all but their nearest and dearest, underline the initial impression that here is a country that could not be more foreign if it were a thousand sea-miles distant. The impression is particularly strong if the first-time visitor also happens to be a driver ... The land mass which makes up the Pas de Calais has enjoyed by turn friendly and bitterly antagonistic relations with Britain through the centuries. Currently we enjoy an amiable co-existence and, individually, friendship between French and British can often be staunch and lasting, especially if the latter tries to speak at least a few words in French. What better place to start practising your 'Franglais' than the gateway to France – Calais – where a large percentage of the natives are bilingual.

If it is your first visit to France, it pays to hasten slowly across this northern terrain, even though it is frequently denigrated by the sun-seekers as a scenic nonentity. This is not the case, since there are some pleasant swathes of coast and hinterland and one or two exceptionally beautiful oases. This region does hold limited appeal for leisure walkers – it really is the domain of the driver – but there is the GR121 which links Boulogne with Arras and continues into Belgium. There is also a regional loop which touches upon the outskirts of Calais, then joins the GR128 which winds east to Cassel near St Omer, again continuing to the Belgian border. These long-distance routes may well be fun to tackle, but only deliberately by purist pedestrians arriving car-less and determined at Calais or Boulogne.

For those who have wheels as well as walking boots, a high-spot in a very strategic location is Arras, about half a day's drive (117 kilometres south-east) from Calais port. It is also one of the most poignantly dramatic towns in western Europe. Arras was a major Allied command centre throughout World War I. To reach it you take a pleasant, easy drive largely along the N43 via St-Omer and Béthune, on a road more or less free of traffic congestion once the busy Channel port is left behind, thanks largely to the *autoroute* which runs parallel. The N43 and D937 is now a genuine holiday route, through undulating wooded country, punctuated at intervals with villages which retain the atmosphere and visual impact of old France.

At the village of Souchez, south of Béthune,

The Pas de Calais landscape is not very alluring for the leisure walker.

you enter a historical arena where carnage occurred on a scale that even today seems almost unbelievable. The evidence is still all around, pin-pointed by the large number of military cemeteries. At Notre-Dame-de-Lorette lie the graves of 40,000 Frenchmen, at Neuville-St-Vaast, the graves of 44,000 Germans. It is, though, the high ground along Vimy Ridge which perhaps captures the essence of the war. Ironically, it is now also a remembrance shrine of surprising peace, where you can wander beneath the trees, among grazing sheep, over a landscape that has been softened by time yet was once the epicentre of a storm of steel. It was here, in the spring of 1917, that 10,500 Canadians were killed or wounded recapturing the Ridge. Given by France to Canada in perpetuity, Vimy is an expansive stretch – about

100 hectares – now a vast memorial ground containing not only the lovingly-tended graves, but a massive cenotaph at the highest point on Hill 45, a network of preserved trenches and tunnels, and even a section of the Front Line; the opposing forces were so close to each other that it seems quite impossible that there were any survivors at all.

Try taking the signposted turn-off to Vimy at the hamlet of La Targette, some 5 kilometres south of Souchez. On entering the Memorial Park, leave your car at the 'tunnels' and walk around the perimeter, taking in the battlefield woodland of pine and beech, the trenches and the Memorial. From this spot there is no mistaking the significance of the ridge. Far below, to the north, are the plains of northern France and the once-great coalmining area of Béthune, the pyramid spoil-

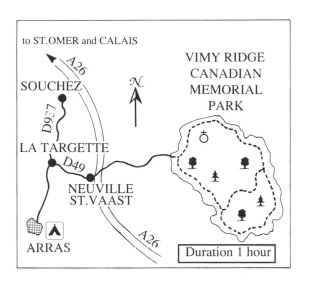

to ST.OMER and CALAIS

A26

SOUCHEZ

D937

LA TARGETTE

D49

NEUVILLE ST.VAAST

A26

ARRAS

VIMY RIDGE CANADIAN MEMORIAL PARK

N

Duration 1 hour

tips now all but cloaked with green. Go quietly and with respect, as requested, completing the circular walk via the cemetery of gleaming white crosses in a secluded corner, a short distance from the worst fighting area. The park is open every day from 1 April to 30 September and is staffed by a team of Canadian students.

In the near vicinity, on the southern fringe of Souchez, is a British military cemetery. This is more formal, but still a poignant and beautifully-maintained tribute to a lost generation – just one of many souvenirs of war along the road from Calais to Arras. The whole area is now a place of pilgrimage for millions of people of every nationality.

Vimy Ridge, and a view across a corner of the 1917 front-line. The killing ground is now an oasis of tranquillity.

The British Military Cemetery at Souchez is just one of over 900 memorial grounds scattered around northern France.

Arras, just 11 kilometres south of Vimy, is an ancient town of tall spires and cobbled squares, and has been almost completely restored after near-total destruction during World War I. For a congenial overnight stop after any battlefield visit, head straight for the town centre and follow the clear camp ground signposts to the rue de Temple. This is a municipal enterprise, small but clean and well maintained, and charging modest fees. There is hard-standing for wheeled units, as well as tree-shaded lawns for tents. Facilities are utilitarian but clean, and there are hot showers and mains electric hook-ups. There

is a supermarket 5 minutes' walk away and you can stroll to the town centre in 20 minutes. To absorb the atmosphere of old Arras, take a walk around the majestic Grande Place, considered to contain the most perfect remaining examples of seventeenth-century Flemish architecture. On a more practical note, there is a Youth Hostel here, clearly indicated among the gracious colonnades. *Gîtes d'Étape* can be found adjacent to the GR121 south-east of Hesdin, at Boubers-sur-Canche and Berlencourt-le-Cauroy. A useful Syndicat d'Initiative is located in place Maréchal Foch, Arras, opposite the railway station.

L'Avesnois

Another area of the Pas de Calais that is not much visited by British travellers is that surrounding the town of Avesnes, in the far south-eastern corner of the region. It is particularly attractive country, and is a convenient stop-over place for those heading towards the Ardennes or Luxembourg.

The forested area begins south-east of Le Quesnoy (Forêt de Mormal), embracing river valleys like the Val Joly (boasting a 180-hectare barrage lake), and continues more or less unbroken to the Belgian border. One particular high-spot, located about 116 kilometres south-east of Lille, is Fourmies, a pretty little market town on the river Helpe, served by an excellent municipal touring site with waymarked forest walks directly accessible. To get there, take the signposted minor road north from the N43, midway between Cambrai and Charleville-Mézières. The landscape here is not at all typical of the region, but more reminiscent of the Ardennes (which is not too far away). Camping des Etangs des

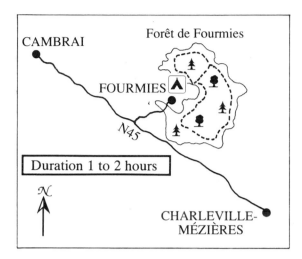

CAMBRAI

Forêt de Fourmies

FOURMIES

N45

Duration 1 to 2 hours

N

CHARLEVILLE-
MÉZIÈRES

Circuit Santé for those who like to take their personal exercise in short, explosive bursts. Log leaps, monkey bars and hop-skip-jump pads have been laid out between short jogging sections – all very invigorating as an early morning tone-up, especially when you can trot straight back to the adjacent Camping des Etangs for a hot shower.

Montreuil – A Walk Around Ancient Walls

Just off the N1, inland from Le Touquet and high above the river Canche, is Montreuil, an historic pearl of Pas de Calais. Unmistakable signposting leads to a quiet and secluded touring site, Camping la Fontaine des Clercs, which is within easy strolling distance of a majestic medieval citadel and rampart surround. The municipal camp ground is green and pleasant, located immediately below the massive old town walls, with lawn pitches among trees and shrubbery over extended terracing. The facilities are clean and well maintained, as one would expect on a TCF site, with good hot water supplies to toilets and showers, and mains electricity if required.

Montreuil-sur-Mer is, alas, nowadays about 4 kilometres from the sea. However, it is ideally located as a first- or last-night stop in France for those using the Channel ports. It is still a genuine enclave of old France, complete with hill-fortress and colourful cobbled streets of stunning impressiveness. The old town centre was used as the location for the original filming of Victor Hugo's *Les Misérables*. There is much visual reward for those taking the 3-kilometre rampart circuit.

There are now tennis courts where once

Moines, efficiently signposted from the town centre, takes its name from the small lagoons nestling amid oak and beech forest which spreads across gently undulating countryside.

It is a modest, 2-star site with charges to match, and pitches are available either under trees or on open lawn. Facilities include hot showers and mains electricity, the outlook is green and pleasant and there is a peaceful atmosphere. The site is open from 15 March to 30 September and covers about 2 hectares of level ground.

The campsite is conveniently close to the town centre, which has a Syndicat d'Initiative in the place Verte. From this office you may collect free descriptive pamphlets of the way-marked footpaths which encircle the forest area. Clear and frequent yellow-band markings on the trees ensure that you won't get lost, and the short walk within this 868-hectare forest takes about 1 hour. There is a longer alternative for the more energetic – a section of GR du Pays, again well-defined with red-marker flashes. There is also a

Le Quesnoy, another Vauban citadel town.

Ready-made film set for the original version of Les Misérables; the Montreuil that very few transit travellers pause to enjoy.

moat waters rippled, but there are still strong old-world overtones, together with some striking examples of seventeenth-century military architecture. Those who have visited Saint-Jean-Pied-de-Port in the Pyrenean Basque country, may have a sense of *déjà vu* in Montreuil; not surprising, since that tireless fortification expert Sebastien Vauban was responsible for the resurrection of the redoubts in both towns, under Louis XIV. Vauban actually modernised about 350 strongholds throughout France in his lifetime from 1633–1707.

From the camp ground, take the right fork and ascend the rue des Moulins to the towering citadel wall, then turn right to follow the obvious, well-marked circular path. There are fine views over the river Canche and carp lakes at first, as the path meanders in and out of the outer moat, always beneath mighty walls of impregnable construction, with rounded watch towers, massive buttresses and ancient archways at intervals. Doubly walled and moated, the citizens of old Montreuil must have basked in lofty, seemingly endless security in those far-off times. The inner citadel is open daily, except Tuesday, and there is a small admission charge.

Other Regional Alternatives

If you do wish to explore the Val Joly and its lake, you will find it north-east of Fourmies,

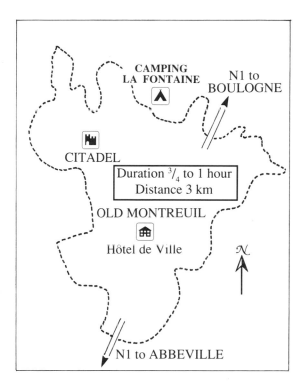

in the Forêt de Trelon. There is plenty of water-sport around the lake and several marked footpaths in the 400-hectare forest. One other oasis of green not far from Lille is St-Amand-les-Eaux. It is a spa, as the name implies, on the river Scarpe, and the town itself is one of ancient charm. The Forêt de Saint Amand, now a nature reserve, is traversed by the GR121.

Basse Normandie

Départements: Calvados – Manche – Orne
Préfecture: Caen

The landscape of Basse Normandie – 'dairy of France' – is made up of patchwork fields and hedgerows, many on a surprisingly small scale considering the overall area of the region. Here there are none of the vast agricultural plains which predominate in the neighbouring regions to the north-east and south. Huge numbers of piebald cattle make up the great Normandy dairy herds, but it is still very much a small-farm region, where most properties are family owned and managed, inherited from generations of efficient smallholders. Over the centuries, land enclosure and, till now, the increasing concentration on dairy produce, have gradually influenced the format of the landscape. Fertility from the cattle population, plus extensive hedging, have created a cosy green hinterland that is almost entirely rural, except for the immediate environs of Caen and Alençon. There is pleasant scenery, but it is predictable and uniform for the most part, and, apart from a ridge or two around Bagnoles in the south, there are few hills of any consequence to break the gentle rise and fall of green terrain. One exception is Little Switzerland (*see* pages 168–69).

Compensation for a generally bland hinterland is provided by a very interesting coastline, plus a history as violent and varied as any in France. Much of the past is still in evidence to surprise and delight both the driver and the pedestrian explorer. If there is a single word that is synonymous with Normandy, especially for the British, it is of course 'invasion'. Wherever you are within the boundaries of this region, you cannot escape from a past – both distant and recent – which has had a profound influence on the course of man's history. At Falaise, in 1027, William of Normandy was born; he was buried at Caen, just 34 kilometres north, about 60 years later. In between he completely changed the face and future of the British Isles – not bad for an illegitimate country boy, even if his cousin was Edward the Confessor!

Perhaps the future soldier-king was influenced by those other invincible invaders, the Vikings, who earlier still had swarmed across Normandy, and then settled and integrated around the Cotentin peninsula, themselves drastically affecting the subsequent seafaring prowess of the Normans.

The coastline's rich vein of history begins at Honfleur, south of the Seine estuary, from where the first settlers sailed to create French Canada. Even today you do not need too much imagination to visualise the sailing ships setting out from the beautiful tiny port. If you happen to be heading for Brittany from the east, do use the coast road, which wanders westwards above Caen, via the latterday invasion beaches of Arromanches, along the Pearl Coast, with Bayeux just 10 kilometres inland.

For a town stroll of consuming interest Bayeux is much recommended – and not only for the tapestry. It has a fine municipal camp ground within easy reach of the town centre, voted one of the best touring sites in Europe as a matter of fact, by the International Cara-vanning Federation. Bayeux is compact, tailor-made for strolling, a maze of cobbled streets, with pedestrian precincts, dominated by a twelfth-century Gothic cathedral, and full of atmosphere and echoes of old France. Miraculously, it escaped major war damage, and the tapestry depicting Harold's downfall near Hastings is now displayed in a surviving gracious seventeenth-century mansion.

Relics of a more recent past are housed in the Battle of Normandy Museum on the edge of Bayeux, while nearby Arromanches has evidence still of that Second Front assault, in the shape of Mulberry Harbour remains offshore. In 1944 this huge artificial port was fully operational just 12 days after being towed and secured into position, the outcome being a major contribution to the subsequent liberation of France. There is pleasant stroll-ing here, along the foreshore promenade and adjacent low cliffs, plus a choice of camping grounds for those who may wish to stay.

If time is not too pressing, consider con-tinuing your journey by probing north-west into the Contentin peninsula below Cher-bourg. Some of the coastal terrain compares favourably with neighbouring Brittany, notably around Barfleur and the Cap de la Hague. If you like sandy beaches and fore-shore walking, you will almost certainly appreciate Port Bail, where fast launches go to Jersey. A few kilometres inland from here

is St-Saveur-le-Vicomte, boasting a prettily situated touring site within the grounds of an impressive ruined abbey. Between here and the sea is the *forêt domaniale*, where there is woodland walking along signposted and marked footpaths.

It is, however, the coast south of Granville which is arguably the most attractive that Basse Normandie possesses. Granville itself, mini-Biarritz of the north, has the style and old-world elegance that befits a bracing sea-air resort developed during the *Belle Epoque*. Built largely over a rocky promontory, it has a lively and interesting commercial port, while the partly-fortified old town is a strol-lers' delight.

No less delightful is the coastal landscape immediately to the south, reached via the D911 coast road to Carolles. Between here and neighbouring St Jean-le-Thomas is the most dramatic scenic corner of the region, one that embraces distant views of Mont St Michel (an obligatory pilgrimage for any first-timer), on the southern side of the bay. Carolles is a quiet and attractive little resort, with a choice of touring sites, all within a stone's throw of the sea. The silver-sand beaches and backdrop of low, wooded cliffs make this an idyllic spot for those seeking a calmer seaside base. Outside August, it enjoys a subdued, therapeutic air, increasingly rare for any coastal holiday spot nowadays. It has, too, the start of a pleasing stretch of footpath, which begins with a steep flight of steps up the cliff from an expansive sweep of sandy beach. The high-level views from the sub-sequent well-defined path are consistently appealing, with rolling farm fields inland, and deep blue sea far below. It continues in this way for the most part to St Jean-le-Thomas, about 6 kilometres distant.

165

Much less visited than Mont St Michel, yet parts of the Cotentin peninsula are just as atmospheric. There is still much evidence of Anglo-French history here.

In between, seaward from the hamlet of Champeaux, is a section which is proudly known – perhaps a little optimistically – as the 'most beautiful kilometre in France'. Needless to say, that there are countless other claimants for this particular title, but certainly it is a lovely stretch of coastline, unblemished by high-rise buildings or excessive numbers of holiday bungalows. Low wooded hills still dominate above the foreshore, the seascape is splendid, and there are glimpses of Mont St Michel on nearing St Jean.

This is another base in the vicinity worth considering, with a municipal touring site that is literally on the beach, nicely landscaped and providing modern, pristine-clean amenities. Level, partially tree-shaded, this is

another camp ground unlikely to be overwhelmed with patrons outside the summer peak. It is open from Easter to 30 September.

The footpath, the Circuit des Falaises, which begins from Carolles beach at la Croix Paquerey, winds its switchback course to the cliff end just south of Champeaux, then continues west and north again along country lanes just inland, back to Carolles township. One interesting feature is the Cabanes Vauban half-way along the cliff path, used by customs men for surveillance of potential contraband entering Normandy. Hence the alternative name for the path as *le sentier des douaniers*. Those responsible for the promotion of tourism are fond of evocative titles hereabouts. Thus, not to be outdone by Granville and its comparison to Biarritz, St Jean-

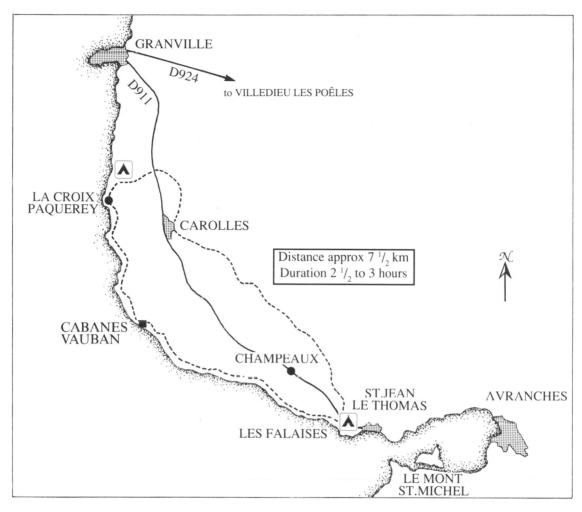

GRANVILLE

D924

to VILLEDIEU LES POÊLES

D911

LA CROIX PAQUEREY

CAROLLES

Distance approx 7 ¹/₂ km
Duration 2 ¹/₂ to 3 hours

N

CABANES VAUBAN

CHAMPEAUX

ST.JEAN LE THOMAS

AVRANCHES

LES FALAISES

LE MONT ST.MICHEL

Mont St Michel.

le-Thomas is sponsored as 'le Petit Nice de la Manche'. Tramping the stretch of richly wooded coast between here and Carolles on a particularly bright and sunny September day, I thought that it was not a bad alternative as a name.

Mont St Michel, after which the Normandy bay is named, is the real draw in the area, responsible for the great majority of visitors from the world over. If you find the pull irresistible, the most direct approach route is from the southern side of the bay at the Pontorson turn-off, where the holy islet is just 9 kilometres away. It is a shrine rising from the shallow sea since the dawn of history, wonderful to some, and a rather over-ornate rockpile to others. None the less, Mont St Michel is one of the treasures of the Western world, a fount of religious and military architecture. Ruthlessly commercialised now, it is still an obligatory objective for any first-time visitor to the area. Find your way to the causeway car park and pay your dues for a memorable ascent. It is possible to walk across the mud flats at ebb tide, for the water recedes for miles hereabouts, but it is not a foray to be undertaken lightly. There are qualified guides available if you insist on taking the ancient and tricky pilgrim route.

Villedieu-les-Poêles is another base, 30 kilometres inland from Granville, strategic for the coast and Mont St Michel, not subject to high-season crowding, and a fascinating township to boot. The town is to copperware what Contrexéville is to bottled water, and examples of the craft shine in almost every window. Villedieu-les-Poêles was created by the Knights of Malta, who established a copper foundry in this 'City of God' within a deep cleft of the river Sienne valley. For all its ancient beginnings, the town is also a shining example of France's second renaissance. The old town was literally crumbling in the 1950s, and today it can display all its ancient streets and buildings with pride, most of them having been beautifully restored without detriment to coveted old structures, passageways and tiny squares. It wears its restored affluence well, is a credit to Normandy and a real haven for the touring visitor.

There is an attractive touring site literally within a few steps of the colourful town centre. Spacious, diligently tended, with the river Sienne forming one boundary, and with green surrounding hills, it provides unlikely pastoral peace just a step away from town amenities. If you enjoy old-town strolling, don't miss Villedieu; you could even come away with a fine pot, pan or kettle that should last a lifetime!

Mortain

If you take the D33 south-east from Villedieu-les-Poêles, in about 28 kilometres you come upon Mortain, an ancient settlement (largely rebuilt after World War II devastation) in a delightful setting of cascades and rock outcrops, on the fringe of the Normandie-Maine Parc Naturel. There is a pleasant camp ground here, appropriately called Les Cascades, which is open from Easter to the end of October. Within Mortain Forest and the adjacent Nature Park, there are numerous pedestrian circuit walks, providing fine high-level views over the surrounding countryside. This is another favoured base of long-distance walkers, since the GR22 Avranches–Paris trail traverses the whole of the extensive Normandy Nature Park.

Normandy's Little Switzerland

Countless countries and regions of western Europe claim their respective 'little Switzerlands', but for the area of Suisse Normande to the west of Falaise, the nickname is justifiably accurate. Certainly, any idea that inland Normandy is flat and uninteresting is dispelled for the traveller exploring this particular part of the countryside. The small enclave formed by the triangle of Falaise,

Putanges and tiny Rouvrou (at the top end of the Gorges de St Aubert, about 19 kilometres south-west of Falaise) encompasses some delightful high-spots. There are good camp grounds at all these places, but they vary greatly in what they offer.

Falaise municipal touring site is quite grand, very modern and romantically located immediately below the tenth-century ruins of William the Conqueror's birthplace castle. Within the town environs, this is a first-class base for any extended stay in hinterland Basse Normandie. An excellent museum nearby houses the history of the 1944 Battle of Falaise Gap, when the town was almost totally destroyed. Putanges, 17 kilometres to the south-west, is a charming old-world village, with a simple but pretty night-halt municipal ground on the banks of the Orne, where the GR36 traces the river course from here to Pont d'Ouilly and beyond; a quite dramatic section of the long-distance trail. For a variety of short walks of equal visual stimulation, try overnighting at the hamlet of Rouvrou on the D43, about 19 kilometres from Falaise and just a short, steep drive up to the celebrated Roche d'Oetre. Be careful of the edges, for here you will see clearly – high above the Orne – why the regional name of 'Suisse' is justified.

Another pleasant short walk in this dramatic gorge country goes from the hamlet of Le Mesnil Villement, 3 kilometres from Pont d'Ouilly via the D167, signposted Le Bateau. Park at the unmistakable viaduct, opposite the cafe, and follow the GR red and white flashes under the arches, and then alongside the river weir and on to the impressive Barrage St Philbert about $2\frac{1}{2}$ kilometres to the south-east. You can pick up the GR36 then and continue back to Putanges if you feel

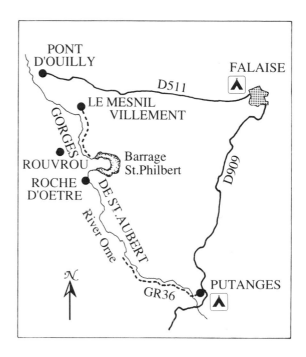

sufficiently energetic and there is someone available to retrieve your vehicle!

A Walk in Lesser-Known Normandy

One of the most popular major roads to the south for British holidaymakers is the N138, which makes a wide western sweep around Paris, between Rouen and Tours. This good road is not too heavily used, except around high summer and during the frenetic weekend of the Le Mans 24-hour road race. Since leisure walkers may conceivably also be motor-sports enthusiasts, the historic circuit could well be an objective for those taking a June break. For others, who simply wish to explore one of the region's hinterland beauty spots, the Parc de Normandie-Maine must be

169

Villedieu-les-Poêles, the copper and brass centre of France, is a fascinating town.

recommended, and in particular the Forêt D'Écouves, north-west of Alençon and some 65 kilometres from Le Mans. This is an especially useful area for a base camp, for those not wishing to mix with the crush of cars and people which constitutes France *en fête* during the Le Mans spectacular.

Sées is the delightful little town to make for, north of Alençon on the N138. It has been largely untouched by progress and boasts a majestic thirteenth-century cathedral and a small but agreeable touring site, open from April to September and located on the Alençon road. The utilities here are basic, but mains electric hook-ups are provided and there is a supermarket immediately opposite. A short stroll takes you to the mellow old town centre and the imposing cathedral square.

Just 12 kilometres south-west of the town, via the D908 and D226, is the centre of what was one of the most ferocious, yet lesser-known combat grounds of World War II. It was here in magnificent forest terrain that the

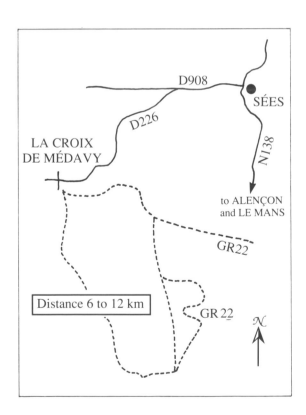

170

German 7th Army was savaged by US tank divisions between 10 and 23 August 1944, during the great Battle of Normandy. Standing at the centre of Le Carrefour de la Croix de Medavy, you can sense the military importance which this elevated forest location once commanded. Today, the panorama to the north is across unbroken forest beauty. Those wishing to see this fine nature park at closer quarters have the choice of several pedestrian routes along forest rides from the Croix picnic place. One of the most attractive winds north-eastwards to join the long-distance GR22, which may be partially followed together with local footpath links to complete a circular route. Distances may extend to 6, 10 or 12 kilometres, depending on personal choice. Map and compass work may be necessary in places, since signposting is not always obvious. If you are in any doubt at all, you should stay on the obvious forestry rides.

The forest ride from the Carrefour de la Croix de Medavy, in the Forêt d'Ecouves near Sées.

Haute Normandie

Départements: Eure – Seine-Maritime
Préfecture: Rouen

The winds that blow so steadily – and sometimes fiercely – across the Pas de Calais invariably abate south of the Somme estuary. The Haute Normandie seaboard, sheltered by the jutting Cherbourg peninsula from the worst of the prevailing westerlies, is quieter climatically than its northern neighbours. Because the area is less wind-battered, vegetation is more luxuriant and profuse and the terrain changes from sweeping plain country to a land of undulating green hills, some of which are surprisingly lofty, notably along the Bresle river valley border with Picardy. The result is a region of distinctive difference. It culminates in some of the most majestic cliff formations to be found anywhere along the northern coast of France, including a section of quite magnetic appeal for those who enjoy leisure walking.

The natural endowments of Etretat, at the eastern end of the Seine Bay, will seem familiar to anyone who has walked in the vicinity of Durdle Door in Dorset, above the Isle of Wight Needles, or across Beachy Head in Sussex. Indeed, so strikingly similar is the area in places, that you could easily concur with the prevalent geologists' view that Britain was once part of the Continental land mass. Certainly the Isle of Wight would slot snugly enough – jigsaw like – into the Seine Bay in the vicinity of Honfleur; while the Seven Sisters between Eastbourne and Newhaven are almost a mirror-image of the cliffs between Etretat and Fecamp. Whatever the origins of the formation, England certainly has no monopoly on white cliffs.

To see the best of the French variety of white cliff there could not be a better base than Etretat, a small, colourful and vibrant seaside resort at sea level behind a pristine pebble and sand beach, almost dwarfed by the towering chalk cliffs which rise to either side. A prime virtue of Etretat is that it constitutes a genuine walking centre. All the attractions are within easy pedestrian reach, including the town itself, the municipal camping ground, and the cliff walks. Here you really can forget all about driving for a spell, and concentrate on the business of putting one foot before the other.

The approach route to Etretat, west of Dieppe, is a pleasurable appetiser too, particularly if you take the minor coast road through St-Valéry-en-Caux and Fécamp. This is country-lane driving for the most part dotted with attractive villages and some up and down ascents and swoops, especially around Fécamp, renowned for its Bénédictine distilleries. There is one set of traffic lights in tiny Etretat, where you turn sharp left for the touring site which will be found less than 1 kilometre along the road from the town centre. This agreeable ground, medium-sized with 120 touring pitches, is fenced, nicely landscaped and admission is primarily restricted to genuine touring units. Richly wooded and quite steep hillsides rise on each side of the valley setting, while the site itself is level in all but one corner. The standard of cleanliness is high and hot water to hand basins and showers is copious and consistent. There are spacious dishwashing and clothes-washing annexes and mains electricity is available. Outside peak months, this is a quiet and pleasant site, open 15 March to 15 October.

The resort of Etretat, something of a mini-Deauville, is geared to tourism, so that the annual swelling of the 1,600 resident inhabitants is not too traumatic (although car parking around the sea-front vicinity is sometimes difficult. However, since the front is only a short distance from the camping ground, this should pose the camper no problems.)

Etretat is an interesting little town, despite the numerous souvenir shops and seaside fun-centres. It is also an ancient coastal settlement, first recorded as 'Estrutat' in AD 1204. Among many intriguing old buildings lining narrow and frequently steep streets is the original town hall. This is a fine wooden structure with a memorial stone over the main door to the 51st Highland Division, which liberated the town in 1944. More practically, there is an excellent choice of food shops, a wealth of cafés and seafood restaurants, a very obliging Tourist Office in the place de la Mairie and a bank adjacent. The pleasant dilemma facing you is which way to walk first from the short promenade – to the majestic summit ridge of the Falaises d'Aval to the south-west, or towards the equally regal Falaises d'Amont to the north-east?

The Falaises d'Aval are closest, offering a brisk and revealing ascent from sea level to the towering chalk formations of arches and pinnacles, charmingly called the Chambre aux Demoiselles and Aiguille Manneporte. It is possible to walk the cliff tops as far as Cap d'Antifer, returning along a choice of footpaths via the high-level golf course. The climb is an easy one, partly stepped, but merits a word of caution if children are in the party: there are a number of unprotected edges, notably in the region of the Manneporte Needle. It is all perfectly safe, provided there is no impetuous straying from the obvious and well-trodden paths.

For a 2-hour walk of landscape contrast, consider the bridleway route to the nearby hamlet of Bénouville and a return via the Falaise d'Amont ('Upstream Cliff'). This route starts in Etretat centre from the rue Jules-Gerbeau and continues along the Chemin Côte du Mont. The path to Bénouville is plainly signposted at the entrance to

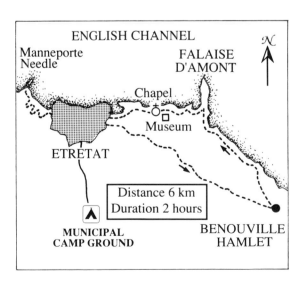

173

Etretat and the cliff path above the town. This is one of the most dramatic stretches of coastline along the Channel seaboard.

the aerial museum. A stiff tarmac ascent is followed by a wide bridle path and farm track, across rolling cereal crop farmland, to the little hamlet about 3 kilometres away, where the tarmac begins once again. For the energetic, this lane continues, as a section of the GR21, into the fishermen's village of Yport, some 6 kilometres from Etretat, another pretty coastal place sandwiched by high cliffs. For others, the pull of the cliff-top path seaward from Bénouville will probably prove irresistible. Certainly, it presents a visual treat after the pleasant but unre-

markable outward walk. There are 3 kilometres of coastal splendour along a well-defined and safe path, with magnificent views in both directions as the cliff structure is revealed from jutting belvederes. Here you are treading the real heart of a 75-mile stretch of towering chalk outcrop, aptly named the Alabaster Coast.

On approach to Etretat along this path, the walker is guided towards the tiny and perfectly-proportioned Sailor's Chapel, now somewhat aggressively overshadowed by the monument to intrepid pioneer airmen Nungesser and Coli, who flew their tiny aircraft across the north Atlantic in the early 1900s. The 'White Bird' is outlined in concrete, rather like Bleriot's even more minuscule craft on the cliffs of Dover. This one is pinpointed by a futuristic landing marker, which appears alien in its surroundings. There is a small and interesting museum here, charging a modest entry fee.

Back at the camp ground you might explore the attractive wooded valley which is adjacent. It looks inviting and there is an alternative footpath route which takes in part of the lushly wooded slopes. Turn left at the camp ground entrance and stroll along the Criquetot road to the signposted cycle path turn-off to Le Havre (about $\frac{1}{2}$ kilometre south). The narrow lane climbs alongside a fenced estate of tall trees, winding gradually west and north to rejoin the coast at the Falaise d'Aval and thus back to Etretat seafront. The round route is of about 2 hours duration, and is a pleasant and varied evening walk, beginning and finishing at the campsite.

The Bresle Valley

The département of Seine-Maritime is well provided with pedestrian routes, especially along the coastline and is becoming quite popular with backpackers, who can begin tramping the long-distance GR network immediately after disembarkation at Dieppe. There is a continuous route from here westwards to Etretat and beyond, to the outskirts of Le Havre. From here, the river Seine may be followed along the southern boundary through the richly wooded country of Parc de Brotonne and around Elbeuf. From here, there is a choice of GR or local trails which

meander northwards back to Dieppe – a fine circuit, of much variety, which should amply fill any 10- to 14-day venture. Indeed, the only part of Seine-Maritime not served by long-distance paths is along the boundary with Picardie; and this is odd, considering the green-hill landscape of the Bresle Valley.

The Bresle Valley encompasses forest, river valley and hill stretches between the ancient and striking township of Eu, just inland from Le Tréport, and Blangy-sur-Bresle, about 20 kilometres to the south-east. Eu has a past going back a thousand years and it has in its time witnessed the best and worst of Anglo-French relations. Here William parleyed – unfruitfully of course – with Harold prior to the conquest of England, while nearly 800 years later King Louis-Philippe welcomed Queen Victoria, distinguishing Eu as the birthplace of the *Entente Cordiale*. The Château des Comtes d'Eu, the great church of Notre Dame et St Laurent and the old hospital (the seventeenth-century Ancien Hôtel-Dieu) are

The hamlet of Monchaux-Soreng on a circuit footpath from Blangy-sur-Bresle, offering hidden delights just off a main arterial route.

An ancient and picturesque watermill on the river Bresle near Blangy – a surprisingly scenic enclave of northern France.

and then through Monchaux–Soreng, a peaceful old-world hamlet of waterwheels. The circuit route continues via an imposing château, another scenic hamlet called Bouillancourt, and then through woodland back to Blangy in the valley below. Blangy is a strategic backwater stopping place, an easy day's drive from the port of Calais which offers an opening scene of rural France along a pedestrian route not trodden by too many foreign visitors.

The Pre-Invasion Beach of Berneval-le-Grand

About 10 kilometres east of Dieppe lies Berneval, seaward of the D925, and its neighbouring commune of Saint Martin en

impressive reminders of an illustrious past. There is pleasant woodland camping here in the Parc du Château, and some interesting short walks, including a botanical footpath.

Follow the narrow and winding river Bresle south-east and you come upon Blangy, something of an overgrown village with some interesting corners away from the N28 which bisects the centre. Among them is a newly-established municipal touring site. From the Syndicat d'Initiative office in the main town square you can pick up a free itinerary of four local walks ranging from 2 to 3 hours' duration, taking in riverside terrain and sections of the Forêt d'Eu. One of the best routes is largely lane walking via Bouttencourt, the uphill village adjacent to Blangy

The Berneval cliffs above a Canadian commando memorial.

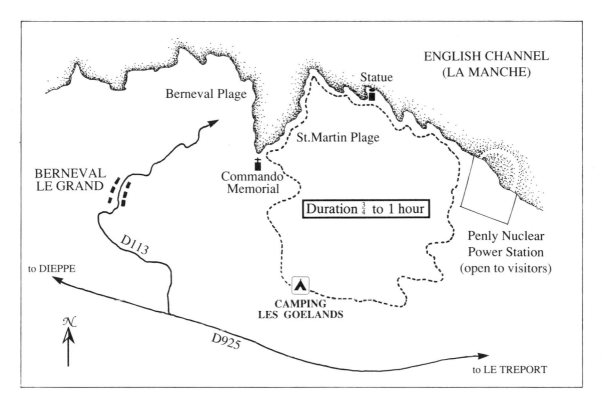

Campagne. An heroic episode of recent history took place here where the waters of the English Channel break against towering 300-foot high chalk cliffs; the valiant but abortive assault by Canadian troops to breach the walls of what was – in the summer of 1942 – Fortress Europe. The story of this gallant foray may be read elsewhere; now there remains only a modest cairn overlooking the sea and a wall plaque inscribed with the names of Canadian commandos. The abruptly sheer cliffs are as spectacular as ever, while tiny Berneval and St Martin have not been grossly developed. The little inlet (a remote and cunningly selected spot for a landing in 1942) still has its inviting footpath, which zig-zags upwards from the seashore to the cliff-top statue of the Virgin and Child and beyond. This is another useful place for those using the Newhaven–Dieppe ferry.

Take the Berneval turn off the D925, continue through the straggly village to the signposted *plage*, and a short distance eastwards behind the cliffs is Camping les Goelands. In a valley fold of sheep-cropped grass, immediately below the cliff outcrop, this caravan park is primarily given over to static units, although there is supposedly room for 100 touring visitors. Modern facilities are housed in several blocks, and all the usual utilities are provided, including mains electricity. Les Goelands is open all year round, and is a pleasant enough night halt for those in transit.

From the site, the cliff path is obvious, although if there are grazing stock in the top fields it may be necessary to detour slightly from the normal circuit route. Another threat to this naturally beautiful terrain is posed by the new (and half-hidden) Penly nuclear power station (open to visitors), which occupies a large section of cliff top and foreshore just to the east of the Virgin and Child monument. For those with time to spare, the GR21 between Berneval and Dieppe is a pleasant pedestrian excursion. One note of warning: the Berneval cliffs are quite safe if walked with care, but there is no fencing, there are one or two deep fissure craters, and a fierce offshore wind should keep every prudent walker well back from the edge.

Seine-Side in Brotonne Nature Park

Approximately 25 kilometres from Rouen, in the heart of a beautiful forested area, there is a splendid first-night stopping place for visitors using any of the major Channel ports. A comfortable day's drive from Calais or Boulogne should find you on the outskirts of Rouen, the great cathedral city, and in a good spot for bypassing Paris on the western side via quieter roads, if you happen to be heading south.

Just to the north-west of Rouen lie Pavilly and Barentin, pretty backroad towns, from where you can take the D143 south-west to Duclair. Suddenly, at Duclair you are confronted by the wide Seine and the first of the tiny vehicle ferries. Do not board, but turn sharp right, following the signposts for the *base de plein air* immediately alongside the river. A superb waterside drive follows, of some 10 kilometres, giving uninterrupted views of the Seine at its most beautiful. The first-class camping park of Brotonne will be found close to the riverside and village of Jumièges le Mesnil.

Here, amid a staggering 40,000 hectares of woodland and heath which make up this large nature park, there are no less than 300 kilometres of marked footpaths and long-distance trails. An area almost unvisited by

The River Seine has mini car ferry fleets readily available. This one is near Mesnil.

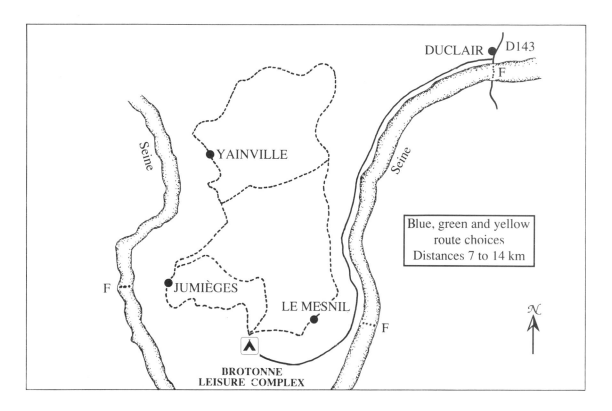

Britons (invariably racing through Haute Normandie in transit), it is a green delight of northern France that should not be missed by any nature lover.

Brotonne Camping/Caravanning Park is just part of a magnificent 45-hectare leisure complex beside the Seine, where facilities include spacious pitching areas in the open or under pine trees, and amenities to suit all tastes, from indoor and outdoor tennis to organised sporting programmes or sailing courses. For those who prefer exploring on foot, there is a great variety of footpath trails in the immediate forest surroundings. Three routes go directly from the leisure centre, waymarked green, blue and yellow and varying in length from seven to fourteen kilometres. All of them take in scenic stretches of the Seine (which encompasses the whole area in a massive loop), fine sections of forest, and quiet hamlets like Jumièges, Yainville and le Mesnil.

When you are ready to continue driving south take the Jumièges ferry across the Seine to the Bourg–Achard road, and go from there to Elbeuf and Louviers where you join the N154 for Evreux. A more direct route south than this is via the Tancarville toll bridge. The cost is about the same but the former is much more interesting for the keen walker.

179

Picardie

Départements: Aisne – Oise – Somme
Préfecture: Amiens

As you drive off the Calais ferry, no matter whether your objective is south, east or western France, Picardie must be touched upon after crossing Nord Pas de Calais. The region is not particularly large by French standards – indeed, it is one of the smallest in the country – but its topography contributes to a stimulating impression of vast space which never fails to make an impact on island-dwelling visitors. The Picardie boundary stretches from Berck Plage near Le Touquet, eastwards to the Belgian border and south, below Chantilly, almost to the outskirts of Paris. It enjoys a short, interesting seaboard to either side of the Somme estuary, with pleasing hill country on the southern side, forming a natural boundary with neighbouring Haute Normandie. Elsewhere, the sweeping agricultural plains are broken by winding valleys of the rivers which give their names to the three départements, which contain a massive 2,600 square kilometres of forest, plus 2,000 kilometres of waymarked footpaths.

Picardie boasts amongst its attractions Amiens cathedral, acknowledged by UNESCO as the finest religious building in the world; Laon, a dazzling medieval town on its isolated ridge high above the plain of Champagne; and Soissons, enviably wealthy in its eleventh- and thirteenth-century remnants, and arguably the place where the notion of France as a cohesive entity was born. Clovis, king of the Francs in the fifth century, enjoyed successive victories over the Visigoths after the Roman departure, became a converted Christian and was virtually the founder of the French nation. His capital seat of power was Soissons – not surprisingly, since at that time Picardie (not so named then) was the political hub of the state.

The fields of Crécy and Agincourt are within the Picardie boundaries, along with one of the bloodiest battle-fronts in the history of modern warfare – the Somme. No region of France has a more tumultuous past, and, if there is one place where history and landscape meet in a fascinating blend, it is surely Compiègne. Here, the enveloping forest is a direct legacy from the mad passion of past kings for hunting. The first written evidence of Compiègne comes from the misty fifth century, when the son of Clovis, Clotaire the First, was killed in a hunting accident within the forest, then called Cuise. For the next 500 years Compiègne was the premier royal residence within the vast territory that eventually become unified France. It was here, during a siege of the Hundred Years War, that Joan of Arc was captured by Burgundians and sold to the British, before being eventually executed at Rouen.

180

The present palace at Compiègne was built by Louis XV and became a favourite court of Napoleon III during the Second Empire. The modern historical importance of the town is indelibly assured, as it is the place where the World War I armistice was signed in 1918, and where Hitler accepted Marshal Pétain's surrender in 1940. Despite heavy damage inflicted during the Liberation, Compiègne retains many treasures within a magnificent setting. The town and its surrounding forest encapsulate a wonderful 2,000-year-old area of French civilisation. Don't miss the splendid palace, the town hall museum which contains a superb Battle of Waterloo diorama, or Joan of Arc's Tower, built to defend the original Oise bridge.

Fittingly, the municipal camping ground, l'Hippodrome, is sited on the fringe of the forest, which is unquestionably one of the most beautiful in France. To get there, take the avenue Royale from the town centre and drive for approximately $1\frac{1}{2}$ kilometres south-east, where the entrance will be found beside the racecourse. The level, part-shaded terrain covers some $1\frac{1}{2}$ hectares and provides 150 pitches for touring visitors. The far end of the ground is reserved for long-stay units, but this does not encroach too much on the allocated casual section. The facilities are adequate and acceptably clean, bearing in mind the turnover of visitors at peak periods, especially during any of the equestrian events. L'Hippodrome is a well-placed base camp, especially for pedestrian exploring. The site is open from 15 March to 15 November, hot showers and mains electric hook-ups are available, the nearest shops are in town, and the tariff is medium.

For those who enjoy cycling, bikes may be

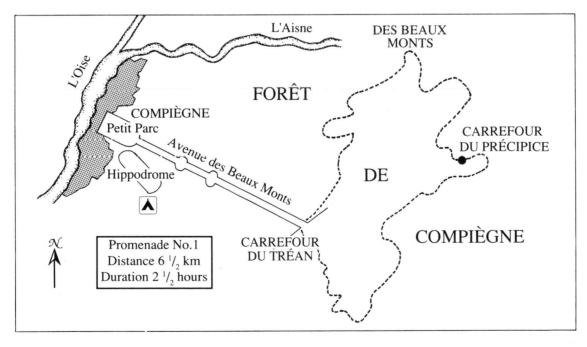

Château Pierrefonds; Napoleonic splendour in the heart of Compiègne forest.

hired in the town. There is a designated cycle track which runs adjacent to the camping ground, from Compiègne centre to the intriguing Château Pierrefonds (built for Napoleon III) about 12 kilometres away. This trail, not unnaturally, is also used by walkers wishing to see the imposing château. This nineteenth-century restoration is something of an architectural indulgence, centuries late with its formidable fortifications, but hugely impressive in structure and setting, dwarfing Pierrefonds village which clusters around the wooded base.

There are also orthodox footpaths which criss-cross the great woodland less directly, ending up at the same objective of Pierrefonds. The choice of walking is wonderfully wide around Compiègne – there are no less than 26 marked circuit paths, totalling 250 kilometres within an area covering some

15,000 hectares. Indeed, if the neighbouring woodlands of Laigue and Retz are included, there is forest of over twice this area for the pedestrian wanderer.

Promenade les Beaux Monts may be equalled for aesthetic and physical pleasure, but it certainly won't be surpassed. It is a nicely undulating route, traversing one of several quite high ridges which rise from the predominantly flat lands of the Oise and Aisne valleys. The path begins from the Carrefour-de-Tréan, meandering through some ancient forest of oak and beech trees, many of which are hundreds of years old. Along the way, there is a picturesque twelfth-century chapel, St Corneille, and some strangely twisted beeches, rather like the faux de Verzy (*see* page 77). The path climbs gradually from here to the summit of the aptly named Beaux Monts. The glades on these lovely wooded slopes are studded by some of the oldest trees in the whole forested area. From the precipice viewpoint, there are fine views across the valley of the Aisne and the adjacent Forêt de Laigue. The path descends from a beech and silver pine ridge, eventually to rejoin the historic 'route Eugénie' at the Tréan crossroads. The summit vistas on this walk are memorable, including the Grande Allée, scythed through the woodland on the order of Napoleon. However, above all, the route is notable for the sheer beauty and variety of the trees, one venerable giant being the Marie-Louise Cedar, planted by the Empress in 1810.

Within the snaking loop of the Aisne river, north-east of Beaux Monts, is one of the most hallowed places in modern French — and indeed world — history: the Clairière de l'Armistice. It was here on 11 November 1918 that Marshal Foch accepted the German surrender. Chosen for its peaceful silence, this natural forest clearing was later landscaped and the Armistice railway carriage positioned here about nine years later. Alas, it was only to be removed and destroyed in 1940 after the tragic reversal of French fortune. Today's carriage is a replica, but there are genuine relics and documents in the little museum. This memorial glade is much visited, yet it retains its tranquil air, and is a dignified and timeless tribute to a lost generation.

The Opal Coast

Just about 100 kilometres from Calais lie the wide flatlands of the Somme estuary. This is an easy opening drive if you are heading for Brittany, and can be pleasantly scenic and relatively traffic-free too, if you keep to the secondary coast roads south of Boulogne through Etaples. This way, the N1 and Abbeville (which can be busy) are avoided entirely, and you have the bonus of seeing the immense and dramatic sweep of the Bay of the Somme at Le Crotoy. The minor road continues right around the rim of the bay, through Noyelles-sur-Mer, before it crosses the river and enters the little port and township of St-Valery-sur-Somme, the most intriguing high-spot along the short length of Picardie coast.

St-Valery-sur-Somme.

The Somme, synonymous with Great War carnage, flowed quietly throughout that conflict, but St-Valery did not escape damage itself during World War II. Indeed, the area has a history of violence and derring-do. For the past alone it is worth stopping overnight. There is also a delightful choice of waterside walks around the bay itself, or alongside the Somme Canal.

There are three camp grounds, all located on the western edge of the town, a kilometre or so from the centre, on the D940 road to Eu. La Croix Abbé is the 4-star ground prominently located at the top of the short hill, followed by La Sablière, and La Garenne, the 2-star municipal site. All three provide adequate facilities, and are acceptably clean but rather crowded with semi-permanent weekend caravans – the penalty you pay for proximity to Abbeville and Amiens. They are, however, salubrious enough for an overnight stop, when you might make time to have a look round the town.

St-Valery old town, perched on its sandstone bluff, must have been a cause of great joy to the original discoverers. It rises sheer and very uncharacteristically from the surrounding sea-level marshes, to provide a near perfect look-out point over the great estuary and a natural patch of defensive high ground. It was fortified very early in the history of man, and subsequently savaged frequently – not surprisingly. Oddly enough, the Greeks were the first recorded inhabitants of St-Valery, using the town as a trading post. The Romans created a camp on the promontory and this later became an abbey, the oldest in Picardie, in the tenth century. Thereafter it was more often than not under siege – no less than 20 times within four centuries – and repeatedly sacked. The town's greatest moment of history was in 1066, when it was the port from which William the Conqueror sailed to invade England. The actual spot where his ship tied up is commemorated by a plaque on an ancient salt warehouse along the Quai Lejoille.

High above the water, massive twin towers form the buttresses of William's Gate (Porte de Guillaume), part of the eleventh-century castle adjacent to the Bénédictine monastery. Through this gate on 20 December 1430 Joan of Arc passed as a prisoner of the English, on her way to Rouen. The squat, powerful towers of the Porte de Guillaume are chilling examples of early military architecture and must surely have stirred presentiments of doom in the girl-soldier.

The sweeping panoramas from the terrace ramparts are of the Somme spilling into the sea, across saltings and pastures where sheep are grazed on rich grasses. Along the water's edge, there is a fine tree-shaded promenade which extends from the town centre seawards, towards Cap Hornu and the lonely lighthouse in one direction, and to the ancient Somme river bridge in the other. From here, where the miniature railway runs between St-Valery and Le Crotoy 27 kilometres away around the bay, there is plentiful free parking and the start of the Somme Canal, a major navigation to Abbeville. The towpath is a much-favoured ramble, a pedestrian route into quiet countryside, visually pleasing and peopled only by anglers and nature lovers – 2 hours or more of waterside walking amid quiet surroundings. For those wishing to explore further, a section of the GR125 runs through St-Valery and is joined by a GR du Pays path to form circuit walks of 10 and 18 kilometres. Detailed information is available from the tourist office, prominently situated.

William's Gate, whose squat towers are relics of an infamous chapter in the town's history.

Champagne – Charly is the Name

The wide and handsome river Marne flows right across the southern tip of Picardie, with Château-Thierry the central point on the N3, which traces part of the river course along the pretty Marne Valley. With many wooded hill flanks separated by manicured arable farms, this Picardie landscape is surprisingly rural, considering the proximity of Paris to the west and the *autoroute* which now slices the terrain just to the north of the Marne. The minor road on the right bank of the river, the D969, between Château-Thierry and Charly, is especially green, while the pedestrian paths right alongside the water between Nogent-l'Artaud and Charly warrant an hour or so of exploration.

There is a good base camp on the outskirts of Nogent (in an area with not too many quality campsites), in a shady and elevated location, with fine valley views in all directions, and with reasonable space for tourers. There is a small industrial zone, well away from the site, which keeps the town prosperous, but Nogent still has the atmosphere of an agricultural market town. This is a very convenient stop for those taking the eastern route around Paris from the Channel ports. Camping les Monts is a 2-star municipal

185

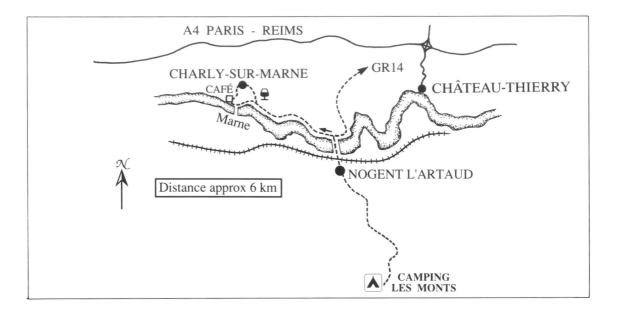

enterprise, open from March to September and the facilities are clean and serviceable, if a little spartan. The ground is nicely landscaped, with wooded terraces providing well-spaced individual pitches, making this an attractive site since it does restrict unit intake to 50 on a 1-hectare patch. There is considerable patronage by weekenders, but space is generally available for tourers, and the limit on total intake means that there is none of the gross overcrowding often found on sites within easy reach of big cities. Mid-week, and at weekends outside July and August, this is an attractive spot. It is well signposted as you enter the little township, and there are a surprising number of leafy arbours on offer, so park and explore before pitching.

Once you are installed, there is a pleasant 10-minute stroll down to the river Marne, via the Chemin de la Champaille ('garlic field lane'), and then the rue Leduc de la Tournelle, following the unmistakable red and white flashes of the GR14 through the back streets of old Nogent, past the medieval church and one or two very ancient dwellings, including a fifteenth-century half-timbered house that is now an antique shop. Over the river bridge and the railway, the GR14 veers away north-east towards a green hill ridge and Château-Thierry. The prettiest short walk is westwards along the Marne towpath for about 2 kilometres to Charly. There is a little café/restaurant by the Charly river bridge, but find time to walk up the road to the little village itself. It is very interesting architecturally and assuredly the champagne capital of the Marne Valley, where almost every house is ready and willing to dispense bubbly to visitors. For its size, there cannot be anywhere else in France that is a greater retail outlet for champagne than Charly. This village is an interesting end to your walk, which also reveals a tranquil reach of the Marne that is normally seen only by locals.

One last comment: if you are coming off the *autoroute*, don't be too tempted to stop at the Château-Thierry camp ground – where the facilities are distinctly unkempt and overcrowding is the norm. The square in front of the town hall, below the ruins of the fourteenth-century château, is the spot to park and look at the best of the town. At the top of the great flight of old steps you can wander around the ramparts, and marvel at the building skills and ingenuity of the medieval stone masons.

Rousseau Remembered

The south-western département of Oise in Picardie has about 40,000 hectares of state forest open to the public. Through these huge wooded areas run some half-dozen GR routes, plus numerous local footpaths, waymarked in red, and the forests of Compiègne, Laigue and Chantilly also have a number of specially signposted walks of 1 to 2 hours' duration. It may seem curious, therefore, that at Ermenonville – on the southern fringe of another great wooded area near Senlis –

emphasis should be on walking in a small public park; but this particular park is something special.

First find an appropriate base camp. Self-containment is really a prerequisite of any visit to the Campeoles site at Ermenonville, for the facilities are primitive and over-used and there are no electric hook-ups. Plus marks are awarded, however, for the setting and for the size of the ground, which covers 12 hectares of level woodland. There are many arbours and shady enclaves despite the predominance of static caravans (inevitable in a place so near to Paris) which are thankfully spread far and wide, and are partially hidden, mostly behind high hedging. Touring patrons are left to choose their own place on this very expansive area. The attractions of this open-all-year base are several: its proximity to both Paris and the Channel ports;

The elegant château at Ermenonville, now an hotel, but once the haunt of Rousseau and Voltaire.

the three great forests that virtually surround Senlis; and the Jean-Jacques Rousseau château park (literally next door to the camp ground), once part of the great forested estate of the Marquis de Girardin (1735–1808).

A precious legacy of France's gracious age, this intriguingly beautiful château park was laid out in the mid-eighteenth century, when the governing élite – and most landscape architects – paid homage to the classic age of antiquity. The Marquis was inspired originally by the concept of the English garden, although what he had created at Ermenonville was essentially French. It is a masterpiece of landscaping, not overformalised but rather a romantic extension of nature around a central lake dotted with carefully-chosen reminders of the world's progression, from a prehistoric grotto to a temple of philosophy. If it sounds rather contrived, it needs to be seen in reality – a creative landscape within a great bowl of beech and oak trees, it is a place that will remain firmly in your memory.

Both Rousseau, a great friend and mentor of the Marquis, and Voltaire fell under the spell of these château grounds. For the privileged few it must have been an enchanting place. (Rousseau died at the Ermenonville château in July 1778 and was buried on the 'Island of Poplars', until the Revolution, when his remains were re-interred in Paris.) Ermenonville has almost 50 hectares of fabulous terrain, enough to occupy an hour or so of contemplative strolling in the footsteps of Rousseau and other eminent philosophers. There is always something of interest along the lake shore, or on the rising ground where it blends with the magnificent woodland glades. The grounds are open every day, except on Tuesday, and there is a modest admission charge.

188

Guise – Rose of Picardie

Above St Quentin the vast plains of northern Picardie roll across the départements of Somme and Aisne, a near-endless carpet of cereal crops, where only a lone combine-harvester or an isolated group of plane trees break an infinite – and usually empty – skyline. However, there are, as with all seemingly monotonous landscapes, interesting pockets. One of these is the small town of Guise on the river Oise, which, on the map at least, appears almost featureless, with little to attract the touring visitor or leisure walker. On the contrary, Guise is delightful, with a rich historic past, a superb pedestrian-only route to an exciting visual objective, and an extremely pleasant camping ground (rather uncommon anywhere in Picardie), plus an option of short-circuit walks around the picturesque old town. It is a fascinating place to visit, within easy driving distance of the Channel ports for a weekend break, in an area of northern France where you can still, in places, find yourself in a turn-of-the-century time-warp.

The name Guise is a clue to the town's antiquity – it was the Duc de Guise who delivered Joan of Arc to the English. Two centuries before that, his ancestors built a mighty fortress above the Oise, a massive and more sophisticated extension of a tenth-century keep. The fortress-château still stands in part today though it was almost destroyed in World War I. It has a history as turbulent and absorbing as France herself, and the contemporary chapter is the most heartening. Since 1952, over 70,000 volunteers, of all ages and nationalities, have pitched in under the inspired leadership of Maurice Duton to restore this great heritage treasure, devoting

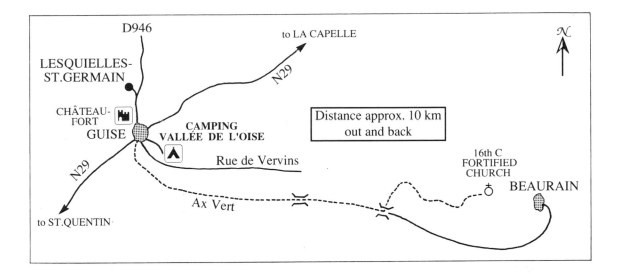

thousands of working days to the gigantic task. The result is that 2,000 visitors a year now come to see the first historic monument in France to be rescued by willing volunteers. The grand total of heritage sites which have subsequently been restored nationwide now stands at 300; Guise castle-château is within easy strolling distance of the town camp ground, Vallée de Oise.

Vallée de Oise is located in the rue du Camping. It is surprisingly extensive, level and agreeably green, a regional club site managed in a diligent and friendly way. There are a fair number of weekend caravans here, but certain areas are specifically reserved for tourers on spacious individual pitches, so there is no close-ranking. The facilities are clean and wholesome, while the common room might almost have been designed by the architect of Versailles! It must be the most intriguing and grand-scale wet-weather shelter anywhere in France, with television, a large kitchen and communal cooking area with full ovens (ready-made for backpackers), a wealth of local information displayed on large placards (especially concerning outdoor leisure pursuits such as walking and

canoeing). There is table tennis, plus palatial space for children; enough to include an indoor play slide and landing mat. All this is housed in a light and airy building which could accommodate a host of people, but which, in reality, is very little used. For a region that is not generally noted for the quality of its camping grounds, Guise gets top marks. It is open 1 April to 25 October, and there are no less than 4 hectares of peaceful space here beside a canalised arm of the river Oise. The site is well signposted on all approach roads.

There is some very pleasant strolling around the old town of Guise; the château-castle is approached via atmospheric cobbled streets and evocative landmarks like the Porte de Paris. In the Place d'Armes there is an imposing and vigorous statue of Camille Desmoulins, a patriot-revolutionary executed along with Danton in 1794. The Chemin de Ronde is an interesting town walk, just one of three recommended short circuits, full details about which are available from the camp ground office.

A little further afield is the village of Lesquielles, 3 kilometres to the north, which

The rare, fairy-tale beauty of Beaurain fortified church.

offers a glimpse of untouched rural Picardie, via a clearly waymarked 1-hour walk, the Circuit St Germain. Just above the tall hill-top church is a large and spacious car park, from where you stroll down to the tiny Mairie, to follow the blue/white arrows along lanes, through woods, past old-style houses and farms, and through river meadows via tracks and lanes. There are many interesting landmarks *en route*, not least the church of Lesquielles, and the Chapelle Ste Grimonie. There is also a variation of the Circuit St Germain, and this is again waymarked in blue and white.

The best walk has to be the 5-kilometres of the Ax Vert, between Guise and Beaurain, which comes as close as any in France to footpath walking at its very best. It starts directly from the camp ground where you turn right at the exit, then first left, then right again. Past the gendarmerie, at the traffic lights on the Laon–St Quintin road, you turn acutely left where you will see a motorised traffic barrier; the wide, emerald-green track with the cathedral-like canopy of beeches is the Ax Vert. The 5-kilometre walk along this marvellous transformation of a one-time local railway line is as enjoyable as any leisure walker could wish, and with just a short deviation you will find one of the most stunning of sixteenth-century fortified churches anywhere in northern France. This structure is unblemished by surrounding build-up, and it stands proud, exuding massive medieval confidence. The cool white interior, beautifully simple, is as exquisite as the chivalrous exterior, and the only embellishment is a series of stained-glass windows in blazing colours. One of these, significant for this locality, features Joan of Arc.

Poitou-Charente

Départements: Charente – Charente-Maritime –
Deux-Sèvres – Vienne
Préfecture: Poitiers

Despite the establishment of long-distance footpaths in the northern part of this region, anyone in transit to the south may well be glad that he or she is behind the wheel. True, there is the GR364 which links Parthenay with Poitiers and the GR36 which traverses the central terrain, but, from the capital southwards, the landscape is one of immense farming tracts, and the road more often than not a straight black ribbon stretching to a near-featureless infinity. The green chequerboard of agricultural endeavour is relieved only occasionally by hamlets or market towns. It's a landscape that is sparsely wooded and which undulates almost imperceptibly.

That is the scene along the N11 and the N150 from Niort, until you begin to near Cognac, the brandy capital of the world. As if to prepare the traveller for something special, the countryside takes on a distinctly lusher look. The terrain becomes rounded, full-bodied, and the tan and gold of cereal crops are replaced by the sharp green of the vine, the vineyards slotted in lovingly-tended order among shady woods. The trees, like the vines, thrive on the moister earth which heralds the fertile valley of the Charente river, imposing in size and luxuriant in growth. After seemingly countless bland kilometres, here is the Poitou-Charente. For those who enjoy finishing a day's walking with a balloon-glass in hand, it is an especially seductive area.

Even the most abstinent, however, will find much of interest in and around Cognac, for production of the heady drink is an ancient, almost mystic craft. The old town reflects this in a most impressive and dramatic manner, and the ancient riverside distilleries are coated with a permanent patina of tannin, the result of fume impregnation.

First, you need a base that is not too far away and which will provide good walking through typical Cognac countryside. You could consider the 2–star town campsite, some 2 kilometres from the centre, but this is not really ideal for touring visitors, although the location is alongside the river. There is a heavy concentration of semi-permanent caravans, the facilities are sad and unkempt, while crowding through the summer months is the norm. More agreeable quarters are available, however, for those prepared to pitch a little further away (about 10 kilometres). Drive into Cognac and out again (east) on the N141 Angoulême road. After 9 kilometres, at the outskirts of Veillard, take the signposted turning for Bourg-Charente. This riverbank camping ground is devoted entirely to accommodating genuine tourists. A simple, 1-star

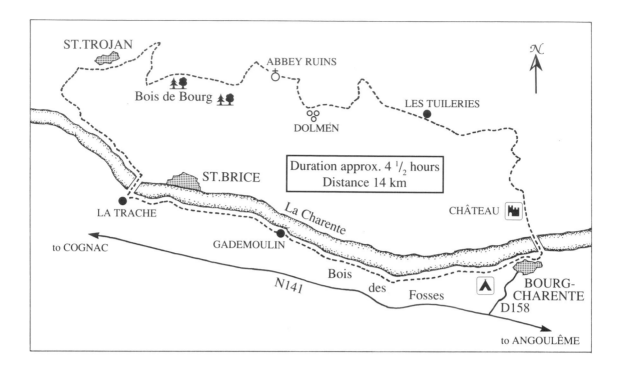

Duration approx. 4 ½ hours
Distance 14 km

municipal site, it is small, slightly sloping and the facilities are somewhat basic. It is clean and well tended though, peaceful and in the heart of countryside that few foreign visitors discover. There are hot showers available, mains electric hook-ups, and the tariff is low. The site is open from 15 June to 15 September (despite tourist office brochures which say it closes in August).

The *bourg* itself has rural charm, and some fascinating features of ancient France, while for the walker the situation could hardly be more strategic. Here at Bourg-Charente is the starting point of a 4½-hour footpath route taking in a superb stretch of the Charente river – the Circuit de Bourg-Charente. The path begins right outside the camp ground on the river towpath.

The adjacent hamlet is a very ancient settlement, a fortified earthworks in the fifth century according to the records, once known as De Burgus. Bourg-Charente still retains a faintly feudal air, with walled farmhouses and once-gracious mansions dotting the riverside meadows in the vicinity. There is a single, all-purpose store (which is also a *dépôt de pain*), plus an attractive, well-patronised riverside restaurant just by the camp ground.

In addition to the circuit walk, there is a pretty stretch of the GR4 winding east for a short distance along the northern bank of the Charente, beyond a lock and a keeper's lodge, where the long-distance path veers away towards Jarnac. To stroll it, cross the river bridge and take the towpath on your right. For the Bourg circuit, carry straight on past the imposing château, which is now a storehouse for maturing brandy, walking northwest via lanes and hamlets like Les Tuileries, for about 5 kilometres. There is an ancient dolmen and ruined abbey before you enter the woods of the Bois de Bourg and turn south towards the river again, skirting St-Trojan. There follows about 7 kilometres of

Bourg-Charente château — preserved, private and now a wine warehouse.

seen in profusion. Courvoisier, Camus, Martell, Hennessy, Polignac and Salignac are all represented, and numerous cellars are open to visitors. Nearer the town centre there is an absorbing museum devoted to Cognac's history. Entry is free of charge.

The French may have invented the golden nectar, but it took a touch of Irish luck to make it demanded worldwide. In 1760, Richard Hennessy, adventurer and ex-soldier, settled here for a spell, sampled the local drink, then shipped a few casks home to Cork for his relatives and friends. The subsequent clamour for more of the same became so insistent that the buccaneering entrepreneur entered the business, and his direct ancestors still hold the reins of the company.

The facts and figures of brandy processing are interesting – it takes 9 litres of white wine to produce 1 litre of Cognac. The distillation is then aged in Limousin oak casks for 10, 25, 50 years, or even longer, till the alchemy reaches its required perfection; a miracle transformation of grape and oak tannin, aided only by heat and time. Of course, it helps if, like the Hennessy family, you have been working the wizardry for seven generations.

After the peace of Bourg-Charente there is another Poitou-Charente high-spot, not far away, that cannot really be omitted. By way of a total contrast, consider the municipal ground of Angoulême, still on the banks of the Charente, and about 44 kilometres east of Cognac. Provided you don't arrive at the height of the silly season, this should prove an agreeable base, not least for its modest charges. Uniformly level and dotted with feathery trees, the grass is kept closely mown, and there are tarmac access roads to all parts

towpath walking now, along a lovely reach of the Charente. A short detour to St-Brice is worthwhile, where there is another elegant old château, amid a venerable cluster of buildings, before you cross the river bridge at La Trache. On the last stretch, past Gademoulin hamlet, there is some beautiful tall-tree woodland, the Bois des Fosses, before you rejoin the tarmac lane and go back to the camp ground.

After this you may feel like a more leisurely exploration of Cognac with your car. The best of the town is the old quarter, alongside the river quay, where you will find easy and spacious parking among the unique string of distilleries where household names can be

of the site. There is a choice of perimeter hedged bays, or more open pitching along the river boundary. There are two toilet blocks, one a super-loo, with individual washing cubicles and hot showers at no extra charge. Camping de Bourgines is open all year and the direction from the west is via the N141, following the green route signs for Angoulême at the city outskirts. Turn left at the traffic lights, signposted Poitiers and Limoges. From here follow the site signs to camp ground entrance. The background buzz of city traffic is constant, but not overly obtrusive. The immediate surroundings are not beautiful, but it is the ancient hill town that forms the impressive backdrop which is the attraction. Angoulême is one of the few cities in France where you can still drive around vestigial ramparts.

It was a redoubt in Roman times, and then a medieval walled town, and there are many remnants of the ancient eyrie remaining. The best way to see them is on foot. Town walking is not really the object of this book, but Angoulême, when the sun is shining, is exceptionally attractive. You need a full day to do the old city justice; it is a wondrous maze of medieval streets and houses all topped by a majestic twelfth-century cathedral. There are some splendid panoramas from viewpoints along the rampart walls. And if your legs aren't aching too much, there is pleasant evening strolling near to the camp ground, by the Charente river.

The Charente flowing through ancient Angoulême – a view from the medieval ramparts.

Two Fine Poitou Forests

To the south-east of Niort there is a welcome splash of green on the regional map of Poitou-Charente – the forests of Chizé and Aulnay which combined make up a regional park to either side of the Boutonne river. This is the terrain that the country-loving French themselves seek to explore on foot, to camp in quiet green places and to commune with nature. The scenery is therapeutic if not dramatic, a mix of arable farms on the grand scale, the gentlest of rounded hills and, of course, splendid swathes of woodland. Part of Chizé forest is a wild animal reserve (and a governmental biology centre), but there is more than sufficient free-range forest for the leisure walker.

An atmospheric backwater base will be found at the hamlet of le Vert, about 5 kilometres south-west of Chizé village, and 4 kilometres north of Dampierre-sur-Boutonne which has – among rustic charms – a grand Renaissance château beside the river. Le Vert municipal camp site is located in the grounds of an ancient mill, immediately beside the tiny town hall, and it welcomes visitors at any time from 1 June (although early arrivals in late May are usually accommodated).

There is a designated round-route walk from le Vert, which wends its way through some nice mixed woodland to the north-west of the hamlet via tracks, lanes and forest rides, revealing some truly venerable oak trees in places. There are alternative trails from this circuit, notably to the west to Boisserolles, and north along the GR36 to the Deux-Sèvres European Zoo. This is a non-profit-making enterprise developed by the National Forestry Office, the Ministry for Education and other organisations. There are some 600

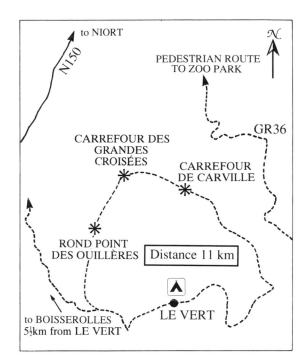

animal species to be seen within the 25-hectare enclosure, which takes about 3 hours to study properly. This is just one local excursion within a forest spread of about 4,800 hectares, all of which is virtually adjacent to the busy A10 *autoroute*. In aspect it is a world apart.

The Arvert Peninsula and the Côte Sauvage

Royan, at the mouth of the mighty Gironde estuary, is now challenging Biarritz as the number-one Atlantic coast resort. It is expanding massively – some would say alarmingly – to accommodate the throngs of holiday-makers drawn by the enormous golden-sand beaches, the bright lights and the 2,000-hour annual sunshine record – one of the highest in France. For the nature-loving leisure walker (who might be forgiven for thinking there is little of pedestrian interest in the vicinity), there remains a gem of Poitou-

195

Forlorn relics of World War II defences still linger on the banks of the Gironde.

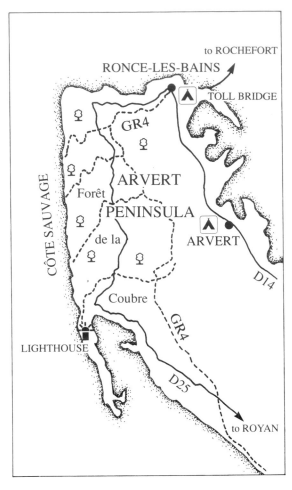

Charente country just to the north-west of this fun-city, at the top end of the Arvert Peninsula and encompassed by the Forêt de la Coubre. Pines planted about two centuries ago to stem encroaching sands, now provide a perfect leisure area over what was once a treacherous and untamed point of land hammered by wild tides and fierce Gironde winds. Today the landscape is tamed sufficiently to encourage visitors to explore more actively than through car windscreens.

Throughout the generous green area that provides protection against the Côte Sauvage, as it is called, there are many designated Zones of Silence, picnic glades, and way-marked walks (with enticing names like Promenade des Demoiselles), of 1 to 2 hours' duration. There are even tarmac cycle tracks in places, which, it must be hoped, is about the limit of forestry sophistication. Those who enjoy wide horizons will appreciate this region, especially close to the foreshore, which is aptly named, and is accessible for much of its length only on foot.

Ronce-les-Bains is one of the more agreeable bases on the peninsula, with a nice choice of pine-wood camping parks between here and la Tremblade. The GR4 traverses the whole forest between Ronce and St Palais, now a Royan suburb. After an invigorating spell of walking, Ronce is also conveniently placed for those who might wish to visit Rochefort or perhaps the colourful port of La Rochelle by way of the Pont-de-la-Seudre toll bridge.

The Vienne Valley between Confolens and Chauvigny

The Vienne is a dignified river – not a mighty one like the Loire or the Rhône – flowing strongly across a great deal of French terrain between Limoges and the point where it joins the Loire near Saumur. Along with the Charente, it is the major watercourse of Poitou-Charente region, and its most interesting reach for those who seek old France, behind the wheel or on foot, is that which begins at Confolens and runs north to Chauvigny.

Confolens sets the mood well for this 70-kilometre stretch of riverside exploration, since it is still visually medieval in the centre, burnished with the patina of centuries and somehow learning to cope with motor cars in its contorted narrow streets. The annual August folk fair is its great claim to fame, when the past is briefly resurrected. Regrettably, the municipal camp site is not too salubrious, but there is an exceptionally good alternative about 12 kilometres further north. On the way, alongside the D729, is an imposing château ruin standing lonely sentinel above the hamlet of St Germain-de-Confolens. At tiny Abzac, take the D99 to Availles-Limouzine (which despite its name is firmly within Poitou-Charente), a one-time fortified village serving a feudal château. The contemporary attraction is a superior landscaped camping ground, part of a municipal leisure park, with pine-tree clusters and close-mown lawn glades immediately beside the river. The utilities here are excellent, but don't confuse the rather hard-worn public toilets at the rear of the administration block with those reserved exclusively for campers, which are immediately beside the reception office. Among other municipal amenities are an indoor swimming pool, tennis courts and open-air table tennis.

For gentler exercise there is an agreeable lane walk (virtually traffic-free), which leads from the camp ground over a nearby hill, roughly following the course of the Vienne, to a secluded and richly-wooded barrage lake. The walk, out and back, takes about an hour and the reward is nice views over Availles' twelfth-century church and neighbouring château. In spring the verges and hedgerows are a riot of wild flowers and the scene for the stroller (apart from the tarmac underfoot), is timelessly rural and peaceful. The Availles touring site is open from 1 May to 30 September and is within a couple of hundred metres of the village centre.

Take a scenic rural drive along the little-used minor roads to l'Isle Jourdain – not to be confused with its namesake just west of Toulouse. This little township is pretty as a picture, reflecting old-world France at river level, especially around le Moulin des Birons, while at the top of the hill is a well-stocked supermarket with easy parking and less expensive petrol. There is another pleasant camp ground here, the Lac de Chardes, which is open from 15 May to 15 September. Again, the local authority has taken full advantage of a barrage scheme to benefit both local people and visitors.

Just north of here, close to the riverside hamlet of Moussac, a short *randonnée* route (designated number 48), has been created from a disused local railway line which more or less follows the Vienne in a near-straight line for 14 kilometres to Lussac-les-Château. Both Moussac and Lussac have municipal camp grounds, so you could consider this walk a two-day venture with an overnight stop at either end. Lussac is the favoured

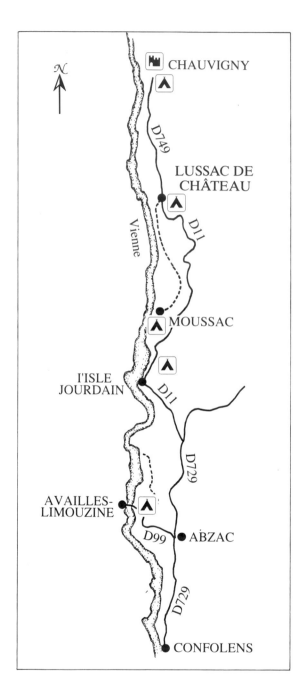

starting point, since the trail is only a step or two from Le Champ Imberge camp ground along the Chemin du Port.

Chauvigny is the historic high-spot, boasting no less than five medieval castle ruins, keeps and châteaux on top of a half-kilometre rocky bluff, high above the Vienne. Dominating both town (and municipal camp ground), this really is an extraordinary feudal ensemble, the centre-piece being the great church of St Pierre (thirteenth-century), with a quite remarkably preserved interior that is bright white and beautifully decorated. Chauvigny camp ground is open all the year round and is itself part of an odd if interesting complex of municipal park, animal menagerie and local allotment patches. Access to the ancient Ville Haute, is virtually direct from 3-star Camping de la Fontaine via old and steep steps.

Footnote

Mosnac is an atmospheric old-world hamlet; the type of backwater settlement appreciated by those who prefer rustic to mainstream France. It is also a very pleasant half-way staging-post between Saintes and Bordeaux. It is located on the now almost unused D134, a few kilometres to the east of the N137 and the A10 *autoroute*.

A tiny huddle of ancient houses around an imposing, if crumbling, eleventh-century church, a *boulangerie* and a general store make up the centre, while beside the Mairie, there is a small municipal camp ground, open all the year round and providing not only basic 2-star facilities, but also a hot bath if you wish! Quaint, green and very tranquil, it has a pitch in a landscaped church garden beside the river Trèfle.

Provence-Alpes-Côte d'Azur

**Départements: Alpes-de-Haute-Provence – Hautes Alpes –
Alpes Maritimes – Bouches-du-Rhône – Var – Vaucluse
Préfecture: Marseille**

This is the region that holds the ultimate holiday allure of western Europe – a sun-bathed place of splendid diversity, from the Roman ramparts of Arles and Avignon, dazzling nobly in the light so beloved of artists, to the frenetic fun-strip that is now almost unbroken from St Tropez to Menton on the Italian border. This is the Mediterranean France invaded by summertime millions. There is, too, another marvellous unsaturated region, away from the Rhône or the Riviera – the high-country hinterland of Provençal centre. This is the Provence of the outdoor-lover, where the natural landscape varies only between dramatic and spectacular and is, for the leisure walker, an infinite joy to experience.

Older hands will have their own mountain favourites, but newcomers may be bewildered by the choice. The driver who is unfamiliar with this terrain may encounter unwanted problems, and should be aware of the potential difficulties of the main holiday arteries of the N75 and N85 south of Grenoble. Both routes converge on Sisteron, which is imposing, but over-commercialised and very crowded in the high season. The N75 can be extremely busy and frustrating for drivers at times, but if you haven't seen Sisteron before, you should not miss this most powerful of

twelfth-century citadels towering over the foaming Durance river. If you have seen it, avoid the traffic by turning east from Gap, escaping at once into near-empty high country via the D900.

There is magnificent scenery almost unbroken along this road, from just outside Gap to the Valley of Ubaye and Barcelonnette. Of medieval Spanish origin, as the name implies, this pretty little resort town is located on the floor of a vast amphitheatre created by nature, with some of the surrounding peaks exceeding 3000 metres in altitude. Geared to outdoor pursuits summer and

Sisteron citadel.

winter alike, it is a much-favoured base with walker-campers, since there is a good choice of pitches both within the town environs and in the surrounding district. The number and variety of pedestrian routes is enough to please all tastes. Notably, there is the GR6 which runs laterally across country to the north-west; the GR5 north–south path which passes through Larche about 26 kilometres north-east of Barcelonnette, and the GR56, which loops through the regal Mercantour National Park to the south, reached via the Col d'Allos or the Col de la Cayolle. It is a drive-and-walk procedure to tackle selected stretches of the high-altitude long-distance trails, although there are some delightful short walks from the town itself.

Camping Du Plan is an excellent starting point for a number of rambles, varying in length from an hour or so to a full day or longer. Within 5 minutes' walk of Barcelonnette (where there is a supermarket, open market, tourist office and an attractive pedestrian precinct), this is a 3-star touring site, small but immaculately landscaped, with level lawns and tree shading. All mod-cons are provided including a cafè-bar and extensive hill-walking information boards displayed outside the office. The site is open from 15 May to 30 September and is one of two in the town vicinity; the alternative, 1 kilometre distant along the same road, is more heavily wooded.

Exploration of the Commune du Lauzet and Jausiers is particularly popular with those who enjoy gorges and steep-sided river-cut ravines. There is a very well-stocked map and guidebook shop in the rue Piétonnée. As an introduction, one suggestion is the walk south from the old town centre, crossing the Pont du Plan and continuing along the minor

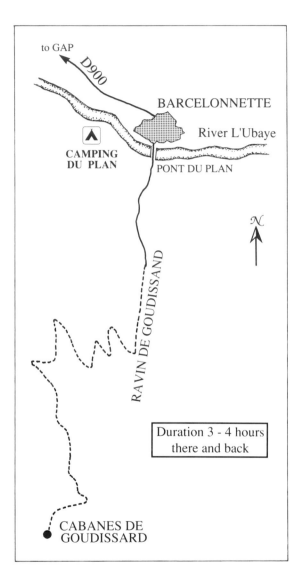

tarmac road for approximately 1 kilometre. From here there is a well-defined track which ascends in zig-zags through some handsome forested slopes rising from 1,270 metres to 1,750 metres at Les Cabanes de Goudissard. From here there are some superb views across

Barcelonnette and the l'Ubaye watercourse. Return the same way and allow approximately 3 to 4 hours; most of it for the outward (and upward), journey.

If you happen to be heading south, Barcelonnette is the starting point for one of the most glorious approaches to the heart of Upper Provence, avoiding the busy N85 between Sisteron and Grasse entirely. It is a memorable drive culminating in the geological jewel of France, the Gorges du Verdon.

Landscape drama begins at once as the D908 is joined for the ascent of the Col d'Allos, which is usually open around early June. This road is a super twister, some 20 kilometres of hairpins to the summit, with astonishing Provence-Alpes vistas the reward. The subsequent descent to the village of Allos is more gentle. The township of Colmars, 8 kilometres, fully deserves its name, which roughly translates as the 'seat of Mars'. There is medieval magnificence in this town of the most splendid kind. Park and stroll around, or, better still, stay a day or two and explore the area on foot. There is a choice of camping grounds and a Syndicat d'Initiative within the fortified walls, where you may collect information about local walking. There is also a *Gîte d'Etape*, at this seventeenth-century guardian-post of the Provence frontier.

At Villars-Colmars nearby there is a Camp de Tourisme, a 4-star family-run site in a beautiful setting of pine forests alongside the banks of the Upper Verdon river. Covering some 3 hectares of level, light woodland, there is a super-modern toilet block (built for all seasons, since this is also a ski resort). With privacy-bay pitches and comprehensive amenities, including a self-service store and restaurant, this is a comfortable base to return to after a day of hill walking. Summer open season is brief, from 20 June to 10 September, but if you find yourself in this area between these dates, it is a lovely spot to stay in.

If you follow the racing Verdon south from here you will find even more historic splendour, after passing the Barrage de Castillon. This is not the most impressive of approach routes to Castellane (you have to ascend the N85 Digne road for that famous near-aerial survey), but beautiful enough, particularly since you are now at the eastern gateway to the Gorge.

If you haven't seen Verdon before, try taking the signposted left bank route from the Pont de Soleils. For the first 10 kilometres or so you may wonder what all the fuss is about then, suddenly you come across the Balcons de la Mescla and an explosion of splendour. Here, some 750 feet below, lies the maelstrom confluence of the Verdon and Artuby rivers, linked, almost impossibly it seems from the belvedere view point, by the contemporary Pont de l'Artuby, which you cross to begin the drive along the Corniche Sublime. For the next 25 kilometres or so, the scenery is stunning in its grandeur, with ravine walls and buttresses soaring sheer from the snaking, vivid green Verdon river. At the north-west end, past Aiguines, the massive Lac de Sainte Croix widens to a distant horizon, while the shoreline at the narrow end is a popular water-sports playground. *En route* you may have cast a walker's eye downward at the ribbon footpath which winds from the Chalet de la Maline to the Point Sublime on the right bank.

The Sentier Martel is a classic walk following a section of the GR4, laid out by the Touring Club de France. It is tough, involving

Provence Alpes, where the higher trails can prove hard going, with long stretches between civilisation. They are not to be tackled lightly.

The river Verdon.

some precipitous ups and downs and a degree of scrambling. If you have a head for heights you'll love it; certainly, it is a ravine route you'll never forget. Allow a full day and don't stray from the white and red markers. This is a trail strictly for the most competent hill walker, who should be fully self-contained, with a powerful torch and extra clothing for the tunnel sections. There is real danger for those who stray from the signposted route, due to power station control of water flow.

For those preferring a less arduous pedestrian introduction to the canyon area there are more gentle alternatives. One popular base is that of La Palud, about 7 kilometres west of Point Sublime on the D952. Here also is the junction of the D23 Route de Crêtes,

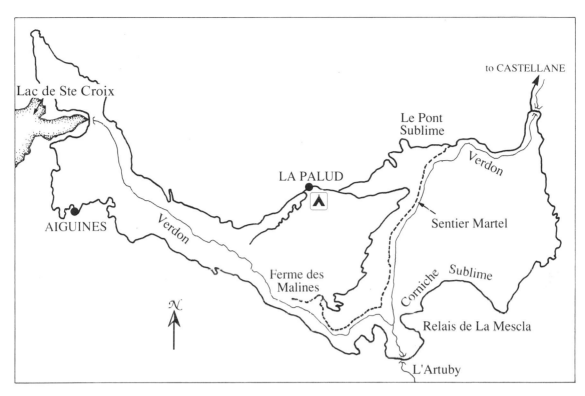

Lac de Ste Croix, Verdon Gorges.

Moustiers-Ste-Marie from Camping St Jean. The monastery is immediately below the left-hand rock pillar.

one of France's most astounding scenic roads, which traces the tortuous lip of the great gorge from Belvédere Baou-Beni to Belvédere Trescaire. At La Palud there are two camp grounds, one private and one municipal, both well patronised by long-distance and local walkers. From here the GR4 which links Moustiers-Ste-Marie with Castellane, diverts to the canyon to join the ravine route already described. The pedestrian approach is dramatic enough and you can then assess your own capacity for further exploration (bearing in mind the return walk), from the Chalet de la Maline at the 6-kilometre mark. This is just one of several footpaths that meander across the plateau of Bois d'Aire from La Palud, a tiny hamlet with basic amenities.

For comprehensive visitor facilities and more sophisticated camping, there is a wide choice in the vicinity of Castellane, all the sites being located alongside the Verdon river west of the town. Castellane itself is ancient, picturesque, interesting and inevitably crowded. It boasts a supermarket (open only in summer to cope with the tourist influx) and its landmark of fame is the Chapel Notre Dame du Roc, perched on a mighty limestone bluff. It can be reached via a challenging footpath which starts behind the church, and is waymarked with Stations of the Cross sculptures. At the western end of the great gorge lies Moustiers-Ste-Marie, yet another architectural treasure blending almost perfectly with nature. Indeed, for a base in this area there could hardly be anywhere more well placed and delightful than this hill town.

There is a choice of camping grounds in the vicinity, but the nearest to the town centre is Camping St Jean. To get there, take the signposted Riez road at the elevated town perimeter and continue for 1 kilometre to the site entrance opposite an Esso filling station. Camping St Jean is a 3-star, tree-shaded ground, open from 1 April to 30 September, nicely level for the most part, grassed, and with tarmac service roads. The toilets are clean and modern, and there are hot showers, while a small provision shop forms part of the site office. There is also a useful selection of local literature of interest to walkers. From here a 10-minute stroll uphill (take the lane signposted 'Interhomes' just outside the site), will take you inside the ancient fortified walls and into the midst of an historical France of intriguing fascination. A fortified stockade in the eleventh century, Moustiers Monastery – a stone eyrie between enormous rock spires – was founded in the fifteenth century.

The town itself, famed for ceramic work, spills steeply to either side of the cascading torrent of the river Roiul, in a setting of craggy beauty. Above all, suspended between those rock pinnacles, is a span of chain carrying a *Croix d'Or*, said to have been hung by a returning crusader in thankfulness for his deliverance. It creates a dramatic finishing touch to a scene of charm.

Shopping facilities are rather limited in Moustiers, but there are all the necessities and the Syndicat d'Initiative is open from 15 June to 15 September. For almost all visitors a couple of hours wandering the steep streets and cobbled alleyways is obligatory. The energetic will also be tempted by that intriguing, half-hidden monastery, and this will be good muscle training for wilder walking around the Grand Canyon.

There are numerous footpaths in and around this town and one of the most interesting is that which winds past the Ravin de Notre Dame, after passing through the age-old remnants of the fortified town gateway. There are some fine elevated views across country from the succeeding hill-top shoulder, high above the mellow Moustiers rooftops.

Around Nans-les-Pins

There is a western corner of this region – something of a Provence paradise – which must be included. Far from any Côte d'Azur conurbations, this high country of gleaming limestone and ancient forest is the Massif de la Sainte Baume. Lying north-west of Toulon, the great French naval base, there is a tract of Provence served only by winding minor roads and small, scattered townships and country villages. One of these is Nans-les-Pins, a venerable settlement around a tree-shaded central square, as Provençal as a Van Gogh painting. To get there, turn south off the N560 between Tourves and St-Zacharie, then take the D80 to the village. On the outskirts, clearly signposted, there is Camping International de la Sainte Baume.

This is a very agreeable touring park in the heart of an oak and pine forest, spacious to a degree and with comprehensive amenities as befits a long-stay site. There are toilets with individual cubicles, hot showers, a food store and a café/bar adjacent to a patio swimming pool. There is even a perimeter horse-riding track since there are stables adjoining the complex. The ground is stony but there is a variety of tree-shaded pitches to choose from on this 3-star site, most of which are level. Open season is from Easter to the end of October, but full services only come into

The oak forest setting of Camping de la Sainte Baume, Nans-les-Pins, a fine base for exploring the great Massif of Provence.

operation from mid-June. Early or late in the year, this camping ground is a subtle combination of that which is best in man-made conveniences and natural surroundings.

For those who walk, the attractions are manifold. Nans-les-Pins is a place for strolling in the evening and since the town square is only 15 minutes' walk away via a pleasant tree-shaded footpath, access could not be easier or more inviting. After some gentle orientation, there is a choice of paths in, over and around the mighty whaleback of the Baume Massif. About 12 kilometres long, this great limestone outcrop is the highest mountain in the Provence chain. Those with limited French will find the camp ground proprietor

Monsieur Reaux helpful, since he speaks good English, possesses equally good local knowledge, and can usually provide useful footpath literature from the site office.

One popular walk, which takes the best part of a day, is the Sentier Rouge de Notre Dame D'Orgnon. It starts from a tiny track immediately beside a chapel at the top end of Nans-les-Pins, then winds around a great wooded bluff past some ancient castle remains, following the course of the river Huveaune. It then ascends to the nineteenth-century hill church and now-deserted village of Orgnon. This is the half-way point of the circuit, which partially coincides with the GR9 as it traverses the forest and finishes as a lane walk on the final stretch back to Nans-

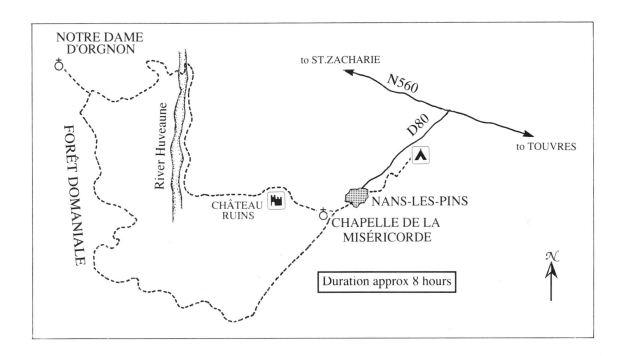

les-Pins. The track is well defined, although the colour-coding (blue for the local circuit, red/white for the GR9) is a bit hit and miss. A compass and a large-scale map are obligatory for navigation.

Other objectives worthy of exploration in this area, again networked by short walks over waymarked routes, are the Pic St Pilon, 944 metres in altitude with fine summit panoramas; and Plan d'Aups, a lofty scattered settlement on the Baume crest more reminiscent of wild California than the south of France. By contrast, there is the lush Parc-de-St-Pons, with its semi-tropical flora and sparkling cascade. All of these high spots are along or alongside the D80 between Nans-les-Pins and Gemenos.

100 Kilometres of Sentiers d'Or

Understandably, in the most popular of French regions, it is not always easy to find the Provençal paradise you seek when half the population of western Europe seems to be doing the same. In the real world, if half of your expectations are realised, then you aren't doing badly. For this reason the Haute Provence walking centre of Orpierre must be recommended, despite distinct reservations about the base camp. Camping des Princes d'Orange has been 4-star rated, presumably for the surroundings, and perhaps for the swimming pool and the on-site restaurant. However, four stars are wildly generous for the very restricted terraced pitches, where desperate touring caravanners and tenters must squeeze between static vans, while the tariff is commensurate with the best 4-star establishments in France. The location is described as '20 hectares of pine forest', when the pitching terraces cover less than 3 hectares! None the less, there are compensations. The toilets are clean (although hot water is in short supply), the atmosphere is friendly and certainly informal, while the patrons (of all nationalities) seem content just to be close to some of the best hill walking in Provence. And *that* is something that Camping des Princes d'Orange certainly *can* offer.

The views in all directions from the 700 metre-high camp ground, are of splendid mountains, while below, just a 5-minute stroll away, is the picture-postcard medieval village of Orpierre, slumbering under the Provençal sun and largely unchanged for the past five centuries or so, when it was a fortified bastide. Walk past the old church where the clock, with charming French practicality, strikes the hours twice, and up the Grand Rue. You are now on the GR946, opening steps of a lovely elevated stretch which will take you to the summit of the lower of the two big bluffs dominating the north-western skyline, Le Gros Doigt (the big thumb).

As you leave Grand Rue and enter La Placette, pause to look at the ancient towered house on your right; this was once the residence of the Princes of Orange, hence the name of the D30 valley road, and the camp ground connection. The start of this half-hour climb takes you through some fascinating once-cobbled alleys, beside incredibly old houses, the GR waymarks leading you through tiny back gardens and terraces at first. Soon you break out to start a steady and quite stiff zig-zag through broom clusters, along a narrow but very well-defined track, past a tiny shrine, and so to the crumbling

wall, once part of a fortified perimeter, capped by a defensive lookout post on the summit of the 'Big Thumb'. The end of the ascent reveals eagle-eye views over the village and, on clear days, the outline of the high alps to the east.

Other Regional Options

Available from the Cannes Syndicat d'Initiative (at the railway station), is a useful information sheet entitled *Alpes Maritimes Hiker's Handbook*. This lists short coastal and inland walks, day hikes and long-distance backpacking routes with relevant accommodation points. If you want walking on the Riviera, this will indicate the possibilities.

The GR51 Cannes–Menton path passes close to the village of Pégomas. There are two agreeable base camps here for walking in the adjacent Tanneron Massif. In the centre of Pégomas turn south on the signposted Mandelieu road and immediately after crossing the Seigne river bridge, turn right to the hamlet of Chabrols. Camping Chabrols is the acknowledged touring park, while next door Camping la Mimosas has holiday caravans for hire under friendly English ownership. (You can book in England before you leave on 0227 372589.) Within strolling distance of these sites you can be in high Tanneron country with splendid views of distant Grasse in one direction and the Mediterranean in the other. The charming (and unspoiled) villages of Auribeau and Tanneron are within a couple of hours' walking via hill tracks.

Pégomas is a quiet backwater place, yet very close to high-society Cannes and the hub of the Riviera. For exploring hereabouts on foot the standard walking map is entitled *Au Pays d'Azur Itinéraires Pédestres*, scale

1:50,000, and covers the coastal region from Fréjus to Menton. (It is also available in England from Stanford & Co, London, as Map No. 26.)

A penultimate trio to this great region are the Cians Gorges, the high Provence Rifts and the Queyras. Drive north-west from Nice along the N202 for 50 kilometres, then turn north on to the D28, signposted Beuil and Valberg. A world of towering red canyon walls opens here. Regal and almost over-powering in places, the Cians Gorges are considered by many to be among the most spectacular in the French Alps, with the rushing white waters of the Cians river plummeting some 5,000 feet in 25 kilometres. The road ascends in a welter of rushing torrents, vivid red walls, and narrow, rock-blasted galleries arched over the defile, so close to the road in places that the sun is momentarily shut out. Suddenly, at the summit, there is lush Alpine pasture, swathes of pine forest, and breathtaking mountain beauty through Beuil and Valberg, a ski resort nestling at 1,670 metres.

After a prolonged and precipitous swoop via a succession of hairpin bends, Guillaumes comes into view, a mountain town that possesses a pleasing patina of time, epitomised by a hill-top castle ruin that is accessible via a winding footpath. This is just one of several high-level or valley walks in this delightful, less-visited area. There is a tiny overnight camp ground here, on the banks of the fast-flowing Var; use of adjacent tennis club showers and toilets is included in the modest fee.

For the Queyras, drive north from Barcelonnette over the lofty and tortuous Col de Vars and you drop down eventually to Guillestre, the principal township of the Parc

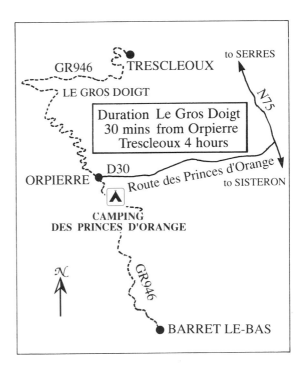

Régional de Queyras. This is virtually a geological continuation of the Ecrins National Park to the west, although it is separated from it by the Durance river valley.

There is more majestic Alpine country here, particularly in early summer (when the passes are just open), when it is a secluded world of wild flowers, pine-clad foothills and a whole cluster of snow-capped mountains close to the Italian frontier. There is quite a wide choice of camping grounds at Guillestres, together with a Youth Hostel, for this is a popular holiday base and the only sizeable town between Briançon to the north and Gap to the south-west.

The more adventurous will push on some 14 kilometres further east, even though this means ascending a sometimes twisting road

From the ascent path to the 'Big Thumb', high above Orpierre village. This is a fine hill walking region.

almost 2,000 feet, to the picturesque mountain village of Ceillac-en-Queyras. There are two camp grounds here (one municipal), both are agreeable and in an idyllic setting. There is splendid walking potential in this area, up to main valleys and along sections of the GR5 and GR58, and this is therefore another recommended long-stay base for the keen walker.

For a fulfilling day walk, you could continue on the GR946, via the summit of Suillet, and down to the village of Trescléaux, where refreshment is available. Those exploring the long-distance route southwards will find an alternative camp ground at Barret le Bas. While the GR946 is the principal footpath bisecting the area from north to south, there is a good choice of local walks radiating both east and west of Orpierre, the majority of which are to the south of the sixteenth-century village. This network of mountain trails is, of course, the Sentiers d'Or and the waymarking colour is yellow. Once again, the 1:25,000 map is recommended for any extended walking in this region.

Rhône-Alpes

Départements: Ain – Ardèche – Drôme – Isère – Loire – Rhône – Savoie – Haute-Savoie
Préfecture: Lyon

One of France's largest regions, actually covering about 8 per cent of the French metropolitan land mass, Rhône-Alpes encompasses no less than eight départements. It is a macro-region, embracing Savoy, part of the Jura, the Lyon area, a large stretch of the Dauphine, plus huge chunks of the Massif Central and Haute Provence. This is almost a country within a country, with an extraordinary diversity of landscape, and it is more or less impossible to single out two or three high-spots. The following are some personal choices, which bear repeated visits and seldom fail to please.

Lyon, France's second city, spreads her influence far and wide around the northern centre of Rhône-Alpes, while the mighty Rhône flows fast and wide from the great city to the southern regional boundary below Montélimar. Some of the finest walking areas – not only within the region but in all France – lie on both sides of the Rhône, amid countryside that could scarcely be more contrasting; to the east is Haute-Savoie and Isère, westwards is the Ardèche.

Rambling territory *par excellence* from late spring to early autumn is pinpointed by names that are universally familiar – Annecy, Megève and Chamonix – all prime ski resorts in winter. Two natural features are the main attraction: the lake at Annecy, and the mountain that towers over all other Alpine peaks, Mont Blanc. Together they form what might be described as a 'French Windermere', but on a much grander scale.

Although some of the loveliest areas of Haute-Savoie have been irrevocably blemished alongside major roads, large pockets of unspoiled countryside do survive, including the Vanoise Natural Park. There is a further problem for those who opt for an off-season visit – mountain passes are often closed to mid-June or even later, denying visitors road access and thus restricting the options for pedestrians.

On an optimistic note, there is relatively untouched high country accessible at almost any season, and some of it is surprisingly close to the bustle and bright lights of Annecy. One place in particular that has all the ingredients to attract the hill walker is Thônes, a pretty little town in a lovely setting, high above and just 20 kilometres to the east of the great lake resort. Take the D909 Green Route direct from Annecy town centre, ascending from Veyrier towards La Clusaz. This D909 is a short but gratifying escape route, and your spirits are bound to rise as the road climbs, the air becomes sharper and sweeter, and the surroundings more rural.

211

There are three camping grounds within the environs of Thônes, all 2-star category. All of them are attractively located and level (surprising and pleasing, considering the mountain terrain), but top marks must go to Le Tréjeux. Le Lachat is atmospheric if quaintly tumbledown, and adjacent to the road; Les Grillons is small and pleasant, but only open from mid-June to August. Only 1½ kilometres from the town centre, and reached via a quiet and well-signposted minor road, Le Tréjeux is secluded, though not isolated, with tree-shaded pitches and the rushing river Fier forming one boundary. Rising majestically on all sides are splendid pine-clad slopes networked by marked footpaths. It is a private enterprise 2-hectare site, efficiently run, with facilities that are clean and adequate and include hot showers and mains electricity. Seasonal opening is from mid-April to the end of September. Access is restricted to genuine touring units only, although there are a few simple camping bungalows for hire. For non-campers there is a *Gîte d'Étape*, 'Les Cat Pat', at Manigod hamlet, 5 kilometres south-east of Thônes.

Thônes, at an altitude of nearly 2,000 feet, has that attractive and definable Alpine stamp, with a central square landmarked by the obligatory domed-tower church. There is some intrusion by contemporary building, but Thônes is not yet too badly afflicted. There are two supermarkets, numerous restaurants and cafés (and lots of retail outlets for the celebrated Blocheron cheese and Alpine honey), a prominent post office and, as befits a mountain resort now highly dependent upon tourism, a tourist office prominent in the town centre. From here you can buy two beautifully produced footpath guides. The first is a 14-part map of marked local

trails all starting from Thônes, and the second is a superb wallet entitled *Tournette Aravis*, containing no less than 17 wanderways through the surrounding *massif*.

This is backpacking terrain of the best kind, a landscape to tempt those who really want to test themselves at altitude. If the local routes provided aren't enough there is in addition the circuit of Lake Annecy via the GR96 (*Topo-Guide* No. 909). Not too far away, either, is the classic circuit of Mont Blanc itself, although since this takes the backpacker into Switzerland it is largely outside the realm of this book. It is covered by *Topo-Guide* No. 001, a loop off the great GR5 Holland–Mediterranean walkway.

Thônes itself and the nearby Plateau des Glières were the scene of a ferocious battle between a German division and the French *Maquis* forces during World War II. The freedom fighters were eventually overcome and there was savage retribution. The town was later honoured with the award of the Croix de Guerre. The impressive Musée de la Résistance and memorial can be seen at Morette.

The Ardèche

In the early 1960s I discovered, more or less by accident, the Ardèche Gorges. Much has changed in succeeding years, and the Ardèche is now firmly on the international tourist route. It *is* a glorious Provençal canyon, not quite as breathtaking as the Verdon Gorge, but coming close to it in places. The best way to see it is not from a car or coach, but from the back of a horse, from a canoe, or on foot. This is not to deny that motoring (especially from Pont St Esprit north-west to Vallon-

The savage grandeur of the Ardèche; le Ran Pointu near Saint Martin.

Pont-d'Arc) along the canyon edge is an uplifting experience – about 40 kilometres of dizzying downward views, of immense cliffs, weird cave formations; a kaleidoscope of nature at its wildest.

The recognised scenic centre of the area is Vallon-Pont-d'Arc, where there are now no less than 26 camping grounds and holiday parks – some of which are over-used (and look it), and others where standards have been set and maintained to a high level of sophistication. There is a helpful tourist office in the small town centre which provides details, locations and charges of all the camp grounds, plus literature on some 21 footpaths in the vicinity, *Promenades sur nos Sentiers Pédestres.*

The Pont d'Arc of Vallon, some 3 kilometres south-east of the town, is a massively-formed natural archway spanning the Ardèche, now a much-photographed rock outcrop and busy canoeing centre. The town itself is pleasant without being spectacular, since the original Vallon has long been deserted. Vieux Vallon is the hill-top ruin just to the south-east of its modern counterpart.

For an interesting short walk of about 1½ hours, consider Le Chastelas Circuit which starts just south of the town off the D290 and winds around old Vallon to give some fine views over 'new' Vallon. The route is easy, with yellow markers. For a 3-hour trek revealing some truly wild parts of this gorge country, the Route le Tiourre is excellent.

One other place well worth exploring is Salavas, the medieval hill village next to Vallon-Pont-d'Arc. Some quiet and loving restoration of a truly ancient stronghold is progressing here and it is a little settlement of great atmosphere and visual appeal. Once a staunch Protestant village (like many others in this region), and the scene of bloody skirmishing at times, there are some genuine remnants of life in the Middle Ages, including massive ramparts and archways, steep alleyways paved with great cobblestones, and a centuries-old water-well, now sealed.

The Lyonnais Rhône-Alpes

It is easy to forget that this vast region of France stretches not only to the Italian border east of Lyon, but also westwards, almost to Vichy in the Auvergne at one point. West of the wide Saône/Rhône valley and its ceaseless traffic flow along the A6/N6 north of Lyon and the A7/N7 to the south, there is an attractive spread of hill country which begins at the regional border with Bourgogne just west of Mâcon. Poule-les-Echarmeaux lies at the heart of this countryside and has two assets: a small, terraced camp ground which has been upgraded to comply with the new 2-star grading, and an adjacent section of the long-distance GR7 which winds north to south through the entire area of deeply wooded and domed hills.

214

The district is also well provided with other local footpaths.

One other pleasant base, towards the southern end of this pretty area, is Camping St Cry, south-west of l'Arbresle and Bessenay village alongside the N89. The country-lane circuit walk to the picturesque hill town of Bessenay provides nice distant views on the gentle ascent route, across grand-scale combe country. There are a number of other hill walks via farm lanes on both sides of the heavily-wooded Brevenne valley.

Another country town that deserves a detour from the *autoroute* (A72) or the N82 is St Galmier, north of St Etienne City. St Galmier, on the river Coise, has an atmospheric, ancient air, and thirteenth century beginnings, and was once home to the Comtes

The famous hanging houses at Pont-en-Royans.

de Forez, a very rich land-owning dynasty. It is just sufficiently far from the principal hill range to escape the weekend affliction. There *are* static caravans on the pleasant 3-star camping ground, but not, as yet, in overwhelming proportion. Also, there are half a dozen attractive local footpaths, all of which start from this municipal site which is about 1 kilometre away from the old town centre, in an attractive river valley setting. Detailed information is available on all the walks from the local tourist office which, like the camp ground, is well signposted.

Parc du Vercors

Between Valence on the Rhône and Grenoble to the north-east is one of the less-populated green areas of the Rhône-Alpes. It also happens to be one of the most ruggedly beautiful within the bounds of the Parc Naturel Régional du Vercors (created in 1970 and encompassing four mountain groups). One of the best bases for exploring this splendid high country is from within the Royans commune, which is centred at the confluence of the Bourne and Lyonne rivers. There is a choice of municipal camp grounds here, at Pont-en-Royans, Choranche, or St-Jean-en-Royans, all of 2-star category. The first is close to the centre of the most picturesque township, which clings in an Italianate way to the ravine rocks above the river. Its rock-perched houses – *les maisons suspendues* – are a celebrated old-world treasure.

The smallest campsite is the keen walker's automatic choice; only a postage-stamp patch of green, but again lovingly landscaped and maintained. The location, at Choranche hamlet, is delightful, on the banks of the Bourne some 5 kilometres east of Pont-en-

Les Petit Goulets in the majestic Parc du Vercors.

Royans, with majestic high country rising close on all sides.

From all of these bases there is some exciting terrain to see, both as a driver and a walker. Once installed at the site of your choice, you might first take a circular drive, starting eastwards and taking in the awesome Gorges de la Bourne on the outward leg, and the spectacular Grands Goulets and Petits Goulets on the return. Les Grands Goulets (translating rather oddly as 'great narrows'), are a series of rock-blasted tunnels and galleries along the rim of a breathtaking ravine; the *'petit'* version, comprising a five-tunnel gallery above another dizzying chasm, is no

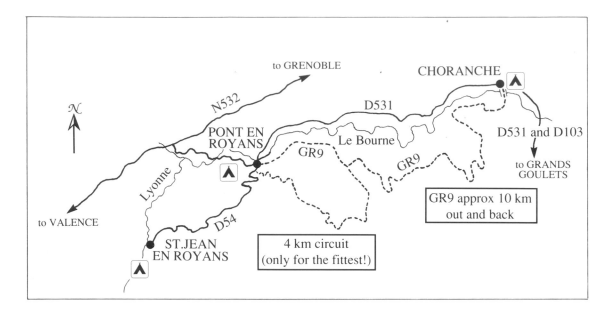

less dramatic, despite the name. This is a drive of roughly 50 kilometres, with as much visual impact in parts as the mighty Verdon Gorges in neighbouring Provence.

Once in walking boots (and having made sure of the precautions always advised when mountain hiking), consider the two fine footpaths which link Choranche with Pont-en-Royans. The first, which starts immediately from the little camping ground, crosses the Bourne on to the southern side, then winds alongside the swift-flowing water before climbing a woodland and mountains pasture route to skirt the mighty granite outcrops. Nearly all ancient hill-track walking, the well-marked path touches upon farm lanes for short stretches, eventually descending, quite precipitously towards the end, via steps directly into Pont-en-Royans opposite the suspended houses.

The second walk is a 4-kilometre circuit, starting and finishing at the Pont, essentially a short but very sharp venture and only appealing really to those with well-developed leg muscles. It ascends steeply at first, then levels out to traverse the mountain flank, ascending again to the tree-line just below the summit of Mont Baret which tops out at 793 metres. The track crosses the high ridge eastwards, then drops down to rejoin the GR9 and so back to Pont-en-Royans. These are just two waymarked pedestrian routes in the area, among a whole variety to attract every walker, whatever their degree of aptitude or inclination. You can, of course, penetrate much deeper into the mountain ranges of this Rhône-Alpes area, but camping facilities are limited and rather basic at the higher retreats like La Chapelle-en-Vercors, or Les Baraques near the Grands Goulets.

Hill Walks from Dieulefit and Bourdeaux

Given good weather conditions, the Royans region could hold you for quite a spell. It is, after all, an acknowledged (if little publicised) mountain resort area. However, when you do leave – if you are southbound – opt for the D70 rather than the more obvious Rhône

216

Valley routes. Scenic beauty begins immediately from the St-Jean-en-Royans camp ground, along a minor road which is well surfaced and wide enough for the largest touring caravan outfit. The D70 takes you almost into Crest, about 54 kilometres away, and is one of the most attractive roads in the southern Rhône-Alpes. It is not spectacularly dramatic, but is continuously delightful to the eye, with forest and pasture unrolling through a very quiet band of sparsely-populated high country. This beautiful and remote hinterland continues south of Crest, along the D538, revealing some regal canyon country near the isolated village of Saou.

Carry on to the distinctive landmark ruins of a medieval château above Bourdeaux, and perhaps beyond, through a craggy defile to Dieulefit, 13 kilometres away. These two picturesque hill towns are the final recommended base camps in the south of the Rhône-Alpes region to the east of the Rhône river. Those who have made themselves familiar with the orthodox route south to Provence over the years (through Valence, Montélimar and Orange), may well wish to try this refreshing alternative to dense traffic and seemingly endless advertisements for nougat. Walking enthusiasts certainly won't want to probe too much farther south in high summer, for as the mountains recede the temperature rises drastically. The terrain around Nyons holds limited pedestrian appeal, while all the camping grounds are likely to be insufferably full from early June to mid-September.

Neither Bourdeaux nor Dieulefit should be so afflicted (at least not until August), for commercial holiday appeal is limited at both places – although they are doubtless on many coach-tour itineraries for their natural charm,

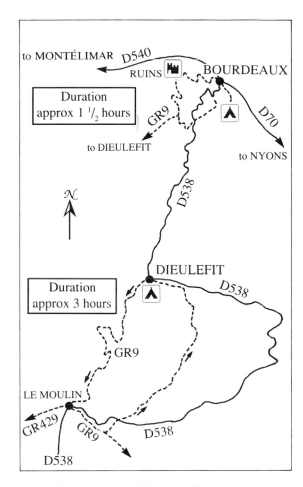

they are happily only of fleeting interest to the majority. Dieulefit is the larger settlement, locally famed for its artist-potter colony and its old town alongside and above the medieval church. The principal river is the clean-flowing Jabron, alongside which is located a level, spacious and well-run municipal enterprise, Camping les Grands Prés, which is open from Easter to the end of September and is for touring caravans and tents only. Generously shaded by tall trees (in part), and with high-standard facilities, the drawback is in finding the place, for the signposting for incoming visitors is confusing. Keep your temper and persevere in your search for the entrance close to the war memorial (Monument aux Morts) on the south side of the town off the Avenue Sadi Carnot, the D540. Once installed, you are only 3 minutes' stroll away from the town centre via a riverside footpath!

There are some sections of the GR9 which invite exploration, ascending both the northern and southern valley flanks rising gracefully and lushly wooded above Dieulefit. The circuits follow well-waymarked tracks along the GR on the outward legs in both cases, returning to the township via local hill paths and back lanes. The climbs from the valley floor are gentle enough, but they are prolonged – these hills may not be precipitous, but they are big. It is lovely walking, especially early in the morning when the cork-oak and pine woods are at their scented headiest.

Each round walk takes from 2 to 3 hours, involving a degree of road walking, and the 1:25,000 map is recommended; despite the good long-distance GR marking, the local path markers are rather desultory. There is a good choice of rambles around Dieulefit, some of which share horse-riding trails, while a popular medium-distance hike with backpackers is the GR9 between Dieulefit and Bourdeaux, approximately 12 kilometres to the north-east.

At Bourdeaux there is another generally uncrowded camping ground for the walker, adjacent to a hill village of colourful old-world charm, dominated by that château ruin which the long-distance path skirts on the final descent. There is an interesting short circuit walk from Bourdeaux, partially along the GR9 towards Dieulefit, easily joined from Le Gap des Tortelles, as the camp ground is called. The utilities here are quaintly rustic, but they are clean and efficient, while the

pitching area is shaded, green and most inviting. The atmosphere is friendly and informal, and the noise level is low both by day and at night. The site is open from April to October and it is about 200 metres from the village centre, which has a few essential shops clustered around two venerable churches.

Walk towards the Salle des Fêtes from the central square and you will already be on the GR9. Follow those familiar red/white flashes up and through the medieval terracing which is the old part of the town, resplendent with delightful archways and wide stone steps being steadily restored and preserved. By the last house on the southern side of the village, the route becomes a narrow footpath which winds up to the broken-toothed ruins of the ancient château. The footpath traces a route parallel to and above the D538, crosses it after approximately 1 kilometre, and continues south for a further half kilometre before veering away from the GR9, south-east on a local hill path, and back down to Bourdeaux. The last stretch goes over a little-used tarmac road.

Parc National des Ecrins

Grenoble, massively and industrially expanded beyond the city's original and rather charming centre, holds scant appeal for most holiday travellers. For the leisure walker, though, the area to the south-east of the city contains some of the best high-mountain country, not only in the Rhône-Alpes, but in the whole of France. The Parc National des Ecrins, created in 1973, encompasses a glorious mountain *massif*, itself occupying much of the land mass (nearly 100,000 hectares) between Grenoble and Briançon. A world of almost undisturbed natural tranquillity reigns here amid a series of snow-capped peaks, untouched as yet (and, hopefully, in perpetuity), by any main roads or settlements larger than one-street hill villages. The whole area is a hiking paradise, and it is all open for exploration from June through to late October most years.

The Valbonnais-Beaumont region is one of the easier corners of the park to reach, since it is only a few kilometres east of La Mure on the N85 Route Napoléon. Valbonnais village, just outside the park perimeter on the D526, has a spacious and level municipal camp ground beside a barrage *étang* of the river Malsanne, which is open from May to September. It is peaceful and uncrowded for most of the season, although there are a few weekend caravans installed; not surprising perhaps, since Grenoble is only 50 kilometres away. The facilities here are simple, clean and adequate.

Even closer to the towering high country, is the neighbouring village of Entraigues, at the confluence of the Bonne and Malsanne rivers, the recognised gateway to the Parc des Ecrins. Here is also a 2-star municipal camp ground, a very small one of half a hectare. It is level, hedged, offers a nice clean toilet block, and usually has space available in spring and autumn. There is a *gîte* here and a national park information office, which will provide detailed maps and guides of the pedestrian routes including the GR50 and GR54 and the Routes des Pays, waymarked red and yellow.

The obvious and most popular opening walk to attract visitors is that from Entraigues village (altitude 810 metres) to the hamlet of Villard, a gentle enough ascent in such high country, following the course of the river Bonne and taking about 45 minutes to reach

The imposing figure of the Little Emperor brooding over his namesake route above Vizille, near the hamlet of Laffray.

the Bronze-Age settlement. It is a beautiful scenic walk, and just an introduction to the 4-hour walk which could take you to St Michel-en-Beaumont (1,217 metres above sea level) where there is a twelve place *gîte* for overnight accommodation.

Parc National de la Vanoise

Spoliation of the area around Albertville, once a lovely green mountain valley, is now almost complete, and you must press on if you seek the white mountains and the crystal air, through Moutiers and on again through Bozel, southwards and upwards via the knotted hairpin sequence of the D915, to the border of a marvellous national park. This now protects the breathtaking splendour of

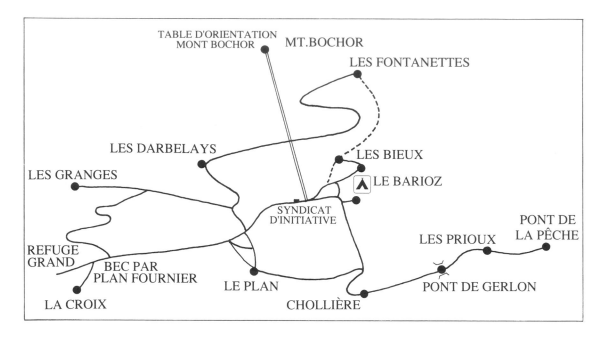

a great wedge of the mighty Massif de la Vanoise, where the king peak of the Grande Casse towers to a gigantic 3,586 metres above sea level, and, like Mont Blanc, its neighbour to the north, is permanently snow-capped. Here, at the dead-end ski resort and summer walking/climbing centre of Pralognan la Vanoise, you *will* find mountain scenery from a picture-postcard, as yet unviolated by developers to any degree, and with some fine mountain walking direct from the camp ground.

Pralognan exists solely as a leisure base – for skiers in winter and pedestrian explorers in summer. Unlike many such places which usually concentrate almost exclusively on the winter game, Pralognan does not wear that forlorn and deserted look once the lower snowfields revert to green. The summer season for this enterprising village on the fringe of the national park begins on 1 June. The flower boxes come out to decorate the main street, and the municipal camping ground is ready to welcome visitors with pris-

tine modern toilet blocks, electric hook-ups and pitching where you like over a high and spacious mountain meadow, as flower carpeted and natural as it is possible to leave a winter skiing ground. All this is just 5 minutes from the village centre, with its excellent tourist information office, providing maps and a specially written guide book on local walks. A variety of shops provides for all needs and there is a choice of cafés, bars and restaurants.

There are more than a dozen short mountain walks within the immediate vicinity of the little resort, ranging in duration from 30 minutes to 2 hours. For middle- and long-distance hikers, there is the choice of the GR55, plus a total of 250 kilometres of way-marked trails between 1,400 metres and 3,000 metres altitude, served by five high-level refuge huts. This spot really is an ideal patch of Rhône-Alpes for hill walkers and mountain lovers, and arriving there is more than enough compensation for the man-made spoliation around Albertville.

Appendix

Recommended Walking Maps

IGN Cartes (Institut Géographique National), Series Rouge 1:250,000, 1cm = 2.5 km, or *Series Verte* 1:100,000, 1cm = 1 km. General map and route planner: IGN Sheet Number 903, *Sentiers de Grande Randonnée* (long-distance footpaths), available from Stanfords, Long Acre, London WC2.
General motoring map Michelin *Series Rouge* Number 989: 1cm = 10 km, available at all good book shops and stationers.

Topo-Guides

Over 150 of these pocket-sized paperback guides are available to those walkers who can read French. All the recognised walking areas of France are covered (encompassing some 40,000 kilometres of long-distance footpaths), with detailed itineraries, places of interest *en route*, methods of getting there, and overnight stopping places. Published by *Fédération Française de la Randonnée Pédestre,* 8 Ave Marceau, 75008 Paris. Available in Britain from McCarta Books Ltd, 122 Kings Cross Road, London WC2 or Stanfords (*see* above).

Useful Addresses

The Caravan Club, East Grinstead House, East Grinstead, West Sussex RH19 1UA.

The Camping Club of Great Britain & Ireland Ltd 11 Grosvenor Place, London SW1W 0EY.

Backpackers Club, PO Box 381, Reading, Berkshire RG3 4RL.

The Ramblers' Association, 1–5 Wandsworth Road, London SW8 2LJ.

The Youth Hostels Association, Trevelyan House, 8 St Stephens Hill, St Albans, Herts AL1 2DY.

French Government Tourist Office, 178 Piccadilly, London W1V 0AL.

General Information

(With acknowledgements to the French Government Tourist Office.)
Value for money Most sites with an official grading can fix their charges, which must by law be posted at the site entrance. Some sites have inclusive charges per pitch, others show basic prices per person, vehicle and space with extra facilities like showers, swimming pool and ironing. In practice, most campsites charge from midday to midday with each part day being counted as a full day. Child reductions up to 7 years of age.
Guidebooks *OFCC Guide (Official French Camping & Caravanning Guide):* 10,500 sites, in French only with English glossary. By post from OFCG (FFCG), 6 The Meadows, Worlington, Bury St. Edmunds, Suffolk IP28 8SH.
Michelin Camping Caravaning: over 3,500 selected sites of varying categories using easily understood signs. From booksellers, the AA and the RAC.
Caravan and Camp in France by Frederick Tingey (Mirador); over 5,000 officially graded sites classed into regions, with maps. In English throughout. Good for touring. From booksellers or post free from BCM Mirador Books, London WC1N 3XX.
Caravanning Through France by Philip Bristow (Navigator): A more specialised guide for caravanners. 2,200 sites plus background information, also in English. From booksellers or post free from Navigator Publishing Ltd, Moorhouse, Lower Kingston, Ringwood, Hants BH24 3BJ.
Camping Associations *Castels et Camping Caravanning:* luxury sites in the grounds of historic houses. Details: Château les Ormes, 35120 Epiniac, France, and Select Site Reservations, 55 Avenue Road, Cranleigh, Surrey. Tel. 0483-277777.
Fédération Nationale de l'Hôtellerie de Plein Air (FNHPA): many first-class sites, several renting caravans and/or chalets. Details from FNHPA, 10 rue de l'Isley, 75008 Paris.
Camping on a farm If you intend to camp on farmland, please remember always to obtain permission from the farmer first. Farms may also receive campers on a seasonal basis, usually 6 pitches or 20 campers at a time (or up to 25 pitches, 100 campers, as an *aire naturelle*). The OFCC Guide (see above) lists 2,200 such sites while 600 farm sites and *aires naturelles* are detailed in the *Gîtes de France 'Camping à la Ferme'* guide, from the Fédération Nationale des Gîtes Ruraux de France, 35 rue Godot-de-Mauroy, 75009 Paris, France.

Camping in the countryside   For casual camping in the countryside, apply on the spot to the local Office National des Eaux et Forêts. Permission is usually granted on production of the appropriate insurance certificate (third party extended to include camping and caravanning) or camping *carnet*.

Camping for naturists   The Fédération Française de Naturisme, 53 rue de la Chaussée d'Antin, 75009 Paris, has a list.

Camping gas   The most readily available is Butagaz from camping equipment shops, ironmongers, Shell retail outlets and many service stations. Camping Gaz is also widely available. Propagaz and Antargaz (red) from Antar outlets.

Disabled campers   Campsites with facilities for disabled visitors are indicated in the OFCC Guide and the Michelin Green Camping and Caravanning Guide.

Motorways   A car and caravan count as category 2, a motor caravan counts as category 3 (but the difference in tolls is minimal).

Caravaneige   OFCC Guide lists winter sites for caravans.

Taking your caravan   Touring caravans may visit France for stays of up to six consecutive months without formalities. Observe these legal requirements:

– any vehicle towing a caravan must be fitted with an adequate rear-view mirror or wing mirror on left-hand side

– maximum dimensions are 2.5 metres wide and 11 metres long (for a vehicle and trailer, maximum length is 18 metres).

– no passengers may be carried in a moving caravan.

– outside of built-up areas, the driver of the towing vehicle is required by law to keep a distance of 50 metres between himself and the vehicle ahead.

– vehicles towing caravans are not allowed to drive into Paris or on the outer lane of 3-lane motorways.

– on narrow roads, you must enable vehicles to overtake by slowing down or pulling in to the side where possible.

– in case of breakdown, whether caravan is on tow or detached, even if the caravan has hazard warning lights, you must display a red warning triangle at least 30 metres behind (and visible at 100 metres).

– you must have written authorisation from the registered owner if the caravan is borrowed.

Speed limits: the same limits as for a car apply provided the maximum gross weight of the caravan does not exceed the kerb weight of the towing vehicle (excluding passengers but including petrol, oil and water).

– caravans which exceed the kerb weight of the towing vehicle by less than 30% must not exceed 65 km/h and must display a disc to this effect.

– caravans which exceed the kerb weight of the towing vehicle by 30% or more must respect a speed limit of 45 km/h and display the appropriate disc.

– respect the 80 km/h limit where posted on some motorways.

Caravans left for more than six months are subject to VAT and must be covered by insurance with a French company.

For information, please contact the Taxation Section of the French Embassy, 58 Knightsbridge, London SW1X 7JT.

Parking your caravan   Overnight parking on a lay-by is not permitted on any road in France. However, in cases of driving fatigue, you can and should pull off the road to rest for a while.

Motorways are well-equipped with rest areas or *aires de repos* which should not be looked upon as alternative camping sites (the toll or *péage* ticket is only valid for 24 hours).

On some road and motorway parking areas, you will find facilities for caravans to take on fresh water, empty toilets and make extended stops. Similarly some towns (details in the OFCC Guide) allow caravans to park on the road.

You will also find towns with notices forbidding caravans to park: these will still have places where you may stop for provisions etc and you can find out where from the local town hall or tourist office.

Where to camp   France enjoys a high reputation for the quality of its camping, with some 10,000 officially graded sites. All graded sites must display their grading and charges at the site entrance. They must have roads connecting with the public highway, be laid out so as to respect the natural site with at least 10 per cent of the ground devoted to trees or shrubs, have adequate fire and security arrangements, permanent covered washing and sanitary equipment linked to public drainage, and daily refuse collection.

The maximum number of people per hectare (about $2\frac{1}{2}$ acres) is 300. At peak periods, when all sites are under considerable strain, there may be some relaxation in the regulations.

Sites graded ** and above must have communal buildings lit (and roads for *** and ****), games areas (with equipment for *** and ****), a central meeting place, points for electric razors, surrounding fence with day guard (night watchman for *** and ****). Sites graded *** and **** also have washing facilities in cubicles, hot showers, safety deposits, telephones and good shops on or close by the site.

Camping *carnet*   Both caravanners and campers will find an International Camping *carnet* useful. Although not compulsory, some sites require that you have one. The *carnet* gives evidence of insurance cover against third party risks and may be obtained by members from the AA, RAC, Camping and Caravanning Club (11 Lower Grosvenor Place, London W1), the Caravan Club, the Cyclists Touring Club (Cotterell House, 69 Meadrow, Godalming, Surrey). If you do not belong to any of the above, you may contact GB Car Club, P.O. Box 11, Romsey, Hants SO5 8XX.

Tourist Offices   You will find these in the centre of town with the international 'i' for information sign. They may be called Syndicats d'Initiative, Offices de Tourisme or Accueil de France. The French Government Tourist Office (178 Piccadilly, London W1V 0AL) can give details of companies offering camping or caravanning holidays to France, and also information on hiring static or touring caravans abroad.

Index

Note: Page numbers of illustrations are indicated by *italic* type.